Francesco M. Bongi[...] and
doctorate in engineering. [...] *Vall St*[...]
and London, [...] *interna-*
tional adviso[...] *night of*
the Order of [...] *deavours*
and biodiver[...]

"It has bec[...] [...]e is in
steep decline [...] y, social
security and international good citizenship has given way to a nightmare of chronic unemployment, unsustainable debt, demographic
decline, political paralysis and street violence. In *The Decline and
Fall of Europe*, Francesco Bongiovanni offers the most perceptive
account to date of a Europe that indulged too many illusions and
is now awakening to bankruptcy."

—**Bret Stephens, Foreign Affairs columnist,
the *Wall Street Journal***

"A thoughtful and provocative cautionary tale that Americans should
read if they want to see how our own increasing regulatory structure, accelerating entitlements and ballooning national debt could
lead to the same decline that the author so clearly describes in
Europe. Francesco Bongiovanni mixes common sense with an experienced eye for the details that show how utopianism overwhelmed
the benign postwar vision of a united Europe and resulted in a nightmare. His description of the EU bureaucracy as an organization of
40,000 souls, a budget of 126 billion euros and the ambition to
control every part of European life is lamentable proof of Kafka's
vision."

—**John Lehman, former Secretary of the Navy
in the Reagan Administration and a member
of the 9/11 Commission**

"In view of the current crisis in the European Union in general
and the Eurozone in particular, the arrival of this book could not
be more timely. It is a comprehensive review of the way the initial
favourable development of the EU has gone wrong and the range

of problems it currently faces. Should be read by every MP in the Union's 27 countries!"

—**Stephen Valdez, author of** *Introduction to Global Financial Markets*

"Revealing. A valuable tool for those who are interested in understanding the roots of the current Eurocrisis and for decision-makers engaged in limiting its bitter consequences."

—**Lucio Caracciolo, editor-in-chief,** *Limes,* **Italian Review of Geopolitics**

THE DECLINE
AND FALL
OF EUROPE

BY

FRANCESCO
M. BONGIOVANNI

palgrave
macmillan

First published 2012 by
PALGRAVE MACMILLAN

Palgrave Macmillan in the UK is an imprint of Macmillan Publishers Limited, registered in England, company number 785998, of Houndmills, Basingstoke, Hampshire RG21 6XS.

Palgrave Macmillan in the US is a division of St Martin's Press LLC, 175 Fifth Avenue, New York, NY 10010.

Palgrave Macmillan is the global academic imprint of the above companies and has companies and representatives throughout the world.

Palgrave® and Macmillan® are registered trademarks in the United States, the United Kingdom, Europe and other countries.

ISBN 978–0–230–36892–7 hardback
ISBN 978–0–230–36891–0 paperback

This book is printed on paper suitable for recycling and made from fully managed and sustained forest sources. Logging, pulping and manufacturing processes are expected to conform to the environmental regulations of the country of origin.

A catalogue record for this book is available from the British Library.

A catalog record for this book is available from the Library of Congress.

10 9 8 7 6 5 4 3 2
21 20 19 18 17 16 15 14 13 12

Printed and bound in the United States of America

To the memory of my beloved father,
a good man who was always there for us,

to my brother Youbi,
who lost his courageous fight against AIDS and
is gracing the heavens with his beautiful paintings,   .

and to my mother,
who whispers to flowers.

Also to the Grand Molvane,
from one Forrest Gump.

CONTENTS

INTRODUCTION

'Qui bene amat bene castigat'
An old Latin proverb

In London for a short visit in early 2006, on a grey and rainy day like any other, I was strolling somewhere in the Regent Street area when I found myself glancing at a bookshop window. Among the many volumes displayed one caught my attention. It was a tiny, brightly coloured book entitled *Why Europe Will Run the 21ˢᵗ Century*, by Mark Leonard. Convinced that it was a prank scrapbook filled with blank pages I entered the store armed with a wry smile, intent on purchasing and couriering it as a surprise to a good friend in Hong Kong. To my astonishment the pages were not blank. It was a 'real' book after all. Its back cover attested to the author being a very serious gentleman, the Director of Foreign Policy at the Centre for European Reform in the UK. Little had I suspected that think tank directors could double as writers of humorous books. The implication that Europe would 'run the 21ˢᵗ century', even figuratively, when everything around me was screaming that it could not even run itself, seemed preposterous at best. Intrigued, I bought and devoured the book. In fairness to Mr Leonard, his argument was not that Europe would dominate in the classical way we expect power to be wielded, but rather that it would lead by example. Another surprise awaited me when I found that in the previous year American reporter T.R. Reid had published *The United States of Europe: The New Superpower and the End of American Supremacy* and trends expert Jeremy Rifkin had written *The European Dream: How Europe's*

Vision of the Future is Quietly Eclipsing the American Dream. A little research uncovered that a couple of decades ago, political scientist Samuel Huntington, author of the essay that was to become the iconic book *Clash of Civilizations*, predicted:

> The European Community, if it were to become politically cohesive, would have the population, resources, economic wealth, technology, and actual and potential military strength to be the preeminent power of the twenty-first century. Japan, the United States, and the Soviet Union have specialized respectively in investment, consumption, and arms. Europe balances all three.[1]

What was wrong with these people and others like them? An epidemic of myopia? I had spent decades outside Europe, witnessed firsthand the dynamism of America and the transformation of China. Upon my return to Europe what I had found was mostly a decaying continent. What a difference from the dynamism I had been exposed to in the Far East! Were Leonard and others like him delusional? Infatuated American liberals? Was I totally off the mark? What was really going on in Europe? To find out for myself I embarked on a long journey of personal enlightenment, the results of which I decided to share with others in this book.

Since I came back from Asia in 2001 I've been telling those within earshot that Europe was going under, a comment that usually elicits curious stares. Now that we've had a full-blown crisis on our hands I increasingly find myself in good company – not that this brings any solace. Among the new prophets of doom, former British Prime Minister Gordon Brown recently pointed out that Europe's output,[2] which used to represent half of the world's total, has fallen to under 20 per cent today and is expected to fall to a paltry 7 per cent by 2050. In other words, by mid-century Europe's economy may be as small as that of Africa. Nobel economics laureate and *New York Times* columnist Paul Krugman lamented that 'Europe's situation is really, really scary'.[3] The *Wall Street Journal*'s Bret Stephens berated a Europe that based itself on the fiction that adding up the GDPs of its disparate countries turned it into an economic superpower; on the fiction that it had developed a model immune from globalization and other world trends; on the fraud of Greece joining the Eurozone when everybody knew it had cooked the books; and on the fraud of getting parliaments to conveniently approve a constitution that had been rejected by the people.[4] New prophets of doom such as these can be excused for focusing on the economic and financial dimensions of Europe's woes because it is there that the most urgent and visible problems and dramatic headlines are found. Indeed, the last two chapters of this book deal with the sovereign debt and Eurozone crisis. Yet the reality is that a rapidly declining Europe is facing intractable challenges across *all* dimensions one cares to analyse, from geostrategic to social. While the Eurozone crisis was a wake-up call resulting in the broad consensus that Europe is standing today at the edge of a financial abyss, there is far more to Europe's broad structural decline than the Eurozone crisis. When former European Commissioner Mario Monti, speaking about Italy, recently said 'From decline we are moving into decadence',[5] his was a judgement that fits most of today's Europe like a glove. To understand what is going on and where Europe is heading one needs to begin to understand the broader picture, which is what this book attempts to do. Politicians like to sound hopeful, and Brown's statement that the decline of the West is 'not inevitable' is unsurprisingly at odds with my own conclusion that the demise of Europe *is* going to happen. Don't misunderstand me: it is not that there are no solutions. There always are solutions. But they would require such profound and drastic changes and adjustments in the mentalities and lives of Europeans, in particular in the south, that they are unlikely to be embraced. Europeans will prefer to continue entertaining their great illusion and to enjoy the last rays of sun, oblivious of their current trajectory of decay and safe in the knowledge that tomorrow is another day.

Let me first clarify my position. I am no scholar, historian or political scientist. Yet I have lived and worked 15 years in Asia and been exposed to the dynamism of this region; I have witnessed firsthand the rise of China; I have worked in Wall Street and also done business in Europe for a decade; and I have also lived in the Arab world – all these experiences have provided enriching perspectives that differ from those most of my fellow Europeans enjoy. The shock of coming back from a dynamic Far East to a decaying Europe played a role in my deciding to write *The Decline and Fall of Europe*. This book is also the result of discussions with people from different backgrounds and origins and of inspiration from scores of books and a great many newspaper and magazine articles from various countries, which gave rise to copious notes taken over the years, the authors of which I am deeply grateful to; I regret that they are too many to pay tribute to properly. Trying to make sense of all the material turned out to be like one of those games where you connect the dots and slowly see patterns emerging. I am no disgruntled former European government official nor a pessimist, and this pen is not guided by a chip on my shoulder, rage or ambition of any sort. I am not even sure I could be counted as one of the possibly many 'concerned European citizens'. I do however feel just enough of a European to be entitled, if not compelled, to say things the way I see them about where our continent is going.

Project Europe remains a noble and indispensable endeavour; yet Europe is clearly on the way down, assessed by any measure one cares to use. It is sinking into geopolitical irrelevance and impotence, and although the aggregate economies of the 27 countries of today's European Union (EU) still make it the world's foremost economic bloc, the quality of life our children will know will be inferior to the quality of life we have enjoyed in the past half-century, and their children's quality of life is likely to be even lower – mostly because of choices made by this generation and the one before. Europe is on the way down in absolute terms as well as in relative terms, compared with a rising Asia and even the US. Decline is bad enough, but that's not all. The one good thing about Europe, the unity carved out in the smouldering ruins of the Second World War that was supposed to put an end to centuries of conflict, cannot be entirely taken for granted any more, and, to make matters worse, the one item supposed to cement this unity once and for all, the euro, has turned out to be the single greatest threat to this unity. Where the responsibility lies is beside the point. Princeton's Bernard Lewis, world-renowned specialist of Islamic civilizations, is fond of reminding his readers that, following the fall of the last great Islamic civilizations and their eclipse by a rising Western world, many Muslims asked 'How did it happen? What went wrong?'.[6] To some extent they had decided to cling to their old ways while the birth of the modern world at their doorstep made them irrelevant. They didn't have the benefit of modern communications to help them realize what was going on;

perhaps they just didn't want to see what was happening around them. On the other hand, today's Europeans have been witnessing the decline of their civilization right in front of their eyes, like a series unfolding on a TV screen. We cannot say we didn't see it coming. Since Europe is the core subject of this book, it will be helpful to agree on what is intended by the word 'Europe'. The reader may be surprised to learn that I am at a loss to find a precise answer. But I am not alone in this predicament. To many, Europe is the collection of 27 nation-states that compose the EU today, together with a few more such as Switzerland. To the former European Commission President Jacques Delors, the EU is an 'unidentified political object'. To others, in particular those who reject the adhesion of Turkey to the EU, Europe is defined to a great extent by its common religious heritage, a club of Christian nations. For the Catholic Church, it is the Christian religion that defines and holds Europe together. To Bismarck, who united Germany in the nineteenth century, Europe was merely a 'geographical expression'. Others, spurred by the recent economic crisis and obvious regional economic divergences, speak of not one Europe, but two: a 'core' Europe made up of a few successful countries centred around Germany and a 'peripheral' Europe made up of the hapless rest. Some perceive Europe as a club of democratic countries with liberal economies; others refer to a shared Judeo-Christian, Greek and Roman historical heritage culminating in the Enlightenment and the Industrial Revolution; and so on. Last but not least, let's keep in mind that Jean Monnet, the true architect of Europe, said 'Europe has never existed; one has genuinely to create Europe'.[7] Since there only seems to be confusion surrounding the meaning of 'Europe', whenever the reader wonders about what is meant by it in this book, I shall politely refer him or her to what Humpty Dumpty told Alice in Lewis Carroll's *Through the Looking Glass*: 'When I use a word, it means just what I choose it to mean – neither more nor less.'

Since we've established that 'Europe' shall come to mean different things in the following chapters depending on the context, it may be useful to point out that, when Project Europe, the EU, immigration or geopolitical matters are discussed, Europe will, by and large, mean the whole of Europe; whereas, when reference is made to economic decline and impoverishment, Europe will mainly be intended to mean the southern part of the continent, the arch stretching from Portugal to Greece, but also comprising Ireland, France and the UK. This latter region is heading for a pretty rough ride, although we shouldn't underestimate the potential of other regions of Europe to end up in dire straits as well. Europe can be seen as a collection of heterogeneous states which have shared some history, geography, culture, and of course religion for a very long time, yet all have their own distinct character, speak different languages and have been fighting each other for centuries. About seven decades ago some wise men came up with the bright idea of intertwining their economies and other aspects of their lives to a point that made armed conflict among them 'unthinkable'. These different countries have nevertheless kept their different characters, and some, particularly in the continent's southern belt, are clearly in multidimensional decline, while others seem not in such bad shape after all, at least from an economic standpoint, and at least for the time being. So when we talk about European decline, it cannot be taken as a process going on at the same rate in all dimensions in all countries, but as something that may be happening more or less uniformly throughout the region in certain dimensions (such as geopolitical capabilities and relevance or even the problems of its new multiracial societies), but in a much more differentiated manner in others (such as economic growth or social well-being).

The argument of this book is that Europe has lost its mojo. It started well but has worked itself into a corner. It has embarked on a road of decline from which there is no return. It has become less than the sum of its parts. The socio-economic model it invented and saddled itself with, the so-called European model (which gave rise to what I label here the 'Civilization of Entitlements'), with its high social costs, rigid labour markets, overregulation and high taxes, when coupled with indifference to economic growth and unfavourable demographic trends turns out to be clearly unsustainable. In some countries the system generally acts as a choke to economic development and entrepreneurship that borders on disdain towards the creation of wealth – as if growth was a natural occurrence, a phenomenon that can be taken for granted or doesn't really deserve attention. In other countries, governments that have made dubious strategic choices find old remedies cannot be applied since their hands are now tied by appurtenance to the Eurozone, and come to the realization that it is 'game over' for them. When high taxes, in the absence of growth, are not enough to fund profligacy, inefficiencies and high social costs, the natural outcome, given adverse demographics, is that many European governments are de facto broke, or soon will be. Having been living beyond their means for a long time and become used to it, they find themselves burdened by unsustainable levels of budget deficits and debt. The shocks caused by the recent economic and banking crisis were amplified into the currency and sovereign debt crisis, which threatened to blow the entire system apart. Not only did the euro reveal its limits, but it turned into the biggest threat to the very Project Europe it was supposed to consolidate. Immigration, indispensable to make up for a declining population, has been so mismanaged across the continent that it planted the seeds of inter-community discord, the severity of which is bound to undermine social stability. The EU organization itself, plagued by inefficiencies and overregulation, has lost credibility, causing Project Europe to lose traction with the public. Necessity has been turned into a virtue with the advent of the soft power narrative, and whatever little power is left for Europe to wield on the geopolitical scene is turning softer by the day, melting like snow under the sun and cementing the continent's growing geopolitical irrelevance. What more signs do we need? The real disease of Europe is that it has learned to content itself with mediocrity. Consequently, Europe's destiny is to be prey to the forces of history instead of shaping them.

The choices that led Europeans to taking the path they chose were not inevitable; and in hindsight other choices could have been made. But the forces leading to these choices prevailed. There was not one precise decision, circumstance or event that led to this situation. Rather, it has been a cumulative process spread over time, all the more pervasive, insidious and inexorable. Civilizations, empires have their own life cycles; they come and go. In a historical sense there is nothing new in witnessing one more civilizational decline, except this one is happening right before our eyes, as earlier pointed out, and the reasons for it are unlike any other case. Yet it is not as if a catastrophe will hit Europe tomorrow morning or next year, or that you won't be able to enjoy sipping your Bordeaux or enjoying the coming new year's Eurovision concert. If you bought this book expecting to read that Europe will be falling down the precipice in a blink, anticipating horror stories, you may need to try for a refund from your bookstore. Things are, thank goodness, not that dramatic or colourful. Europe is rich. It has been forging ahead economically since the Industrial Revolution, and it comes as no surprise that a survey by *Forbes* magazine indicated that 70 per cent of the world's richest individuals are still found in Europe. If Europe has become so prosperous and peaceful it means that the European model works after all, or at least it worked for a while in the particular context of the decades immediately following the Second World War when Europe's GDP was growing at a rapid 5.5 per cent pace. Unfortunately the growth rarely topped 2 per cent after a couple of decades, and the model failed thereafter to adapt to the fundamental changes in local, regional and worldwide environments. As a consequence, what we are witnessing today is a process of inexorable decay, one that will take time – although it is not entirely impossible that the fall could come swifter than anyone might expect. The foul smell, the signs are already here, clear for us to see – if we care to open our eyes. The question is not what should be done to stop or reverse the process, for it is already too late. Europeans would never agree to the extraordinarily huge collective sacrifices and changes that would be needed to attempt a *real* reversal, assuming they were conscious of the need to do so and assuming a reversal was theoretically possible. More practically, one should rather wonder about the speed at which this decline will happen and what should be done to anticipate and manage its consequences, limiting the damage rather than being overwhelmed. But this sort of issue is for another book to address in appropriate detail. *The Decline and Fall of Europe* undertakes a brief journey of exploration to understand where Europe comes from, the causes and consequences of its broad multidimensional decline, and how we may be affected in the years to come.

The year 2005 was a watershed: it was the year in which Europeans citizens, asked for the first time (after Maastricht) to have a say on Project Europe by means of referendum votes on the so-called EU Constitution, rejected it en masse. It was a wake-up call for Project Europe, by which we shall mean the ambitious, historical and indispensable unification project launched by eminent and creative thinkers after the Second World War based on the idea that Europeans should find better things to do than to keep slaughtering each other. 2010 was another watershed year, the year in which the euro, the last brick on the edifice of Project Europe and its proud symbol par excellence, turned out to be in danger of causing Europe's demise. You will thus find frequent references to 2005 and 2010 in this book. I conclude by saying that I sincerely wish I shall be proven wrong and that this book will, in the end, turn out to be ridiculous. At least you'll have had a good laugh. Regrettably, the odds seem heavily stacked in my favour on this one.

ONE

THE RIGHT STUFF

How Europe was Created and the Good Things About It

Big guns and little islands

In order to understand the unique value of the political unity that post-Second World War Europe achieved in a short period of time and its appropriateness as a model for the rest of the world, let us start by turning our sights East, to what was going on in the People's Republic of China in mid-September 2010. Protesters had been gathering for days outside the Japanese embassy in Beijing and Japanese consulates in Shanghai and elsewhere. Tempers were flaring. This was not just because of the anniversary of the Japanese occupation of Manchuria in north-east China in 1931. Anti-Japanese feelings, always existing below the surface, saw their flame rekindled after the arrest of Chinese captain Zhan Qixiong, whose fishing boat collided with Japanese coastguard vessels in the waters surrounding a few islands the Japanese call Senkaku and the Chinese call Diaoyu (which mean the same thing, 'fishing islands'). These barren rocks, a few hundred kilometers west of Okinawa, are the object of territorial claims by both countries as well as by Taiwan. They were annexed by Japan in 1895 just before the end of the first Sino-Japanese war, as the Qing empire ceded Taiwan to Japan,[1] a move denounced as illegitimate in China. Chinese fishing boats based in the coastal waters of Fujian province facing Taiwan often operate as convenient substitutes for the Chinese Navy; so the Japanese Navy keeps a close eye on them. The row over these islands has been made all the more venomous by the close presence, a few hundred kilometres away, of the disputed Chunxiao gas field. In Shanghai and Beijing, Chinese protesters were shouting 'Get out of our islands!'. It was about old and new territorial disputes. More ominously, it was also about the 'peaceful' rise of China in the region.

A few generations after the end of Japanese occupation, you would think that people on both sides have no more need to reminisce about old conflicts. But the old ghosts have not been fully laid to rest. The fishing trawler incident was resolved peacefully, with Japan backing off and releasing the captain and his crew of 14; but this was only after it had triggered the most serious Sino-Japanese dispute in five years. This is just one among the many unresolved territorial and other disputes hanging like dark clouds over the prosperity this region recently acquired with hard work and thrift. There exist today many such disputes involving China, the region's rising power, and its neighbours: with Taiwan over its return to the motherland; with Vietnam, the Philippines and other Southeast Asian countries over the Spratly Islands (located near an international trade shipping route vital to China and Japan); with India over territory in the state of Arunachal Pradesh (it is worth remembering that the two countries fought as recently as in 1987, that an incident, albeit a minor one involving the Indian Navy and China, took place in July 2011 in international waters off Vietnam, and that India recently reinforced its military presence along the Tibetan frontier with China),[2] to name only a few examples.

In Southeast Asia, where national maritime boundaries are particularly complicated to define, many nations have been doubting China's 'peaceful rise' (*heping jueqi*) doctrine. China's traditional enemy Vietnam is one of these: with their last military fight having taken place as recently as 1979, Vietnam is irritated by Beijing's increasingly assertive claims over most of the South China Sea (which some Chinese officials recently seemed to upgrade to the status of a 'core' national interest of the same importance as Taiwan and Tibet).[3] Statements by Chinese military and civilian officials in early 2011 to the effect that China's sovereignty over the Spratly Islands is 'indisputable' and that China's permission was needed for hydrocarbon exploration, didn't help to calm the nervousness of the other claimants. These countries are, as expected, moving closer to the US, still the foremost Pacific power, as a counterweight to China; this prompts Beijing to feel that the US is trying to use other nations to encircle and contain it. Determining who is right and who is wrong is very difficult.

Yet China is by no means the only nation concerned with pending territorial disputes, and, while it looks for its own interests first, it has, by and large, been behaving as a status quo power rather than a revolutionary one intent on destabilizing the existing world order. India and Pakistan, which have fought three wars aggregating over 15,000 dead, are at odds over the province of Kashmir. There is now a nuclear dimension added to their antagonism. The infamous demilitarized zone separating the Stalinist dictatorship of North Korea from South Korea is a sad reminder of a conflict never formally resolved and which could ignite at any moment. Various military incidents took place in 2010, including the North's sinking of the *Cheonan*, a South Korean warship, and its firing of a deadly volley of artillery into a South Korean island, allegedly to get attention, with some more incidents a year later. The just-below-the-surface animosity between many Chinese and Japanese is only matched by that between many Koreans and Japanese. Farther south, the border between Cambodia and Thailand near Shiva's Preah Vihear temple, built by the Khmer a thousand years ago, is still the object of disputes involving both countries that recently saw exchanges of fire leaving people dead.[4] And Japan and Russia never signed a peace treaty ending the Second World War because of a territorial dispute over the Kurile islands, a dispute still simmering today as demonstrated by Russian President Dimitry Medvedev's well-publicized visit to the islands.

A regional arms race is quietly going on in East Asia, one that prompted the Stockholm International Peace Research Institute to point out that military expenditures increased by 71 per cent between 2000 and 2009.[5] This arms race shows no sign of abating: China's National People Congress approved a 12.7 per cent military spending increase in early 2011 and launched its first aircraft carrier, with two more commissioned, attesting to its desire to expand its power projection capabilities to back its growing clout. The race continues, with Malaysia having bought Franco-Spanish submarines, Indonesia getting Russian fighter jets, Japan, South Korea and Vietnam launching ambitious military programmes, and even Singapore launching its second Swedish attack submarine.[6] With its acquisition of power projection assets, including aircraft carriers and IL-78 airborne refuelling tankers, India is increasingly positioning itself as a power to be reckoned with in the Indian Ocean region, not only with its traditional foe Pakistan in its sights but, increasingly, China and the bases China has been building in an arch stretching from Myanmar to Pakistan. This general build-up, coupled with the uncertainty over China's own military expansion, means that the threshold for potential miscalculation by any party is dangerously lowered. Nationalist passions in this region can be rapidly rekindled and get out of hand. In the case of China, popular nationalism was in the recent past promoted by the authorities attempting to increase central legitimacy in the wake of dwindling communist ideological fervour; but the jinny is out of the bottle and the danger is that nationalism could take a life of its own, become uncontrollable and ignite a conflagration from which Chinese leaders may find it difficult to climb down in the face of a militant public opinion. Asia may be the one region of the world where economic development and miracle are one and the same word, a region that today, on the surface, appears peaceful. But when you consider these simmering disputes, add in the ingredients of a resurgent China, competition between China and India, throw in a weakening America and a greying Japan and a wide variety of political systems, you end up with an explosive mixture. Can economic interdependence alone really result in stable relations in this region? The jury is still out on this one.

But, you will rightly ask, why are we digressing so far from European shores?

An engine of peace

We have appeared to digress because of a question that relates to the essence of Project Europe itself: in the case of Asia, will China, Japan and other 'antagonists' find the wisdom and the resolution to bury the past forever as the Germans, French and other antagonistic Western European nations did after the Second World War? Samuel Huntington pointed out that

> In the late twentieth century Europe has been bound together by an extraordinary dense complex of international institutions: the European Union, NATO, Western European Union, Council of

Europe, the Organization for Security and Cooperation in Europe, and others. East Asia has nothing comparable except ASEAN, which does not include any major powers... in contrast to Western Europe, the seeds for conflict among states are plentiful in East Asia.[7]

Project Europe may contain serious flaws, but one virtue is undeniable and priceless: the locomotive of integration, central to Project Europe, so intertwined the economic and socio-political lives of countries it touched that armed conflict between them has truly become unthinkable. This is one of the rare instances in the history of the human race when swords have been turned into ploughs. For this alone Project Europe, as an ideology of peaceful integration, deserves the highest praise. This achievement, unique in the troubled history of mankind, is often forgotten by the generations of Europeans born after the Second World War. It has not been easy to come by. Project Europe is a child born of catastrophe, exhaustion, necessity and vision from the ashes of war. Its implementation required courage and wisdom. It is still work-in-progress and probably always will be. It may have many flaws, but has undeniably brought peace and prosperity.

Former Korean President Roh Moon Hyun saw Europe as a model for regional cooperation based on a community of law and a commonality of values, correctly capturing its essence as subjecting relations between sovereign states to rules. Could it be a model for regional integration anywhere else on the planet? A model for Asian integration for instance? Or is it unique to the circumstances of Europe? It may be argued that the only interest China, as the upcoming power in its region, may have in the EU is as a counterweight to the power of its American rival rather than as a model to emulate in its region. Or that China's true intention is to recover its historical position as the central regional power surrounded by tribute-paying vassals, a far cry from the integration model concocted by 'foreign devils'; or it may be that Asia will devise its own Project Asia. Geography, history and social, political and economic circumstances undeniably play an important role in such an endeavour. In Europe, the sheer proximity of countries, the sharing of so much history and conflicts, of so many borders and cultures, resulted in exasperatingly competing interests – though these very factors may have made possible such an unlikely undertaking in the first place, once the region had turned into a wreck of countries that were *all* exhausted and on their knees at the same time and had *all* finally had enough of war (and Uncle Sam was here to help tidy things up).

The geography and history of Asia are quite different. Some countries lie oceans away from others and share little in terms of history, culture and political-economic systems, some are on the way up; others are declining. These factors do not play in favour of such a common undertaking. The ascent of China (and to a lesser extent India), at a time of declining US and Japanese power, will inevitably lead it to assert this power one way or another at the expense of others, at the very least in terms of developing power projection capabilities to protect its interests abroad and along shipping lanes. In the economic sphere China is already quietly paving the way to turn most of Asia into a renminbi zone (renminbi is the Chinese currency, popularly known as the yuan). Intra-Asian trade is increasing by leaps and bounds, and the yuan is increasingly used between China and its regional trading partners (as well as with other countries such as Brazil). This raises the question of how long the US dollar will maintain its primacy in the region. Asian economic integration may, in a sense, increasingly look like that of Europe, but, if this is the case, it stems from different premises. Today's relative peace and integration under the American security umbrella and tomorrow's eventual Pax Sinica, amounting to integration of vassals under a Chinese umbrella or to a mere co-prosperity sphere, however peaceful it may turn out to be, have little to do with the core philosophy of the Project Europe model. There is no hint of an Asian Monnet or Schuman, as Yoon Young-Kwan, a former South Korean foreign minister pointed out.[8]

Beyond economic interests, the ideological underpinnings are not there. The twenty-first-century question for Asia will be whether it finds a peaceful way to accommodate competing ambitions based on an irreversible voluntary regional integration model such as a 'Project Europe with Asian Characteristics', or whether the seeds of instability will remain. For French geopolitical expert Dominique Moisi, there is no cause for alarm and the seeds of Asian instability are likely to remain just seeds:

> The rivalry among China, India and Japan will not shape the future of Asia as the rivalry among Great Britain, France, Russia and Germany shaped Europe (and the world) in the nineteenth and early twentieth centuries, nor will the Asians tear themselves to pieces through nationalistic warfare, as some Western commentators believe.[9]

In any case, Asians have nothing to lose by at least looking into the Project Europe model and its lessons. It is now time to take a closer look at the birth of modern Europe.

A dangerous place

To gain a better understanding of where the ideology of European integration came from we need to briefly dip our toes in the currents of history. As far back as can be recalled, Europe, as a region, was for much of the time a battleground between warlords, tribes, nations, states, powers and empires. The only time it has been 'politically united' was a couple of millennia ago under the Roman Empire. The empire anchored the region for centuries under its rule and imposed foreign-born Christianity as a common religion. Even 'barbarian' nations on the outer fringes of the empire such as the Germanic tribes beyond the Rhine or the Goths beyond the Danube existed to a certain extent in a symbiotic relationship with the empire, to which, when they were not fighting, they provided manpower for military and agricultural purposes; yet they too were eventually Christianized. The Roman Empire of the West fell with the deposition of the last Roman emperor, Romulus Augustulus, in 476, when Europe entered the Middle Ages. To facilitate its management, the empire had in the third century been divided into a Western Empire, centred on Rome, and an Eastern Empire, centred on Constantinople (Byzantium) – this latter continued for almost a thousand years. With the breakdown of the Western Empire, in the fifth century, Western Europe reverted to a collection of separate nations with different languages and aspirations, sharing only a recent religious and imperial past. No subsequent intra-European empire, even those carved out by Charlemagne with his Holy Roman Empire, Napoleon Bonaparte or the Habsburgs with their Austro-Hungarian Empire, came close to the Roman Empire in terms of European geographic coverage or duration, although some of these empires covered large areas outside Europe. The Great Schism of 1054 between the Roman Catholic Church and Constantinople's Eastern Orthodox Church split Europe along a cultural faultline running from the Aegean Sea up to the Baltic Sea. The Eastern Orthodox half of Europe was thereafter viewed by Western Europeans as an almost alien world. A piece of Europe was even lost to a foreign power from the East, the Ottoman Turks, who conquered Constantinople in 1453, took over the entire Roman Empire of the East and occupied large parts of today's Eastern Europe for centuries.

It is easy to take for granted the notion of 'countries', that is, modern nation-states, sovereign entities within their own well-delineated frontiers, distinct people with a distinct language, history and laws, represented by differentiated colours on maps. But it was not always like this. Historically, Europe went through the centuries with a never-ending succession of wars, conflicts, invasions, alliances and revolutions involving empires, kingdoms, principalities and city-states with frontiers that expanded and retracted. It experienced feudal times, warlordism and other eras in the process of getting nations built, wars between secular powers and conflicts involving or inspired by the papacy. It is said that the origins of the modern nation-state were first defined in the Treaty of Westphalia concluded at the end of the bloody Thirty Years War in 1648. Designed to rein in religious and other passions that had led to wars in Europe, the Treaty embedded the notion that a country was a sovereign entity entitled to well-defined frontiers and to do whatever it wanted internally. The notion of sovereign nation-states, taken for granted today, was a result of the dismemberment of empires, emerging from the fragments left in the wake of disintegration; and they turned out to be very efficient organizations, as we shall see below.

At the beginning of the twentieth century Europe was still, by and large, a mosaic of empires, principalities and other polities. The natural outcome was balance-of-power dynamics among various competing states. Countries constantly jockeyed to prevent any one from dominating. For any given nation the aim was to secure prominence, by force if necessary, at least to thwart the ambitions of rival powers, or simply to survive. This was, by definition, an unstable state of affairs, with no real order. A war was always waiting to happen. Europe became the stage for a ballet of brutal conflicts between nations, alliances established and broken, multinational empires born and dismembered, choreographed by ambitious visionaries. Nations were in frequent conflict with each other even while they were busy expanding their competing empires beyond Europe. In the nineteenth century, not content to fight wars only at home, European nations also fought abroad for the mastery of the world; the entire planet had turned into their battlefield. Nations such as France developed state-like identities and cohesion early on, while others, such as Italy or Germany, carried on as mosaics of city-states, principalities and other polities until relatively recently. Prussian statesman Otto von Bismarck subverted the affairs of Europe when he united a fragmented and weak Germany in the late nineteenth century, creating a country big enough in terms of size, population and industrial power to redefine Europe's balance of power forever. Sure enough, as this new Germany replaced France as the dominant power in Europe, the question of its place on the continent and of its containment became the foremost issue (especially to the French). Three wars took place between France and the new power of Germany in the eight decades preceding the birth of Project Europe, of which two became known as world wars because of their global dimension. The question of Germany's place in Europe is one that persists today.

No wonder that a region so fragmented has been a conflict zone. Territorial ambitions, religious conflict between Catholics and Protestants and rivalry among secular rulers carried the seeds of bloody wars. In modern times the situation became worse and worse. As Europe raced ahead of the rest of the world in industrialization and technological prowess in all sectors including the military, the extent of devastation brought on by conflicts, with entire societies and industries mobilized to fight, reached unprecedented levels. 'Never have so few been able to do so much harm to so many,' said British statesman Sir Winston Churchill. The 1870–71 Franco-Prussian War (which spurred Bismarck to create Germany) caused fewer than 200,000 deaths, while the First World War topped

8 million and the Second World War more than 40 million. These two world wars, the central issue of which was to keep German power in check, ended the various European colonial empires and the balance-of-power dynamics that had prevailed for centuries. Europe, which had dominated the world for five centuries, had now effectively committed suicide: the economic, military and geopolitical supremacy it enjoyed was now over. The First World War, a war that saw the end of several European empires and the birth of new independent nation-states, was followed by a short-lived liberal democratic impulse throughout Europe. Yet the efforts of the Société Des Nations (a precursor of the United Nations) to put an end to intra-European conflicts came to naught as Europe seemed intent on finding yet new ways to run itself to the ground. Conflicts in Europe entered a new dimension in the first part of the twentieth century as the totalitarian universal ideologies of fascism and national socialism on the right and communism on the left, powered by an ambition to remake the world according to their visions, were now driving entire nations. Never short of new ideas, Europeans had invented more reasons to be at each other's throats. Between them, the two dictators who epitomized the extremes of these European-born ideologies, Joseph Stalin and Adolf Hitler, caused the deaths of tens of millions people and untold damage in Europe and beyond. Europe had developed the means to devastate itself and the rest of the world and was not shy about using them. Due in great part to Europe, the earlier part of the twentieth century was the bloodiest period in the history of mankind.

It is easy to assume that the default setting for the political landscape of Europe is a blissful mosaic of peaceful liberal democracies. Of the three political ideologies Europe had produced in the twentieth century, the Second World War buried fascism, and the collapse of the Soviet Union eliminated communism, leaving in place democracy as the benign political ideology that defines today's Europe. Yet this was not entirely new. Europe had flirted with democracy before. The end of the First World War had brought about the elimination of an *ancien régime*, ushering in an era when liberal democracies flourished. This era was, however, to last no more than two decades as the Great Depression of 1920 started pushing governments to the right. The far right assumed power in Italy and Germany not by *coups d'état* or revolutions, but through elections. It is easy to forget that the Nazis rose to power in Germany backed by a massive electoral wave. 'National socialism,' wrote British historian Mark Mazower, 'fits into the mainstream not only of German but also of European history far more comfortably than most people like to admit...today, it is hard to see the inter-war experiment with democracy for the novelty it was: yet we should certainly not assume that democracy is suited to Europe.'[10] So if today's Europe, with its mixed economies, soft power and welfare state is your friendly neighbour, let's not forget that yesterday this Dr Jekyll was Mr Hyde.

Genesis

The vicious circle that had gripped Europe and turned it into a frequent battleground for a good part of the past two millennia was finally broken after the end of the Second World War. The crucial new element was the rise of the United States. America's involvement as a catalyst and sponsor of European unification would change the face of Europe forever. Now undeniably the world's foremost power, a rich and non-European giant of European origin towering over the smouldering ruins of Europe, America had decided that its interest and its heart was in rebuilding a strong Europe as a partner in its struggle against the Soviet Union. According to the new paradigm, intra-European rivalry had given place to American–Soviet rivalry. The pre-war structure of Europe had ceased to exist, with its dominant nation, Germany, cut in half as Europe became divided between East and West. This resolution of the 'German question' was not displeasing to all: some cold-blooded politician at the outset of the Second World War had said that it was better that Russia should dominate Eastern Europe than Germany dominate Western Europe. And the French statesman Charles de Gaulle was the prime opponent of a unified Germany.

America helped to rebuild Western Europe as a counterweight to Soviet ambitions and as a future economic partner. Vast sums of money were directed by the Americans to Europe's reconstruction through the Marshall Plan and other vectors, which were conditional on Europeans working together. American troops remained stationed in Europe as ultimate guarantors of intra-European peace as well as peace between Europe and the Soviet Union. America led the way to form the United Nations (UN), the International Monetary Fund (IMF) and the World Bank, and set the basis of a new world order and international financial system. The North Atlantic Treaty Organization (NATO) was established to cement an intra-European military alliance under American control, with the Soviet Union in its sights as a clear and present danger. With its aggressive instincts finally checked, and with its security outsourced to the US, Western Europe could now safely turn to the task of rebuilding itself under the American umbrella. The presence of American 'boots on the ground' in Europe was undeniably a critical ingredient of launching Project Europe: it was a security guarantee against German military resurgence inside Europe, and against the Soviet Union outside. Under these circumstances the nations of Western Europe had all the right incentives as well as the time to shift their energies into the reconstruction and economic spheres. Project Europe is to a great extent the child of a French desire to contain Germany (and also a later desire to create a counterweight to the US) and an American desire to contain the Soviet Union.

Immediately after the end of the Second World War Winston Churchill had advocated the creation of a United States of Europe centred on a partnership between France and Germany. The eighteenth-century Austrian statesman Klemens von Metternich had spoken of Europe as one single integrated republic that could be achieved by the cooperation of the various states, an idea far ahead of his time. In the twentieth century, visionaries comprising intellectuals, politicians and business leaders, informally known as the European Movement, started to advocate the unification of Europe, with the active support of America. The stage was set for the next and most important step. Rivalry between France and Germany had been at the origin of recent European conflicts and it is only fitting that the last nail planted in the coffin of intra-European conflicts should have been hammered in by a genial French economist, Jean Monnet. Monnet was not one to pay much attention to grand talk of political union in Europe, an idea that was floated but didn't gain much support at the time. His approach was far more practical and subtle. To conduct modern warfare governments needed quantities of coal and steel and the ability to mobilize and control these industries. Take away the power for any given government to unilaterally commandeer these resources and you permanently emasculate the threat. That is precisely what Monnet set out to do in the early 1950s. The solution proposed was clever: coal and steel production from both countries was brought under the purview of the European Coal and Steel Community, a supranational organization (comprising France, Germany, Italy, Belgium, the Netherlands and Luxembourg) that functioned on the basis of cooperation between France and Germany and which Monnet came to head. Monnet drafted the 9 May 1950 declaration read by French Foreign Minister Robert Schumann and which contained words such as 'War between France and Germany would become not only merely unthinkable but materially impossible.' The Schumann Declaration, signed by France and Germany, made one thing clear: there were no plans or blueprints; this was to be a step-by-step process. Europe was to be work in progress *ad aeternam*. The process of cooperation was seen as more important than where this cooperation would lead to. The text of the Schumann Declaration made it clear that 'Europe will not be made all at once, or according to a single, general plan. It will be built through concrete achievements, which first create a de facto solidarity.' Monnet was only too aware that an openly political agenda would be resisted by nation-states but that a process of myriad incremental agreements binding these countries in growing day-to-day ties would sail through – death of sovereignty by a thousand cuts. Apart from Monnet and his associates in the European Movement, early visionaries such as Germany's first post-war chancellor, Konrad Adenauer, or the Italian Alcide de Gasperi shared the mantra that nation-states would not need to be done away with: countries would continue to function as countries, but they would have to work together. France and Germany, the main powers of continental Western Europe, were now 'forced' to cooperate. They would share a common interest in Project Europe.

This was the beginning of an irreversible process of more and more integration and cooperation in a variety of sectors, a process still at work today. The rationale for the integration of the continent by means of harmonization of tariffs, commercial practices and other measures was naturally attractive to all. A sense of common purpose was born, resting on the foundation of a gradualist programme.

After the advent of the coal and steel pact, Project Europe took on a life of its own. The Treaty of Rome was signed in 1957 by the six founders of the coal and steel pact, only 12 years after the end of the Second World War, creating the European Economic Community (EEC), which established a common customs union that would serve as a foundation on which greater unity would be built and committing European countries to seek an 'ever closer union'. The ideology of integration and enlargement was born. What started as a series of negotiations between sovereign countries took off with the federalist impulse of the 1980s. The web was made tighter with an endless succession of treaties and agreements. The 1992 Maastricht Treaty, for instance, established the European Union (EU) as successor of the EEC, effectively heralding the advent of a single market with the free flow of capital, goods and people, and paved the way for the euro single currency. In a further blow to the sovereignty of nation-states (something which always pleases Brussels's Eurocrats), Maastricht recognized a few hundred 'regions' throughout Europe that would obtain direct representation in Brussels.

Project Europe inherently intruded into areas of sovereignty these countries had previously jealously guarded, but the new buzzword for these 'postmodern states' was cooperation. They had decided they had had enough of empires, wars and conquests, and that interdependence would henceforth remove any security threats from within Europe. The only existential threat from outside Europe was from the Soviet Union, but this was now handled by a US-led NATO, with the added benefit that Germany would no longer be compelled to keep its own large armies from fear of France and Russia. A military resurgence of Germany was thus naturally prevented. European countries came to redefine themselves as part of a broader Western construct anchored by the US and NATO instead of as individual rival entities. Ironically, Europe's stability and prosperity owes a lot to the Soviet Union. The Cold War divided Europe in two, and life in the Soviet-dominated half was certainly no fun. But the Cold War meant that Western Europeans were united by a clear and present danger and could cooperate to an extent they had never done before, under the safety of the American security umbrella. The French President François Mitterrand had said of the order imposed by the Cold War that it was 'an unjust order, but it was an order'.[11] The New World Order ushered in and guaranteed by America in the aftermath of the Second World War, coupled with the ideas of Jean Monnet and other visionaries, brought Western Europe in the course of the following few decades to a level of material and social prosperity and peace that the continent had not previously dreamed of. Necessity had been turned into a virtue and Project Europe became a fully fledged ideology, a model, a new recipe to link modern democratic liberal nation-states into a prosperous collective system. Participating nations gave up important aspects of their sovereignty and accepted that their lives should become increasingly entangled with the other member states; in exchange for this they could share in the panacea of long-term peace and prosperity. This was no dream, this was tangible reality, and Europe became a continent of peace and the world's foremost economic power. Today, the combined economies of the EU's 27 members exceed that of the US by more than a trillion euros.

Project Europe and its promise of never-ending peace and prosperity gained more and more allure, to the point of turning into an irresistible magnet for nations at the periphery of Western Europe that has led to the challenging enlargement process witnessed in recent years, particularly after the break-up of the Soviet Union. Everybody in the neighbourhood wanted to be in. By the end of 2010 Project Europe had absorbed 27 countries, with additional applicants waiting in the wings. The lure of membership to this club of wealthy democracies was too much for nations at the periphery to resist after they were freed from the Soviet grip, and is undeniably a force for evolutionary change for the better. Applicants have to review their systems, abandon nationalist ambitions, turn into real democracies governed by freely elected politicians and the rule of law, improve their governance and reform in a 'good' sense if they want to join the club. Olli Rehn, EU Commissioner for Enlargement, stressed that 'Enlargement is one of the EU's most powerful policy tools: it exemplifies the essence of the EU's "soft power", or the power of transformation, which has helped to transform countries to stable democracies and more prosperous societies, with higher levels of economic development and social welfare.'[12] American columnist Roger Cohen labelled Project Europe the most compelling and transformative of the last half-century.[13] The Project has doubtlessly acted as a locomotive, pulling countries in the right direction in terms of human rights, democracy and the rule of law.

We've never had it so good

Growth and well-being became the creed of Europe. Article 1 of the Organisation of Economic Co-operation and Development (OECD) established in 1961 declared that the organization's objective was 'to achieve the highest sustainable economic growth and employment and a rising standard of living in member countries'. This was Europe's new raison d'être, and it worked. In the first few decades after the Second World War Europe underwent a period of sustained and unprecedented economic growth which transformed the continent. As rising prosperity became a way of life and full employment the default position, layer upon layer of entitlements and benefits piled up, but high growth made them affordable. Europe got busy building the welfare state while America was busy building the national security state.

Let us take stock: an entire continent has, in the space of just two generations, reinvented itself, morphed from a battlefield zone to a land of blissful peace and prosperity. Sir Winston Churchill aptly summarized what had been taking place: 'We are asking the nations of Europe between whom rivers of blood have flowed to forget the feuds of a thousand years.'[14] Throughout Europe, in the past half-century, quality of life indicators such as per capita income, life expectancy and the average holiday time steadily rose to the world's highest levels. Europe is number one in the world in terms of economic size and comes just after the US in terms of per capita income. Europe is rich. Project Europe has delivered the goods, and many agree that one would be at a loss to find a place on the planet where quality of life, in quantitative and qualitative terms, is better.

It reminds me of the time when, as a student, I took off on a summer holiday, a low budget backpacking trip, criss-crossing Europe armed with my student rail pass, a foldable tent and just enough money to buy food, necessities and to cover camping fees. Every time I crossed a frontier (and there were many in Europe) I had to show my passport and find a place to change cash – lira, drachma, franc, kroner, peseta . . . The same student today would not even need to carry his passport – he would just have euros in his wallet, and that would work for most of his trip. A small step for a student, a giant step for companies and businesses. The free flow of goods, capital and people throughout most of the continent is a reality. Business thrived in the process, creating the world's largest free trade zone with 2.5 trillion euros in 2008 intra-European trade. We are still far away from America's homogeneous market in terms of language, regulations and opportunities, but also quite far away from the frontiers of the past. On the geopolitical chessboard Europe may have become emasculated, renouncing ambitions and hard power, it may remain firmly anchored in the camp led by the US, but it has, by and large, become an independent force for good and stability in the world, one that promotes peace and is the world's largest aid donor with 53.8 billion euros in 2010 (more than half the world's total official aid) – an achievement not to be ashamed of.

The reader will have surmised by now that this book is not in the least extent intended to be an indictment of Project Europe. Project Europe and the EU have received heavy doses of criticism from many quarters over the years, some founded, a good deal unfair. As an ideology based on peaceful and willing regional integration, the goal of which is to create long-term peace and prosperity, as an engine promoting the free flow of goods, money and people across the continent, Project Europe undeniably remains a necessary and noble cause. It may be an experiment, it may be work-in-progress, it may carry substantial flaws, it may not make everybody happy all the time, but there is no denying that it has brought significant benefits.

If Europe faces inexorable decline and impoverishment today, it is not due to Project Europe or the ideology behind it. Rather, the seeds of this misfortune have been planted by a series of broad, dismal socio-political choices made by European countries, their leaders and their citizens during the past decades. Particularly in the southern part of the continent it is as if Europeans have been just as busy creating wealth and prosperity with one hand as they have been busy planting the seeds of their destruction with the other. The origin of these unfortunate choices has nothing to do with the ideas of Monnet and Schumann and everything to do with the mentality and shortcomings of modern Europeans in general, as we shall see in the following chapters. Monnet never said the French should work only 35 hours per week or should send 15-years-old children to the barricades to protest against raising the retirement age from 62 to 65. Monnet and Schumannn had nothing to do with the excesses of the Civilization of Entitlements that has bankrupted most of Europe or with the causes of today's Eurozone crisis. It is granted that the uniformization implicit in Project Europe may have helped accelerate the dissemination and institutionalization of some of these choices, but Project Europe itself was not the original driver behind them.

Bye bye Hobbes, hello Kant

Mark Leonard, author of *Why Europe Will Run the 21st Century*,[15] recognizes that, while the birth of the EU may have owed a lot to America, Europe went its quiet way to bring about something Americans had not foreseen: a revolution in the essence of what power is, what he calls 'transformative power', which he considers as important a development as the advent of the nation-state. For Leonard, clinging to an outdated definition of power leads many to conclude that Europe is weak when in fact it is not. Europe transcends classical definitions of power and moves on to the idea of a community of nations based on the rule of law. The power of Europe, according to this line of thought, is not in conquering or dominating anything but in transforming the countries it touches for the better because they want to be included, which is what has actually been happening at the periphery of Europe with the enlargement process. Europe is and can be an agent of positive transformation in the world.

To Jeremy Rifkin, author of *The European Dream*, Project Europe represents 'a beacon of light in a troubled world',[16] a true revolution, nothing less than the birth of a new type of economic system and government that is 'as different from market capitalism and the modern territorial state as the latter were from the feudal economy and dynastic rule of an earlier era'.[17] Contrasting the European Dream with the American Dream, he finds the American Dream an 'old dream . . . too centred on personal material advancement and too little concerned with the broader human welfare to be relevant in a world of increasing risk, diversity, and interdependence',[18] and the European Dream a new paradigm 'with its emphasis on inclusivity,

cultural diversity, universal human rights, quality of life, sustainable development, and peaceful coexistence'.[19]
In 2005 American journalist T. R. Reid was considering Europe as a 'second superpower that can stand on equal footing with the United States',[20] and ventured to say that 'the Euro was specifically designed to challenge the global hegemony of the US dollar',[21] and that 'in the twenty-first century, the rules that run the global economy are largely Brussels's rules.'[22]

Whether or not one subscribes to these messianic views, one can only agree with Leonard's view that this is the first time ever that a great power has arisen without others joining forces to oppose it; this is due to the fact that Europe is perceived not as a state but as a sort of benevolent community or network.

How deep is your love?

Bringing European countries together is something that would have been unthinkable a century ago. Transforming this fragmented continent into a single market was one of the greatest market-opening endeavours ever undertaken, even if much work still needs to be done. It took several wars and the complete exhaustion of the continent to get there, and it was done against the odds of clashing histories. The end of the Cold War and the fall of the Soviet Union in 1989 (a cataclysmic but mostly peaceful event which few had predicted) and the end of terror-induced stability spelled the end of balance-of-power dynamics and imperial ambition by powers on the continent. European empires within Europe had cut across nationalities, and it had been a constant throughout European history that, whenever an empire crumbled, nationalisms were revived and with them intolerance of minorities. The fall of the Soviet Union was no exception and had the effect of bringing back to the surface in its former zone of influence the old nationalisms. Countries and nationalities suddenly seemed to emerge from the fog of long-forgotten Eastern Europe. Yugoslavia was an example of a state that disintegrated, leading to conflict and ethnic cleansing in Croatia and Bosnia, and in Bosnia between Serbs and Muslims. Yet the most important consequence of the fall of the Soviet Empire in relation to the equilibrium in Europe was the reunification of Germany, which brought the German question back to centre stage. Pessimists would side with those speaking of a 'return of history' and a revival of Europe's old demons and nationalisms, and optimists with Francis Fukuyama, who had spoken of the 'end of history' in the sense of a democratic future by default. Which would it be?

Moved by self-interest, nation-states have generally been efficient constructs when marshalling a country's resources and energies and mobilizing its society. Nation-states are naturally reluctant to relinquish sovereignty or to put the interest of other nations or of a club of nations before their own narrow self-interest. But that is precisely what Project Europe has been asking them to do. The EU is the most radical example of a pervasive 'de-sovereignization' trend among nations that has been gaining momentum worldwide in the past 50 years. As the world is getting 'flatter', nations have become increasingly linked to each other, collapsing distance, through the explosion of trade and globalization, a web of international non-governmental organizations, instant communications and other 'stickiness factors' such as world public opinion. Interdependence means that a country will suffer if it finds itself suddenly marginalized by the 'system'. Anything happening in or done by a country can be instantly seen or perceived by the rest of the world, live, on TV. Any government acting unilaterally to the detriment of others will rapidly feel the wrath of many other nations and find itself penalized. No country, except for a few pariahs voluntarily living outside the system such as North Korea, can enjoy for long the advantages of being part of the international system if it flaunts the rules. The independent, self-contained nation-state that the world used to know has been gradually losing its sovereignty and giving way to a new type of nation-state that depends on others for its well-being and is forced to play by certain rules.

Project Europe may have its flaws, but as I will continue to point out, it has delivered peace and prosperity to a continent in which conflict was the default setting for centuries. In such an endeavour the forces of integration have always to contend with centrifugal forces, and there is no knowing how serious are the Eurozone challenges that are currently confronting European countries and will confront them tomorrow and whether they will succeed in pulling some of them away from the Project. The danger is that, as time goes by, things be taken for granted. Success and prosperity may lead to complacency and make Europeans forget what it has taken to arrive at this point and what the alternative could be. Difficulties may breed resentment and make some European nations think they can do better by themselves. The euro crisis is the perfect example of such a danger.

First, things could be taken for granted on the political integration front. We may think that conflict among today's nations of Europe is unthinkable – one cannot, for instance, imagine Germany invading France and Germans enjoying the beaches on the Côte d'Azur and sitting outside at cafés in the Champs-Elysées as if they were theirs anyway. And although one can imagine instability and conflict at the periphery of Europe, in the Balkans, this would be unlikely to represent a serious threat to Europe itself. Today's invasions within Europe are the work of tourists. Yet we should not forget that peace on this continent is only about seven decades old. This is a very short time, a drop in the ocean compared with the centuries of conflict that the continent has endured. But it is long enough for old rivalries and nationalism to come back to the surface should Europeans be confronted by very serious challenges that make them forget the reasons why such people as Churchill and Monnet launched Project Europe in the first place. Populist and nationalist politicians are always waiting in the wings of history for the proper occasion to rouse crowds. It has happened before, and it can happen again.

Secondly, there is a risk of matters being taken for granted on the economic front as well. Problems related to the differences in Euro-zone economies and to the accumulation of unsustainable amounts of debt and deficits were boiling below the surface during the relative calm of most of the first decade of the new millennium. These problems exploded, unleashing forces that threaten the entire European structure. It is undeniable that, despite the strides made towards integration, individual countries still place their own narrow interests ahead of the collective good when push comes to shove. They may some day forget that a good deal of the prosperity they are enjoying today came as a result of the free flow of goods, money and people inherent in Project Europe. Hard times may push countries to look inwards and revive the spectre of protectionism. Paul Krugman reminds Westerners in general that 'Our grandfathers lived in a world of largely self-sufficient, inward-looking economies, but our great-great grandfathers lived, as we do, in a world of large-scale international trade and investment, a world destroyed by nationalism . . . so, can things fall apart again? Yes.'[23] Such tendencies are bound to be reinforced as Project Europe loses popularity and legitimacy (as we shall see in later chapters). Recent upheavals within the Eurozone have led several 'peripheral' countries to ponder loud and clear the opportunity of leaving the Monetary Union in order to be free from the shackles of the single currency; that is, to return to their own currency and devalue it to gain the competitive edge they are unable to obtain from the structural reforms they have been avoiding. Talk of leaving the euro is not new, despite the Monetary Union being like the Roach Motel: you can get in but you can't get out. Should a country leave the euro, or should the cost of keeping this union together become unsustainable for the larger economies (such as Germany), or should a two-tier euro economy develop, it could very well lead to an unravelling of Project Europe, or at least many of its components. The German question, for one, would be back on centre stage. Will the balance of power painstakingly put together after the Second World War to contain Germany survive these tensions?

Europeans would be remiss to take Project Europe for granted. The question is, then, what is the true default setting for Europe? Is it the centuries-old way, with its never-ending conflict-prone rivalries or the new way, just decades old, with the EU acting as a glue that keeps countries interdependent? Is Project Europe truly irreversible? As Europeans grow disillusioned by the Project's limitations, frustrated by its encroachments, as they get spoiled by a prosperity that now seems to be a given, as crisis after crisis comes and they feel their jobs threatened, there is a risk that the lessons of history and the original ideals behind Project Europe be forgotten, that forces hostile to it take the upper hand and old rivalries re-emerge. Former French president Valéry Giscard d'Estaing pragmatically pointed out that people's passions could not be roused for something that is 50 years old. Should such hostile forces predominate, one could envision many scenarios, including one where the first to lose interest in Project Europe might be the 'Great Powers', with Germany increasingly looking East, the UK instinctively reaching across the Atlantic and France towards the Mediterranean. Given such fragmentation, the EU nations of Eastern Europe would probably want to strengthen their security relations with the US, possibly involving the UK as a conduit, unless they decide to throw in their lot with Germany and Russia. Europe would be ripped apart. While not entirely implausible, such a scenario remains far-fetched. There seems to be a consensus that Europe is better off being European than not. Moreover, Project Europe is probably so advanced already and the nations involved so interdependent and symbiotically related that backtracking is simply not feasible in practical terms. All evidence points to Project Europe having become today an integral part of the modern landscape of the continent, likely to remain so in the long term, for better or for worse. In the aftermath of the disastrous 2005 popular referenda that said 'No' to the proposed European Constitution, former German Chancellor Helmut Schmidt said: 'the fact that so many diverse citizens and cultures have combined to create a union of their own free will and without violence is a unique achievement in world history'.[24] Yet complacency should not set in and vigilance is no luxury. The peace and prosperity brought by Project Europe are precious: maintaining them requires unyielding attention and sacrifices, particularly as the environment becomes increasingly challenging. A return to the past, even partial, is not an impossibility and could have disastrous consequences for the continent and for the world. Undeniably there are forces today pulling Project Europe apart. Such forces ironically originate for the most part in the success of a Project Europe that seems to have gone too far too fast, an issue we shall turn our attention to in the following pages.

TWO

ARE THERE ANY EUROPEANS IN EUROPE?

The limits of Project Europe's acceptance by Europeans

The wake-up call

The only thing that should have caused 29 May 2005 to be a little different from any other sunny and lazy Sunday in France's seasonal march towards the long summer holiday period is that it was Mother's Day. One thing is sure though: few people are likely to remember it as Mother's Day. What this particular Sunday will be remembered for is that it was the day French citizens kicked Project Europe in the teeth by shouting a loud *'Non'* to the so-called European Constitution that had finally been submitted to popular referendum after a long period of gestation and heated debate among EU members. The French didn't care in the least that the Constitution they rejected with so much gusto had been written by Valéry Giscard d'Estaing, a former French President (technically the term *constitution* was incorrect since Europe is not a country, the document was in fact a *treaty* among nations). Adding insult to injury, another popular referendum, held in Holland, resulted in yet another rejection a few days later. Together these constituted a knock-out victory for 'No'. The British, sensing there was no particular need to court embarrassment, wisely let it be known they wouldn't proceed with the referendum they had planned to hold. Popular enthusiasm with Project Europe had taken a hit. UK Foreign Secretary Jack Straw's statement 'the European Union does now face a period of difficulty' may very well be remembered as the understatement of the year.[1] The 'No Debacle', as it became known, turned 2005 into a watershed year in European politics.

This was not just an isolated case of Eurofatigue gripping jaded old-timers by now tired of the EU 'thing'. A year earlier, in the summer of 2004, elections for the EU parliament recorded the lowest turnout ever (under 45 per cent), and the lowest of the lowest didn't come from the old-timers but from new members of the club – the 10 Eastern European countries that had joined the 15-member EU club in May 2004 after being freed from decades of Soviet subjugation following the fall of the Berlin Wall. The newcomers couldn't care less about the EU just one month after they had joined. Dublin, where the ceremony marking admission of these new members took place, was filled with Europhoric crowds in May: just a month later these same people didn't even bother to go vote for the EU Constitution. Was this a case of apathy, which historian Arnold Toynbee defined as the penultimate stage of civilizational decadence? Another hint that something was not quite right came a few months later from a TV interview of Giscard d'Estaing who commented (as head of the Convention that would write the Constitution), that all would be well because 'French logic' would be applied to drafting the document. That Giscard assumed that today's France was still the France of Descartes and of 'la grandeur' could be seen as amusing. That Europe had selected the most pompous (or, shall we say, aristocratic) of its former heads of state to carry out the job was not necessarily a harbinger of doom. What was, surely, a bad sign was that the person in charge of writing the treaty that was supposed to cement the (then) 25-country union was still thinking in nationalistic terms. Unable to bring himself to say '*European* logic', he had said instead '*French* logic'. Giscard could be forgiven for the lapse. Like any other good schizophrenic European, he was sincerely in love with Project Europe in broad philosophical terms but had said that it would take at least 20 years before the EU would speak with a single voice. This meant that, in the meantime, he would always first identify himself and his interests with those of his home country. Yet, if the man in charge of writing the European Constitution is not European first of all, we are hardly starting on the right foot.

In a more general sense, the No Debacle was symptomatic of a growing malaise within the nations of Europe that went beyond Project Europe and covered many areas. This was not really surprising: a year before, the French daily *Le Monde* had pointed out that 'The governments of the 25 members lack enthusiasm for the European project'.[2] Some grievances directly related to the Project while others had little to do with it and were just frustrations over home-grown problems inside the countries themselves. A common grievance cutting across country lines was the perception that their destinies increasingly depended on important decisions taken by faceless EU bureaucrats, these Eurocrats operating outside the countries' internal political systems. Another source of EU-related concern was the standardization of ways of life throughout Europe – inherent to the integration project – the side effects of which included a dilution of national identity and sovereignty, of certain competitive advantages and national characteristics. Others were concerned that the protective social model they had become accustomed to was being threatened by the process of EU enlargement as more liberal-minded economies joined in. Others still were worried about immigration and the EU letting Turkey, a poor country of 70 million Muslims, join the club. The Netherlands voted No partly because of its frustration, as the largest per capita contributor to the EU budget, with the propensity of the 'Great Powers', France and Germany, to indulge in profligacy, ignore the rules of the Eurozone's Stabilization Pact and generate deficits over the agreed 3 per cent limit whenever it suited them. Some voted No fearing a general erosion of jobs not specifically related to Project Europe. Any excuse was good for people to vent frustrations now that they had been given the chance.

Project Europe has never been a bed of roses, and in a sense Europe was used to hearing *No*. In fact, Project Europe had collected countless *No*s in various languages over the years. The French had said *non* to British demands to join Project Europe in the 1960s; Denmark had at first said *nej* to the Maastricht Treaty in 1992; and another *nej* to the euro eight years later. The Irish said No to the 2001 Treaty of Nice; not to be undone by the Danes, the Swedish added their own *nej* to the euro in 2003. Yet this new collective *No* had deeper implications, as we shall see.

An embarrassing piece of paper

Where the American constitution is a short, inspiring piece of writing which put fire in the belly of a newborn nation and inspired it to rapidly become the most powerful on earth, the 2005 European Constitution was a 265-page monument of legalese containing almost 500 Articles.[3] It was the epitome of arcane bureaucratic thought, as inspiring a reading as a telephone directory. Former German Chancellor Helmut Schmidt said of this labyrinth: 'not one of the 25 foreign ministers and 25 heads of government today has a complete grasp of these texts .... they are an exemplary illustration of bureaucratic chaos'.[4] To be fair, this document was not supposed to make people thump their hearts and sing the European anthem (there is indeed a European anthem, straight from Beethoven's Ninth Symphony, the part featuring a poem from Schiller). It was intended to be a rules book, a treaty among various nations pertaining to a club and written by Eurocrats after years of give-and-take negotiations. 'The Constitution was supposed to provide clarity to some of our organizational problems,' said Schmidt. The aim had been to define the detailed rules governing the day-to-day affairs of a 25-nation club, give it a president, a foreign minister and, in pure democratic tradition, a voting system based on population size. As such it would inevitably turn out to be complex and arcane and, apart from a few inspired specialists, not a single EU citizen was really supposed to understand or identify with this technical document. Yet, with the EU intruding more and more into the lives of its member states, this document was intended to regulate many aspects of the life of the average EU citizen.

As an experienced politician Giscard recognized that European leaders had done a poor job at selling Project Europe to the Europeans. A '*Oui*' could have been secured by bypassing the people and having the Constitution ratified by the French parliament (controlled by the party of then President Jacques Chirac) instead of risking a popular referendum. As a very good politician he could not resist hinting the *Non* had not been so much a rejection of the Constitution (written under his purview) as a rejection by French voters of the government of his former rival, Chirac. Giscard was right on one point at least: in France and Holland, where the Constitution had been submitted to a popular referendum, it was flatly rejected, whereas in Spain and Germany, where it had been submitted to parliamentary approval, it was ratified. Tactically, approval of such a complex document should have been left to parliamentary politicians, and, where it was not, the people, who could not be expected to read or make sense of the document, seized the opportunity of the vote to deride their own governments and an ever-intruding EU and to express their frustrations with anything that they didn't like in connection with Europe and life in our world in general. Incidentally, the only time Europeans had been asked for their collective opinion on European matters was with regard to the Maastricht Treaty in 1992: it is interesting to note that this treaty, which ushered in institutional reforms and paved the way for the euro, was rejected by two Danish referenda and was only narrowly ratified in other countries. But political shenanigans were now beside the point. What Giscard and most of the European political class could not understand was the extent of the chasm separating the political elites of the EU from the common people when it came to European matters. In this respect the No Debacle could be seen as a necessary pause in a process that had got out of hand and would, it was hoped, usher in a healthy debate about where Project Europe was heading. Needless to say, Eurocrats went back to the drawing board, but even in its watered down version the Constitution, now morphed into Plan B, or the Treaty of Lisbon, tailor-made to avoid embarrassing referenda, was rejected by Ireland, this time in 2008. It took one more year of negotiations and watering down before it was finally agreed.

The forgotten people

Contrary to what one may think, Project Europe did not start as a grassroots project. After the Second World War people were busy reconstructing their lives and countries. They had more pressing things on their minds than paying attention to lofty pan-European ideals. Project Europe was effectively the brainchild of political elites who went on developing it on their own, an endeavour separated from the common people's daily lives and even from the internal political lives of the individual countries. Much has been said in hindsight about Project Europe's 'democratic deficit'. People were aware that strides towards European integration were being made; they understood and approved the broad ideology behind Project Europe, which they instinctively perceived as being something good that would make their lives easier. Eurocratic political elites instinctively felt that there was no overwhelming necessity to make an effort to 'sell' the Project to the people or to involve them in its development, because people were instinctively in favour of it in any event and its complex development was a matter for politicians and technocrats in their ivory towers. The people of Europe were not really involved in the making of Europe.

Gradually, however, people's perception of Project Europe began to change. The more the Project turned into reality, the more it produced a plethora of new rules and regulations impacting on daily lives. It didn't help that Eurocrats (whom I venture to also call Eurognomes) were carried away with regulatory zeal, going so far as to impose rules about the curvature of imported bananas or the size of condoms. And we are not talking about just a few laws and rules here and there: almost 40 per cent of all laws introduced in any given country in Europe originated one way or another in Brussels since that country became part of the Union. They were not the outcome of national political debates, the result of give-and-take democratic processes people were used to in their own countries. They came, instead, top down, from Brussels-based faceless Eurognomes, a source of power and laws that was increasingly looking alien, disconnected from people's daily lives and needs. Further, Eurognomes vested themselves with privileges such as high and tax-free salaries, chauffeur-driven cars, subsidized apartments and similar perquisites, privileges that would not endear them to the people and would exacerbate the disconnect, especially in times of austerity. These rules and regulations were made for *all* citizens of *all* countries but were endorsed by *none*. Nor did it help that, with the process of enlargement resulting in the EU gobbling up country after country, with no end in sight, the whole thing smacked of having got out of hand. To the people it started to feel like unwelcome interference and diktat emanating from a 'foreign' entity out of control, operating from a parallel political universe in Brussels. Former British Prime Minister Tony Blair said, in the aftermath of the No Debacle: 'The crisis is about the failure of Europe's leaders to reach agreement with the people of Europe about the issues that concern them.'

This issue goes to the core of Project Europe and its limits. The EU is not a country or a state. There is no such thing as the United States of Europe. The EU remains today a heterogeneous 'club' of 27 nations who decided to link their destinies and share many things but who never agreed to give up their sovereignties or identities altogether. No politician in Europe can claim to have a cross-border constituency and speak for more than one country. The constituencies of European politicians are limited to their own home turf, which means that the interests a European politician promotes remain more often than not narrowly nationalistic, even when he or she is seconded to Brussels and directly involved in Project Europe, as happens from time to time in their careers. In truth, there is no such thing as a 'European politician' or a European leader of any stature. It started to dawn on people that decisions taken in Brussels were impacting on their own countries' socio-economic fabrics from job creation to enlargement, from immigration to other fundamental issues. Nothing illustrates better the disconnect between national and European politics and the ambivalence today's Europeans feel about Project Europe than the 2010 election, for the first time, of a president (and a foreign minister equivalent) of the EU. The candidacy of Tony Blair as president never had a chance: I met him in Singapore, where he came across as brilliant, charismatic and independent. He had his own ideas. Paris and Berlin (and London) would never condone a strong EU presidency where the centre could challenge their national interests or turn into an alternative centre of power. Instead, it was Herman Von Rompuy, a capable but perfectly grey and faceless career bureaucrat who likes to take his holidays in a eleventh-century Benedictine monastery in Belgium and write Japanese haiku poetry, a man few people in Europe had heard of before (other than in Belgium perhaps, where he was prime minister for less than a year), who in November 2009 was sworn in as the EU's first president. But that is precisely who the major capitals wanted at the helm of the EU: grey bureaucrats with no political power or following, 'reassuringly dull' as a British politician put it. And who can blame them? The last thing the elected heads of government in Europe's 27 countries, in particular the larger ones, want, is a challenge from Brussels. The EU is to continue being a supranational bureaucracy whose authority will remain limited by the national interests of the 'Big Powers'.

Last in first out

It may be seen as understandable that, given the chance in 2005, the old-timers, the nations that originally drove the Project, would decide it was time to slow down and see where the experiment was leading to. But what about the newcomers, those nations that had bent over backwards to join the club later on, as soon as the Iron Curtain fell? Why didn't they seize the opportunity to make their voices heard when given the chance? That Project Europe and its ideology of integration and shared prosperity had been delivering what was wanted was not lost on the nations at its periphery. Moreover, those in charge of Project Europe were happy to proselytize. Europe's statue of liberty carried no book or torch as it was too busy opening its welcoming arms to its returning children. Enlargement was inevitable. There is little surprise that nations such as Spain and Greece, already part of Western Europe, joined the club in the 1980s. Eastern Europeans, on the other hand, had to wait for the fall of the Berlin Wall to free themselves from the shackles of Soviet domination before they could eagerly jump on the bandwagon. Their motivation, however, was primarily driven by security considerations: after the devastation of the Second World War and after Roosevelt had given away so much to Stalin at Yalta they had found themselves abandoned and stuck into the Soviet orbit, a very unpleasant experience indeed. The USSR was now gone but Russia remained, and you never knew with the Russians. These nations would thus do anything to anchor themselves firmly once and for all and as soon as possible to Western Europe – especially to US-led NATO, whose raison d'être was to be a bulwark against the Soviets. Secondly, a poor man is always keen to join the next door millionaires' club given the opportunity: there is always the hope that some of the wealth will somehow rub off.

For these countries, anchoring themselves to Project Europe was the natural thing to do after the fall of the Soviet Empire. One would be tempted to add one more motivation for them, in line with Sam Huntington, the idea that the nations of continental Europe would inevitably gravitate towards a common European cultural heritage – except that the cultures are different enough (such as differences between Catholic and Orthodox nations) that it would probably take at least a generation for Eastern Europeans to truly feel culturally close to Western Europeans, and vice versa. Instead, the newcomers' motivations for joining were practical rather than ideological. What they wanted first of all was protection, an insurance policy. There's nothing wrong with that, except that once these new members had securely boarded the EU train and tucked their freshly signed insurance policy papers in their pockets, they refocused their attention to the pressing task of rebuilding their own countries and didn't feel a particular urge to actively participate in the politics of Europe. Someone else was running the EU show in any case. They could let their enthusiasm for the EU slacken. It's no surprise, then, that after having joined the club and obtained their membership card they didn't pay much attention to European parliamentarian elections: one year after Poland joined the EU, Polish President Lech Kaczynski did not hesitate to say 'What Poles are interested in is the future of Poland, not that of the EU'.[5] Having just recovered their independence, they wouldn't readily give it away, even to a 'good' cause such as Project Europe – so much for European ideals from the newcomers.

Sharing the pie

It is probably clear to the reader by now that different members of the club harbour different interpretations of their memberships. To be convinced that competing national interests remain the driving force behind EU debates we need look no further than in the area of budgets. It's always the money. As the system works today, member states contribute sums (like club membership fees) for the most part proportionate to their GDP that add up to form the EU budget: they then jointly decide how this pie will be split among members. The result is that there will inevitably be winners and losers, countries that are net contributors (such as Germany, England and the Netherlands) and countries who are net beneficiaries (such as Spain,

Greece and Portugal). Each country will inevitably perceive the exercise as a zero-sum game and fight accordingly. Net contributors try to minimize the overall pie to spend, and net recipients fight tooth and nail to try to increase everybody's contributions to make the pie bigger. Agreeing on a budget becomes a process of old-fashioned horse trading, as anywhere else in the world: there is nothing unusual in this, except that lofty collective European ideals are nowhere to be seen in this process. It is everyone for himself. After 2004 further complications were injected into these discussions as the number of participants around the table jumped from 15 to 25. They are 27 today, which doesn't make it any easier. Immediately after the No Debacle, discussions were taking place regarding the 2007–2013 budget, and one would have expected that politicians would have striven to find some unity and salvage a modicum of face. But it wasn't to be.

French President Jacques Chirac (with some assistance from German Chancellor Gerhard Schröder) made a public show of asking the British to abandon the more than 4 billion euro rebate privilege former British Prime Minister Margaret Thatcher had skilfully extracted from the EU in 1984. Naturally, British Prime Minister Tony Blair replied that France was the greatest beneficiary of the EU's Common Agricultural Policy (CAP), a set of subsidies France extracted from the EU in 2002 in exchange for endorsing enlargement to 25 members. CAP was effectively initiated as a sort of giveaway to the many small farmers who were an important part of the electorates of France and Germany; it then morphed into subsidies to fewer but larger farmers. At a cost of more than 43 billion euros per annum, CAP was gobbling up over 40 per cent of the EU's budget, and France received nearly 25 per cent of this bonanza, fuelling a sector representing no more than a small percentage of EU GDP and one that was hardly a source of new technologies and growth. Moreover, the subsidies and protectionist tariffs involved in CAP have been acting as an impediment to world trade, especially for developing economies. Chirac's quip is worth remembering: 'the only thing that Britain had done for European agriculture is the mad cow',[6] referring to the mad cow disease that had hit Britain. The tone was set, and another horse trader entered the fray, Italian Prime Minister Silvio Berlusconi, who clamoured for more subsidies for southern Italy's 'economically challenged' regions. Germany, as the biggest contributor to the EU budget and the one who habitually got the shortest end of the stick to the tune of a net loss of over 8 billion euros per annum, entered budget debates worried about how much more it would be required to contribute to fund Europe's enlargement drive. Since the interest of EU newcomers at that time was to see the money coffers prized open as soon as possible to get their first share of the pie, it is not really surprising that they were the members who extolled the virtues of compromise for the collective good: they were ready to make concessions just for the sake of a deal, any deal. It might have been thought that, following the No Debacle, European politicians would have tried to find common ground and save further embarrassment. But compromise appeared too much to ask for, and budget talks collapsed. Can any of these politicians be called a real *European* leader? Hardly. But what could Chirac, elected by French voters, be expected to do, or Blair, elected by British voters? The first will obviously fight for France, the second for the UK. That is their job. Politicians entering such debates hang up their European hats with their coats, just outside the debating room. This was and this still is the modus operandi today. Bickering, infighting, horse trading and the formation and unravelling of ad hoc alliances are likely to be constants in the life of the EU.

All for none, none for one

French statesman Charles De Gaulle famously predicted that European solidarity would take one or two *centuries* to materialize. The limits to European solidarity and to how little *European* are Europeans are, alas, not confined to the economic sphere. The free movement of people and immigration is an example. In reality there is no such thing as a coordinated, coherent pan-European policy. It is true that the Schengen Treaty signed in 1985, one of the crown jewels of Project Europe, is a remarkable achievement that makes it possible for 400 million Europeans from 25 countries to freely move from one country or another and even to settle there. Yet, with the rise of national populist parties all over Europe, Schengen ominously came under direct assault in the summer of 2011 from the Danes (from the Danish People's Party) intent on reinstating controls along their frontiers; and the Finns (from the True Finn's Party) followed not far behind. Increasing anti-Polish feelings in the Netherlands mean anti-immigrant attitudes apply not just to Muslims but to fellow Europeans as well. Economic crises have the nasty habit of awakening national populist instincts in nations, and, since European economies are generally in for a difficult time, one can expect the liberalization achievements epitomized by Schengen to come under increasing pressure across the continent. As a result, Europeans are likely to become even less *European* in the years ahead.

Intra-European solidarity took another hit when confronted with the thorny question of what happens when a country lets in many immigrants who, by virtue of moving freely within the Schengen space, end up in another Schengen country that didn't really want them in the first place. Following upheavals in Tunisia and Libya in early 2011, Italy's tiny island of Lampedusa, by virtue of being located the closest to these countries, was subjected to tens of thousands of illegal boat people overwhelming its shores. France, which led the military intervention in Libya, steadfastly refused to share the burden of 'welcoming' these immigrants. The row was finally resolved, but not after a public upset. Lack of solidarity is blatant among European nations unable to agree on common asylum policies, on burden-sharing among countries closer and farther from the source of illegal immigration and on management of the Schengen area in relation to multitudes of asylum seekers.

Labour mobility is key in this respect. Considering the map of Europe today, on one side are countries with very high unemployment, such as Spain, Ireland or Portugal, and on the other countries that need manpower, such as Germany. In a later chapter we'll point out that Germany, for example, needs *millions* of new workers in the coming years and that today's Spain has an unemployment rate of over 20 per cent. It would seem logical to try to match the needs of some EU countries where people struggle to find jobs with the needs for other EU countries where jobs struggle to find people. Only very recently did Germany start making timid moves to import young workers from Spain's 'lost generation', and only in May 2011 did it open its labour markets to citizens from the Eastern European countries that joined the EU in 2004 – after seven years. Contrary to what happens in America, European labour mobility is still, by and large, a pipe dream, especially among Western Europeans. Admittedly, language and cultural barriers get in the way, and people still find it difficult to think of Europe as their 'country'. A Frenchman who can't find a job at home may as quickly look for employment in the US or in Shanghai as in the Netherlands or Germany.

Later chapters examine the birth of the euro and the paradox that this single currency, which was supposed to be the final touch to the Project Europe edifice and to cement its unity, exacerbated divisions, threatening instead the whole edifice. The 2010 sovereign debt crisis, which started with the near financial collapse of Greece and ended up threatening the euro and the cohesion of Europe, became the ultimate test of how *European* Europeans really were, a test they failed miserably. Germany, Europe's powerhouse, was now in control of Europe's future: without it there was no possible rescue of Greece, Ireland or other countries threatened by financial collapse. Yet, despite the clear and present danger of a domino effect that could engulf other weak European countries and threaten Europe and its single currency, and despite the fact that Germany benefits from the euro, Germany played for time and postponed decisions until faced with catastrophe, an attitude that further unnerved the markets and aggravated the crisis. Understandably, the German electorate saw no point in spending its own hard-earned resources to bail out a country that had brought profligacy and indiscipline to the level of a national sport, and was even more reluctant to contemplate having to rescue others as well. Some German politicians came to publicly advocate a realignment of Germany, on the basis that convergence of Eurozone economies was unachievable in any case and that Germany might as well ditch the Eurozone and form a DM zone with nearby and like-minded countries, thereby advocating nothing less than the end of a European Germany. No wonder that whenever Germany acted during the Eurozone crisis, it was not out of conviction but because there was no choice. According to the financier George Soros, Germany carries a good portion of the blame for the Eurozone's current woes and its lack of solidarity has pushed Europe towards 'disintegration':

> The euro crisis had its origin in German Chancellor Angela Merkel's decision, taken in the aftermath of Lehman Brothers' default in September 2008, that the guarantee against further defaults should

come not from the European Union, but from each country separately. And it was German procrastination that aggravated the Greek crisis and caused the contagion that turned it into an existential crisis for Europe.[7]

In truth it was not only the Germans who demonstrated the limits of their *Europeaneness* in time of crisis. In usually placid Finland large election gains from Timo Soini's True Finns nationalist party in April 2011 were based in no small part on a campaign platform opposed to the bailouts of troubled Eurozone countries. In early 2011 Merkel tilted in favour of French proposals involving more 'economic government' within the Eurozone, and her proposal for a 'competition pact' aiming at ensuring better economic management throughout the Eurozone, now revived as 'pact for the euro' and rammed through in mid-March, came with a twist: regular summits of Eurozone members. To European countries outside the Eurozone such as Britain and Sweden this smelled of a Franco-German plot to split Europe's 27 countries into 17 members of the Eurozone to be led by the plotters and involving more *dirigiste* government, and ten outsiders comprising more liberal countries, including Britain and Sweden. There was fear that regular summits exclusively reserved to Eurozone insiders would result in a loss of the outsiders' influence on overall EU decisions, and tilt Europe towards a decidedly non-liberal economic future. The row prompted Polish Prime Minister Donald Tusk to publicly scold French and German leaders: 'Why are you trying to show divisions? Are we getting in your way? You are humiliating us!'[8] In 1990 British Prime Minister Margaret Thatcher, who was against Britain joining the Eurozone, had famously warned the House of Commons that 'If you hand over your sterling, you hand over the powers of this parliament to Europe.'[9] Nothing can be more Eurosceptic than that, and in hindsight the British are quite happy today that they did stay with the pound.

However, if you harbour doubts about European solidarity, about the willingness of a country to sacrifice itself for the good of the other members of the club, there is no need to look further than Ireland. In 2007 Irish national debt stood at a very respectable 25 per cent of its GDP. By 2013 it was expected to reach 125 per cent. How did that happen? A good portion of this increase is due to a decision by the Irish government to save the German, French and other banks and lenders who recklessly poured money into the country, as we'll see in more detail later. These foreign lenders merrily funded Irish banks, which fuelled a property bubble that, like all bubbles, imploded and brought the country's banking system down. With its banking system on the verge of collapse, in 2010 Ireland reluctantly decided to accept the hand extended by the rest of Europe in the form of a 85 billion euro rescue package from the European Financial Stability Fund (EFSF), to be used to repay the debts Irish banks owe these foreign banks. To save these foreign lenders, every man, woman and child of Ireland will, in other words, now carry a debt burden which they had very little to do with, and which they'll be toiling most of their lives to repay. The government destroyed its own country's credit to save that of other EU countries – a fine example of real European solidarity, some might say. But after Ireland had shot itself in the foot this way, grateful countries such as Germany and France politely asked Ireland to reload and shoot itself in the other foot for good measure by increasing its corporate taxes (which at a low 12.5 per cent level, had been attracting companies from all over the world to Irish shores) up to the crippling levels of French and German corporate taxes for the sake of the lofty ideal of 'tax harmonization'. And when the newly elected Irish Prime Minister, Enda Kenny, refused to play ball, France and Germany told him to forget about getting some relief from the crippling 6 per cent interest rate Ireland has to pay on the EFSF package.

All this is testimony to the mutual mistrust, parochialism and lack of solidarity still pervasive among European countries when key prerogatives of sovereignty are called into question. French Socialist Prime Minister Lionel Jospin properly summed the dilemma up when he spoke about the difficulty of 'making Europe without unmaking France'.[10] Here is one last example: just as the euro crisis reached its peak, members of the Eurozone had to nominate a new head of the European Central Bank (ECB) to replace Frenchman Jean-Claude Trichet in late autumn 2011. One might think that, since the crisis threatened the entire European edifice, leaders would have shown decisiveness and swiftly nominated the man most capable for the job. It was not so easy. The best candidate for the job, following the withdrawal of Germany's Axel Weber, was widely recognized as being Mario Draghi, the 63-year-old governor of Italy's central bank, holder of a PhD in Economics from MIT (the Massachusetts Institute of Technology). Yet something impeded his nomination, something that should not even have been taken into account: his nationality. Draghi happened to be Italian. There was already a southern European, Portugal's Vitor Constancio, in the number two position in the ECB, and two at the top would have been too many.[11] Since, in Germany's view, the ECB's primary mandate is to fight inflation, German newspapers couldn't resist pointing out that in Italy inflation was a way of life, despite the lack of any evidence that Draghi was soft on inflation. At a time when the ECB needed the best possible man at the helm, old European habits of stereotyping would have meant that the ECB would probably have got a second-rate candidate were it not for the fact that the intensity of the crisis brought a stop to months of bickering and Draghi was finally confirmed. Regrettably, most decisions in Europe continue to be made by compromise and juggling national interests and priorities instead of promoting the best solutions, a system that results too often in promoting the lowest common denominator.

A bridge too far

One would be at a loss to find a significant number of 'true Europeans' today who would place EU interests ahead of their own country's. Europeans remain fragmented and ambivalent about some of Project Europe's directions, about how far it has gone and should still go. Despite its being a child of political elites and technocrats, Project Europe was welcome as long as it was offering benefits that were easily understood by all, such as travelling around the continent without a passport, or, for businesses, the free flow of goods and services, and, of course, peace. But with the actual implementation of Project Europe came the perception that it had taken a life of its own to the detriment of national interests, that it had morphed into an intrusive supra-bureaucracy and that not all the goods it delivered were beneficial. In truth, everybody wants Project Europe to succeed but nobody wants it to succeed to the detriment of their own interest. These are difficult propositions to reconcile, especially with 27 nations around the table. What is the situation five or six years after the No Debacle? We are undoubtedly witnessing a reversal of the attitude of European countries which, during the past decades, had accepted the sacrifice of some of their sovereignty to the collective ideal of Project Europe and the euro crisis has thrown oil on the fire. Political life throughout Europe is going in reverse mode as one country after the other wonders if the Project has not gone too far, what it has really done for them, and attempts to reclaim some of this lost sovereignty.

In this context, the most worrying trend may be found in Germany, Europe's *indispensable* nation, which defined itself for decades as the most European of all Europeans. The road to Brussels goes through Paris and Berlin, and Germany was, with France, *the* original co-founder and co-leader of Project Europe. But how European is Germany today? If Germany falls prey to centrifugal forces, then the entire edifice of the EU risks being compromised. Economics are a key factor here. Germany has always been critical of the high costs of enlargement and has in the past been footing 20 per cent of the EU budget bill, resulting in a net yearly cash outflow. That Germans have had enough of systematically getting the short end of the stick was obvious during the Greek debt crisis of 2010. A weak euro may have helped fuel Germany's recent export boom yet Germans see the bottle as half empty, not half full: they see the high price hard-working and disciplined Germans have to pay to bail out undisciplined countries. Unsurprisingly, polls conducted by Germany's Infratest Dimap in December 2010 showed 60 per cent of Germans feel that the euro had disadvantaged them and 57 per cent are nostalgic for their beloved D-Mark, echoing Finance Minister Wolfgang Schäuble's worry about the possibility of an 'anti-euro party' coming into the German political landscape. The unravelling of the euro that was supposed to cement Project Europe has had instead the effect of a cold shower on Germans in general, planting doubts that their country has much to gain by deepening its involvement with things European. Frank-Walter Steinmeier, foreign minister of Germany and minister of finance, decried a lack of political courage endangering the euro and asked for a signal that Germany wanted a more European Germany rather than a more German Europe. Given the German people's lack of enthusiasm, Steinmeier's idea that Germany should plunge deeper into Project

Europe may not have been very realistic. Another question was could Germany, instead, mould the rest of Europe more to its image. For the smaller countries in its immediate periphery, already gravitating towards Germany, the answer is a qualified affirmative, but a definite no for the irreducible southern Europeans. Germany's loss of interest in Europe is a reality.

As intra-EU solidarity fades away, politics based on narrow national interest are bound to take the upper hand across Europe; and the trend feeds on itself. The recent rise of right-wing, nationalist, populist politics throughout Europe cannot be attributed only to the issue of immigration. It is also fed by a resurgence of nationalism, which defines itself in opposition to the dilution of identity, national character, autonomy and sovereignty that is part of the Project Europe package. The advent of the euro and the consequences of the economic crisis in Europe have made Germany more dominant than ever, yet they have confirmed some of its misgivings about Europe. Reunification a couple of decades ago was a necessary first step towards forging a new German identity. Now it is its economic strength that sets Germany firmly above its peers and has given it reasons to assert a newer, more independent identity. On the political side, with the enlargement of Europe and growing frustration with things European, Germans have markedly lost some of their earlier enthusiasm for Project Europe. German Chancellor Angela Merkel, facing daunting political difficulties at home, wasn't going to rush into supporting Eurozone weaklings, and, as Germany is a federal state, she had to constantly negotiate among the country's fragmented power centres – no easy task. As a result, Germany and France in time of crisis move according to different political rhythms, something that does not help provide cohesion to this *pas de deux*. To Germany, the partnership with France is not as useful or indispensable as it used to be before the Franco-German axis lost its power to set the European agenda in an enlarged Europe. With French economic credibility now in question, the relationship is likely to be further weakened, which will not make it easier for Europe to resolve the Eurozone crisis, speak with a coherent voice or undertake sweeping reforms. In the end, while Germany is unlikely to become introverted, let alone nationalistic, it is likely to give less importance to its role as anchor of Project Europe and tend to become more of an independent actor on the global stage, a development bound to worry many inside and outside Europe, including Russia. This fear may be mitigated by Germany's need of Russia's natural resources and Russia's need of German know-how: a Russo-German entente is not as far-fetched as it may at first seem.

In 2005 Europeans woke up for the first time to the fact that Project Europe may have taken them further and faster than they had cared to go – and they slammed on the brakes. Their message was relatively simple: there should be a new debate about where Project Europe should be heading before it resumes forging ahead. This was not a bad proposition in itself, except that, in 2011, the perception that nothing has changed means people increasingly think it cannot be fixed. Indeed, the Eurozone crisis has exacerbated tensions. And once ordinary Europeans start questioning the appropriateness of Project Europe the road is short to the simplistic assumption that the EU should be blamed for everything (when in reality the national policies of individual countries are just as much to be blamed for their ills). As the EU becomes the scapegoat, the Project is bound to keep losing traction with ordinary Europeans. The disconnect between them and EU political elites is bound to grow wider. Monnet and Schumann will easily be forgotten by the generations that have not known wars. An October 2011 rebellion by 78 British Conservative MPs to force the Cameron government to hold a referendum about leaving the EU was a sign that the unravelling of Project Europe, though highly unlikely, is not impossible. It also represents the most fundamentally dangerous challenge facing Europe and the world today. What is certain is that Europe's existentialist crisis is chronic, and is unlikely to be resolved soon. At the very least this crisis will mean that it will be even more difficult for Europe to speak with one voice and forge a common policy on most major issues, in particular where structural reforms are needed. Turmoil may loom ahead if Project Europe transmutes into something that is European only by name as its members become irresistibly drawn to Europe's natural default setting: a bunch of competing countries.

THREE

WHICH EUROPE
IS IT ANYWAY?

Visions and limits of what Europe could be

In search of an identity

Jean Monnet famously said that European unity would be forged through crisis. The Slovenian intellectual Slavoj Zizek went a step further when he stated Europe will need to go through no less than a political catastrophe before it can put together a unified political vision.[1] Someone once said that peace between Israelis and Palestinians would only be possible after a civil war in Israel *and* a civil war among Palestinians. It is to be hoped that the analogy will not apply to Europe. For Zizek the European system, with political democratization as its core philosophy inherited from ancient Greece, is the only valid alternative to the American and the authoritarian capitalistic Chinese. But the danger is that core European countries will lose interest in Project Europe and go their own separate ways if political unity is not achieved soon. Can the EU become something more than a mere club of nations? What sort of *Europe* should Europe be?

One positive consequence of the No Debacle of 2005 was the emergence of the first truly public debate of what Europe should be. Competing ideologies attracted unlikely bedfellows. On one side, the quintessentially Eurosceptic British, ambivalent from the beginning about Project Europe and always in favour of a looser union, joined Scandinavians and the Benelux in recognizing that, since individual countries' national interests would make political integration impractical, it would be more realistic to promote a vision of Europe short on political integration and long on the free flow of goods, services and people. Geographical enlargement was acceptable to them since, if handled without too much infusion of political integration, it resulted in enlargement of the common market without substantial political consequences or loss of sovereignty. This line of thinking, realistic rather than idealistic or ideological, recognized the limits to the loyalty Project Europe exercised on citizens of individual countries. It echoed Paul Kennedy, who wrote, two decades ago, in *Preparing for the Twenty-First Century*:

> Is it not utopian to imagine twelve or fifteen nations, each with a tradition of acting as a sovereign unit, ever becoming a United States of Europe as the early federalists once hoped? Is it not more practicable to undertake modest reform measures... and be content with a loose federation of peoples possessing close cultural ties and more consistent industrial practices, without wasting energies pursuing the chimera of turning Europe into an integrated world-political player?[2]

On the other hand, voices were heard, mainly in Germany, France and Italy, promoting a vision longer on politics, a federal political integration anchored by the euro common currency. They were closer to the idea floated by Churchill after the Second World War of a United States of Europe. For this, Europe's destiny should be more than just a free trade zone or a mere club of countries. It should become more cohesive, ambitious and regulated. For them geographical enlargement had already gone too far and should thus be slowed down to allow for more profound political integration of the countries already in. The newcomers from Eastern Europe, on the other hand, wanted to maximize political as well as geographical integration since a greater intertweaving of destinies meant less danger from Russia.

Benghazi blues

Had one segmented the debate along security and geopolitical lines at the time, France and Germany were again sitting on the same side of the fence, favouring a decrease of Atlanticism and an increase in the international role Europe had to play; whereas the rest of Europe remained more attached to the US and was less interested by an active and independent European role on the world stage. But would Europe truly have had the means to turn such a concept into reality or would it be trying to punch above its weight? The debate at the time was not made easier by the suspicion many countries in Europe, and in particular the newcomers, felt over the Chirac–Schröder couple. This may have had its positive qualities, but it was arguably the most divisive tandem of leaders modern Europe had known, having flouted the euro's Stability and Growth Pact, ditched the Lisbon Agenda and made every effort to weaken Europe's Atlantic link by playing on European feelings against the unpopular US-led Iraq quagmire. Moreover, they treated the newcomers with lofty arrogance (Chirac said Eastern Europeans had lost a good opportunity to keep their mouths shut). The Chirac–Schröder plan was simple: to take joint control of the European security agenda, decouple Europe from the US and position Europe as an independent strategic player (led by France–Germany, of course) in opposition to the US. Then French Foreign Minister Michel Barnier put it plainly: 'Our American friends must understand that we are going to build Europe, not only as a market but as a power.'³ Given the recklessness shown by the US in international affairs in recent times it is no wonder that some European leaders were thinking that a dose of separation would be healthy. Such a plan might have had a small chance of working given the extent of popular anti-Americanism at the time. Chirac–Schröder, however, and others, had failed to grasp that Europe had just turned into a club of 27 members with different dynamics. It now included nations from Eastern Europe who regarded America as their saviour from Soviet subjugation. For the newcomers NATO's integrity was sacred: they would be (and still are today) suspicious of any Franco-German attempt to push Europe towards more independence from the US or to create a home-grown EU defence architecture in competition with NATO and with the risk of weakening American commitment. To construct a powerful Europe, Chirac–Schröder would at the very least need to bring in the third 'big power', the UK which, being traditionally pro-US, wouldn't be likely to play ball. This attempt to unify Europe by defining it in opposition to the US achieved little more than division. Cynical observers said Chirac–Schröder had been intent on playing 'big power' with the ultimate delusional objective of turning Europe into an independent geopolitical player and counterweight to the US *without* the means to take on that role effectively.

Following the Chirac–Schröder era, Sarkozy–Merkel took over, a couple shorter on ideology, longer on realism and Atlanticism, above all conscious of the shortcomings of the Chirac–Schröder plan. Gone was the Bush II administration, an easy target for demonization, supplanted by the more popular figure of Barack Obama. It was now clear that in a 27-member Europe the Franco-German axis would no longer be able to set the agenda as freely as before. Talk about a 'Great Atlantic Schism' quickly abated. Some powers outside Europe, including China, which had been hoping to see Europe evolve as a counterweight to the US, saw their hopes dashed.

Today's Europe is too fragmented and does not have the teeth or the will to play an independent geopolitical role. Sarkozy's boldly taking the lead role in Western military intervention in Libya in early 2011 had more to do with the reassertion of French power in the southern Mediterranean neighbourhood than geopolitics, following domestic complaints that France had been doing nothing to assist pro-democracy movements across the Maghreb (and French elections were looming on the horizon, with the far right gobbling up centre right votes in polls). David Cameron, possibly loath to let the French take the limelight, followed suit. But a more self-confident Germany, together with the countries in its immediate sphere of influence in Eastern and Central Europe, refused to cooperate with France, preferring to shy away from a new military adventure, particularly in the southern Mediterranean when its interest is increasingly in the East. Germany abstained from voting on the issue at the UN, the first time since the Second World War that it publicly denied its support to its allies, a watershed event in the history of the EU, attesting to Germany's growing distance from Europe. It is difficult to understand what Germany wants except that it no longer seems satisfied with the status quo and is ready to assert its self-interests to the detriment of European cohesiveness. Merkel's decision was approved by 65 per cent of Germans polled, to the despair of newspaper *Suddeutsche Zeitung* which lamented a 'historical mistake' on Germany's part,[4] prompting former Foreign Minister Joschka Fischer to label it a 'scandalous mistake'.[5] Some observers said the episode may dent German ambitions to hold a permanent seat on the UN Security Council. Only 7 of Europe's 27 countries decided to be part of the operation. With intervention under the EU umbrella impossible because of Germany's well-publicized dissent with France over Sarkozy's forceful application of UN Resolution 1973, and with an increasingly marginalized Italy threatening to deny use of its air bases if the operation continued under French leadership, the remaining participants insisted on NATO taking over the lead; the NATO intervention thus became a coalition of the willing.

NATO means America, and the last thing Obama wanted was to get involved in yet another Arab conflict. But he could not deny help to his European allies in the case of Libya and, at the same time, expect that they continue helping him in Afghanistan. So America reluctantly intervened in a military operation launched by France and the UK. Libya turned out to be a rare case of these Europeans being from Mars and the Americans from Venus. The operation was transformed into one more NATO intervention outside Europe, significantly the first one in which America took the back seat. The Libyan operation would, by the way, have floundered without American air defence suppression capabilities and ammunition stockpiles. Europe's own capabilities were so depleted that France and Italy had to pull out their aircraft carriers because of repairs and budget constraints. No wonder it took half a year for NATO to 'win' against such a third-rate military power as Libya. One of the lessons from the Libyan campaign is that nothing has changed since the Balkan wars in terms of European dependence on US military capabilities. Even the French daily *Le Monde* had to recognize that France no longer had the military means to match its political ambitions.

Libya found Europe deeply divided on the issue of intervention, something which is likely to leave scars for a long time. Notwithstanding the end result of the campaign, Libya will be remembered as the graveyard of the idea of a common European foreign, defence and security policy. European countries are likely never to trust each other enough for such an idea to work beyond the occasional ad hoc alliance such as that of France and UK in the case of Libya. Moreover, the Libyan episode brought to the surface the newfound independence and assertiveness of two key European actors, Germany and Turkey, which, having made their own calculations, declined to assist their allies. It is difficult to envision such a fragmented Europe defining itself in opposition to the US or turning into an independent power at any time in the future. The Franco-German axis is unlikely to be as cohesive or wield the power it once did, although a Franco-German entente is a prerequisite for European stability since a reassertion of their rivalry would tear Europe apart. These realities suit the US (and the British) well but do not mean that European powers will be content with automatically aligning themselves with the US on every security issue. European popular opinion has never been *fully* Atlanticist. A large swathe of the population of Old Europe subscribes to leftist political tendencies and will always look with hostility, or at least suspicion, at anything the Americans do. The right is not necessarily pro-American. Even the Atlanticist Sarkozy has not shied away from moves to get closer to Russia, as well as Germany. Moreover, the electoral pendulum in most European countries is bound to usher in from time to time parties or leaders less keen on Atlanticism, whether from the left or even from the nationalist right.

27 visions and growing

Coherence and clarity in working out a definition of what Europe should be today are not assisted by the wide difference separating the vision that the 'joint leaders' of Europe, France and Germany, have for it. Each of them favours a Europe that is an image of itself or reflects its core political philosophy. Historically France achieved unity centuries ago and rapidly moved on to become a strong centralized state with a pervasive bureaucracy; so it favours a centralized bureaucratic Europe operating as a mega-state. Germany achieved unity quite recently, by cobbling together independent regions that kept substantial powers to themselves; so, as a federal, decentralized state, today's Germany does not favour a centralized Europe where the state plays an omnidirectional, omnipresent role, but prefers the EU to concentrate on those things that it is equipped to do best while leaving substantial independence to countries in running the rest of their business. The recent euro crisis has changed that to some degree, as paramount German concerns for the stability and governance of the Eurozone met the French desire for greater control of Eurozone economies, resulting in the two countries jointly sponsoring various initiatives aimed at increased governance. But this has hardly led to a revival of the Franco-German axis. Where France likes to lead from the front and make a show about it, German leadership is quieter. It has been said that France needs Germany to hide its weakness and Germany needs France to hide its strength. It used to be that France was useful to Germany as a vector to regain legitimacy lost in the Second World War; Germany was walking a step behind. Today's Germany, however, is far more self-confident, independent and assertive in promoting its own interests and has been growing stronger relative to France. In England, Margaret Thatcher promoted early on a liberal Anglo-Saxon vision for Europe favouring free market ideals and against integration politics, a stance that still colours Britain's European politics today.

Within any given country different currents and political parties with different visions of Europe may co-exist, which means that a country's vision of Europe can change over time following swings of the electoral pendulum. Ana Palacio, former Spanish foreign minister and head of the Spanish parliament's joint committee on European Affairs, said in 2005 that Europe was pioneering a new world order, a multi-network Europe based on a shared institutional framework. Whatever that means, there was no clear definition at the time of what Europe was to be – and we are not closer to a definition six years later. Following the No Debacle in 2005 geographical and political integration slowed down. Yet with 27 member countries now in the club, each one with its own interests at heart and its own view of where Europe should go (or not go), the debate between 'federalists' (preaching for an expansion of EU government authority and centralization) and 'nationalists' (preaching for less) is likely to continue, and we cannot expect a clear direction to be found soon, if ever. Europe will probably remain weak and fragmented, and Project Europe remain work-in-progress.

Surprisingly, even the political stability of some European countries can be questioned. Belgium, whose capital, Brussels, is the seat of the European Parliament, took on the rotating EU presidency in 2010 while in the middle of a long drawn-out crisis that saw the country on the verge of splitting in two: one country for its Flemish, Dutch-speaking population, and the other for its French-speaking Walloon population. Will Belgium still be Belgium a few years from now? In Spain it is the region of Catalonia around Barcelona that has been striving to split from the centre. In Italy, Umberto Bossi's independentist and powerful Lega Nord party vociferously advocates dividing the country's poor south from the richer north, where it has a strong following. Northern Italians are, by and large, fed up with their perception that they have to carry on their shoulders a much less productive south that has represented a black hole engulfing massive government subsidies for decades, all the while underpaying its share of national taxes. A leading Italian business newspaper published an article showing that, in order to gain its independence, the productive north-western part of the country could itself absorb the *entire* national debt of Italy, repay it in 35 years and still show some growth.[6] Will Italy still be Italia in ten years' time? The political stability and cohesion of individual European countries may seem cast in concrete, and the idea that any of these countries would split up, disintegrate or depart from Project Europe may seem far-fetched. But it is not entirely impossible, and further fragmentation would not exactly increase Europe's stability or make it easier to find a common European identity.

The new and the less new

In 2003 the former US Secretary of Defense, Donald Rumsfeld, not one to mince his words, famously pointed to a cleavage between what he called Old Europe and New Europe. Such segmentation has its rationale, not only when viewed through the prism of security interests. Old Europe (mostly Western Europe) made a dramatic recovery from the Second World War and turned into a peaceful, free and prosperous zone. New Europe (the former Soviet satellites which joined the EU after the fall of the USSR), by contrast, went mostly straight from life under the Nazi boot to life under the Soviet boot. The reasons they bent over backwards to join the EU club were practical, driven by security and money. In their view, the more former Soviet satellites (such as Ukraine) could be integrated, the stronger Europe would become, and a stronger Europe meant less danger from Russia. The 'soft imperialist' ideology of Project Europe was naturally attractive to them. Who could blame them? Today's Russia may have shed its totalitarian ideological mantle and may have opened up to some extent, but it is still perceived as an autocracy, a dictatorship capable of violence when silencing dissent at home or imposing its will on neighbours when it feels its interests threatened, particularly in its 'near abroad' periphery. Russians welcomed a strong government after the chaotic 1990s and there is hope that, as Russia modernizes, it will change its ways; but the newcomers will need time before they can trust the bear. It thus comes as no surprise that these nations have been pushing for Project Europe to forge ahead with its ideals of geographic expansion and integration. For the nations that compose Old Europe, which did not share the same experience, security concerns are generally overshadowed by socio-economic ones. Old Europe considered that absorbing poor nations had a cost that they would have to bear. In addition they feared the generous welfare and quality of life they had become used to would inevitably take a hit, while jobs might be lost to the hungrier Eastern Europeans.

As soon as they freed themselves from the shackles of communism, Eastern European countries that joined the EU had to decide which way to go. These countries wanted to make up for lost time. Having had enough of communism and rigid socio-economic structures they enthusiastically adopted models promoting free enterprise, with lower taxes and business incentives, and they were less concerned with social benefits. Until 2004 Old Europe was comfortable and content with its social model, even if it was unsustainable, built on limited working hours, generous welfare, retirement and health benefits, strong unions and a vital public service sector. Suddenly New Europe catapulted itself on this scene with its multitudes hungry for work at any price. The best-kept secret is that some Old Europeans would probably have preferred the newcomers to be somewhat lazier. There is no underestimating the amount of concern Old Europe, in particular countries such as France, had when it came to the attitude of New Europe towards work, as, among other concrete signs of a hungrier and more flexible workforce from New Europe, the European Industrial Relations Observatory disclosed in 2005 (as Old Europe was voting No to the EU constitution referendum), that the workers of New Europe, having joined the club only a year earlier, were working three weeks more per year than Old Europe's. Old Europe did not care about the fact that these countries had just freed themselves from poverty and communism and were keen to work. Inevitably, reaction from Old Europe came swiftly, with accusations of 'social dumping'. In other words, Old Europe wanted New Europe to raise its wages and burden itself with the same labour market rigidities that it suffered itself. The attitude resembled the 'fiscal dumping' accusations Old Europe levels at countries such as Ireland which maintain low taxes to attract businesses. Anything that threatens the benchmarks Old Europe established around the lowest common denominator of mediocrity is anathema.

In realistic terms, New Europe will probably have forgotten its communist past within a generation. If Russia is no longer viewed as a threat, then New Europe's ties to Old Europe may grow stronger, to the detriment of Atlantic ties. New Europe may increasingly be seduced by Old Europe and become more like it, instead of the other way around. Eastern Europe does not have the capacity to pull the rest of Europe towards whatever vision it may have for Europe's future, assuming it has one. Former Eastern European countries at the periphery of Germany may coalesce around a Germany that is increasingly likely to look east for its future. Europe is unlikely to find its identity in Eastern Europe.

A fickle old lady

Former American Secretary of State Henry Kissinger's famous line 'When I want to call Europe, what number do I dial?' held true when he said it years ago and holds even more true today with a 27-member Europe. For security issues and international affairs, when the going gets tough Europe is difficult to find or understand because it cannot speak with a single voice. Moreover, depending on the particular topic of the moment, subgroups and alliances tend to be formed by those European countries whose interests or inclinations will, at that time, see them sitting on the same side of the fence. These alliances are bound to shift over time like a kaleidoscope, depending on the topic and interests at play. Sorry Kissinger, but you won't get a phone number today or tomorrow for Europe, and don't even think of calling Lady Ashton, who was sworn in as the EU's first foreign minister in late 2009 (her official title is High Representative for Foreign Affairs and Security Policy) because she cannot give you a definite 'yes' or 'no' until she has spoken to Paris, Berlin and others, and tried to get them to come to a consensus. If there is any doubt about who's *not* in charge one needs to remember that in early 2011 Lady Ashton was publicly scolded by British Prime Minister David Cameron who criticized her weak reaction to the 'Arab spring'.[7] Later she was chided for not doing enough to move Europe towards a unified foreign policy. In other words, the same European leaders who insisted on placing grey bureaucrats at the top were later complaining that they got little action from them. Working out where Europe stands on any given foreign policy and security issue depends on when the question is asked, the European country addressed and who is governing it at that particular time.

Doubts over such fickleness disappear when recalling Spain in 2006. At that time the centre right government of José Maria Aznar, an Atlanticist, was in power, and Spain was unquestionably an ally of the US in the Bush II invasion of Iraq. Aznar lost Spain's national elections because of his dismal handling of the 2004 Madrid terrorist bombings. When José Luis Zapatero and his socialist party were elected they immediately proceeded to pull Spanish troops from Iraq and join the Chirac–Schröder tandem and their strident anti-Americanism – a 180 degree turnaround over a major foreign policy issue in a matter of a month. The same would probably have happened in Italy had a group of Italian hostages been killed by the terrorists who kidnapped them instead of being released at the time: such an incident was likely to have cost centre right coalition leader Silvio Berlusconi his premiership and ushered in leftist leaders such as Romano Prodi or Massimo D'Alema who would have jumped at the opportunity to 'do a Zapatero', pull out of Iraq and perhaps join the Chirac–Schröder bandwagon. Particularly in Old Europe, there exists a profound cleavage within the constituencies and political classes alike between the ideologies of the right and of the left. Although extremes have been, by and large, marginalized (in spite of a marked resurgence of the right today), the reality is generally one of centre right versus centre left; yet ideological differences between the two camps run far deeper than those between Republicans and Democrats in the US, for instance. The implication is that swings of the electoral pendulum in a given country can have substantial and immediate consequences on that country's stance regarding any given issue and on its impact on the European agenda. The result for foreign policy and security can sometimes be as spectacular as the Zapatero turnaround. At the very least it makes for a frequently shifting mosaic of views, priorities and policies from the governments of the individual countries. Such fickleness tends to turn Europe into an inconsistent and ineffectual player in world affairs, one difficult for outsiders to understand.

This fickleness has implications for the way Europe's principal ally, the US, regards it. As noted earlier, the US was historically keen to see the building of a Europe as a trading partner and as a counterweight to the Soviet Union. Civilizational kinship, as defined by Sam Huntington, may have had something to do with it. The US interest is in a Europe that possesses enough strength and cohesiveness to be a useful geopolitical partner, but not too much to become an independent one. In the eyes of many Americans, today's Europe is a fragmented, weak, indecisive player difficult to deal with and an economic weakling with no military teeth, of limited practical assistance to America's grand geopolitical designs. A good portion of Europe's population is of leftist ideological tendencies and in any case has been no friend to the US, no matter what the US did during the Cold War when America was the ultimate guarantor of Western Europe's security. The fall of the Soviet Union has not done much to change these perceptions. If one then extracts the nationalists one eventually reaches the subset of the hard-core friends of America, who are likely to form a minority, dwindling after the recent wars and financial crises. Although in the end Europeans may turn out to be more Atlanticist than expected, when real challenges arise, to what extent America can count on Europe to help advance its agenda is by no means clear.

Some like it soft

Europe finds it hard to act decisively on any given issue, the more so when it involves the use of 'hard' power. However fragmented Europe may be, there is one area where the majority of its members are consistently likely to find common ground: the use of 'soft' power, a term coined in the 1990s by Joseph Nye, former Assistant Secretary of Defense in the Clinton Administration. Project

Europe represented, after all, the *ultimate* use of soft power to resolve a chronic conflict situation between the nations of the continent. Unsurprisingly, modern Europe as a whole tends to abhor the use of force and privileges the use of dialogue, diplomacy and other tools of soft power in international relations. Cynics will say that this is a case of necessity made a virtue since Europe, having limited hard power at its disposal and neither the political will nor means to project it effectively, has no choice but to recognize that its foreign policy has no teeth and play the soft power card by default. Robert Cooper, former British diplomat and head of External and Politico-Military Affairs for the Council of the European Union, wrote in *The Breaking of Nations*:

> To put it crudely, the United States is unilateralist because it has the strength to act on its own; Europe's attachment to treaties, the rule of law and multilateralism comes from weakness and wishful thinking. Rules exist to protect the weak and Europeans like them... in this postmodern paradise it has been easy to forget that force matters.[8]

In 2003 Robert Kagan wrote in *Paradise and Power*:

> It is time to stop pretending that Europeans and Americans share a common view of the world... Americans are from Mars and Europeans are from Venus... when the European powers were strong, they believed in strength and martial glory. Now they see the world through the eyes of weaker powers.[9]

Few countries are more representative of the desire to shun hard power than Germany. When US President Obama publicly said he stood for a nuclear free world, he found a listening ear in Berlin and raised eyebrows in Paris. Germany is not a nuclear power and has been pushing for the US to remove its tactical nuclear weapons still kept in bunkers in the Rhineland Palatinate. Having none of its own, Berlin sees nuclear weapons and nuclear deterrence as outdated and obsolete and the American missile shield project in Central Europe as something that takes away the rationale for keeping any. France is a nuclear power, has stated its firm intention to remain one since the time of Charles de Gaulle, and perceived America's new missile shield project as *complementing*, not replacing, nuclear weapons. Eastern European nations are anxious when they hear about a decrease in American or NATO's military power, nuclear or conventional, in Europe. Yet, apart from the debate on whether or not to keep nuclear weapons, Europeans seem to agree that their future lies with soft power.

Positioning itself as world champion of human rights; proposing a universalist ideology of peaceful integration; posing as the ultimate wielder of soft power and as the inventor of the doctrine of forceful intervention for humanitarian purposes; advocating negotiations at all prices – all this is well and good but it raises practical questions for Europe. First, Europe is likely to find itself confronted from time to time by the dilemma of whether or not to intervene with hard power, particularly in its neighbourhood, when human rights are trampled on or atrocities committed on a large scale. Can a Europe that claims the moral high ground afford to sit idly and wash its hands of responsibility when its public and the world at large are confronted with daily TV scenes of civilian massacres in, say, neighbouring Bosnia or Libya? To look the other way and carry on with business as usual would imply a callousness that may result in a loss of moral legitimacy. Second, if Europe does intervene, should it be left to individual nations, to a coalition of the willing, to NATO or to the EU? Third, is the EU ready to go defend human rights with force if necessary *anywhere* in the world, or only in its neighbourhood? And where are the limits of neighbourhood in this case, given that it intervened in Libya? Fifth, will the EU intervene only when economic or other interests are involved? How legitimate can the moral underpinning be if intervention is conditional upon mercantilist interests being at stake? Sixth, granted that soft power is the EU's first response, what if, as was the case with Libya in early 2011, there is no more room or time for diplomacy and only hard power can have effect? What if endless negotiations with Iran over its development of nuclear weapons simply buy time for the Iranian regime to complete this development?

The Balkan wars of the 1990 took place right in Europe's backyard. The Kosovo conflict was a humiliating reminder that Europe on its own was not able to stop even by military means a low-grade conflict involving third-rate powers, so run down and ineffective was its military machine. In other situations in the Balkans, Europe was paralysed and could not bring itself to intervene. It was only when US-led NATO decided to do something that Europe finally took coordinated and organized action. The Libyan episode was not dissimilar. Confusion arose as to what political umbrella the intervention should be placed under. If Europe risks being confronted with similar situations in the future, it should devise beforehand a political and military framework for such interventions lest it appear confused and callous and finds itself taken over by events. The problem is that Europe, as a whole, is unable to think in strategic terms.

Batman and Robin

The US, by contrast, can calibrate its actions and use hard power (for better or for worse), as in the case of Iraq or Afghanistan, as well as soft power, to date as with Iran and North Korea. Whether of necessity or wisdom, the natural tendency of Europe will always be to maximize the use of soft power tools such as multilateral forums, negotiations and aid. Other than the occasional Libya-type neighbourhood intervention, situations requiring the use of hard power are likely to arise as a consequence of strong pressure from the US, and will rarely meet approval with the European public, except when there is a clear humanitarian or peacekeeping dimension to the military campaign. The US, for which security is always at the top of the agenda and the use of hard power a way of life, would have hoped to be able to count on Europe as its junior partner in security matters. But Europe has clearly chosen butter over guns, soft over hard power, feels comfortable under the American security umbrella and has little incentive to change. To the US, Europe can only be perceived as a weak and unreliable ally, one that does not take defence matters seriously and whose military forces can barely be used even for peacekeeping operations. From a purely military standpoint, the quantitative and qualitative capabilities and the interarms services capabilities of European forces are so far behind those of the US that to US military leaders European forces can often be more of a hindrance than aid. The American inclination would thus be to do without Europe as a geopolitical ally, except that the US gains international legitimacy when it involves Europe in its military operations. Such legitimacy is priceless in today's world and will continue to be sought by the US, however reluctantly, even as the US loses interest in Europe.

American loss of interest in Europe is likely to accelerate as Asia, Central Asia and the Middle East become increasingly important – and volatile – in the geopolitical chessboard relative to Europe. Why should the US divert its attention to Europe when these other regions represent tomorrow's biggest challenges and prizes? 9/11 and the US's perception of a global conflict with Islam (a perception not shared by Europe) has further diverted America's attention away from Europe. Changes in American demographics make its population less European in character, contributing to long-term cultural and spiritual decoupling. Europe has a deep-seated fear of a loss of interest from the US, but can do little to address the issue. The alliances that defined the relationship between Europe and the US in the recent past, against Nazi Germany and then against the Soviet Union, were based on unequivocally clear and present dangers. Today, with no obvious external existential threat to Europe, the importance of the security alliance with the US recedes for both sides.

However, different parts of Europe respond more enthusiastically than others to American requests for involvement in military campaigns. The countries of New Europe, for reasons pointed out above, are naturally more inclined to stand by the US when asked to. That is why they didn't hesitate when asked to send troops to Iraq: the Bulgarian foreign minister, Solomon Isaac Passy, said at the time: 'Iraq needs our help'. Nevertheless, their readiness to join in is likely to cool off within a generation when these New Europeans have forgotten about their years under the Soviet boot and tasted instead the fruits of EU-led prosperity. Interestingly, while the US favoured Project Europe from its inception, Washington has never promoted the idea of a strong and independent European military force or a strong European polity, concepts which would dilute Atlantic ties and American influence. The interests of the US are in effect best served by a Europe that is militarily strong, but acts within the US-led NATO framework, and whose political fragmentation makes it weak – a Europe subservient, or attached to American interests.

Does Europe need a foreign policy?

Europe is in decline by all criteria of power, and to define itself as a 'Great Power' would be delusional. Europe has trouble knowing what it is and what it wants. It is unlikely that Europe would at any time be able to articulate a coherent strategic approach to any major international issue. At the UN every single European country has its own separate voice (Europe wields 27 votes) and will generally vote according to its own sovereign interests of the moment. No European country is willing to give away its sovereignty in matters of security and foreign policy. Europe is a new type of entity on the world stage, a new animal in the menagerie, one that defies classification. It is a fact that, despite its many shortcomings, it has become a force for the collective good of the planet. Should its foreign policy also break the classical mould and be something entirely new, a geopolitical force of inspiration for the collective good?

It is easy to criticize Europeans as being ineffectual. But there is one case of the undeniable success of their use of soft power: the enlargement of Europe. This 'soft imperialism' works. It is voluntary, not imposed, it is unprecedented in the history of humanity. It transforms potential threats and instability at the border by absorbing countries and putting them on their best behaviour. Does Europe really need to fill the shoes of a classical power? Does it really need to set geopolitical objectives, articulate a foreign policy and develop the means to achieve them? In a sense, Europe has done it all in the past, including creating empires that covered the globe. What can today be characterized by some as a spent force can be seen by others as wisdom. Security is at the top of America's agenda: it is at the bottom of Europe's. China feels like the phoenix reborn: Europe can say, 'Well done, and please buy some of our bonds, machines and handbags.' Europe does not see the need to flex muscles. It does not even see the need to have muscles to flex. Since the fall of the Soviet Union Europe's radar screen has not displayed any real existential threats; its security has in any case been outsourced to the US, which makes it possible for Europeans to spend as little as possible on guns and save money for butter. Its own 'near abroad' has been in general pacified, and even truculent Balkan countries have now turned their energies to trying to join the EU instead of fighting among themselves.

There are no imperial ambitions left in Europe's make-up apart from the soft and benign imperialism of enlargement. Apart from the occasional and reluctant participation in military and peacekeeping operations as a junior partner alongside the mighty US or the occasional mopping-up operation by the French in Africa, Europe does not see the need to grow teeth, let alone use them. It is a benign status quo power in that its overwhelming interest is to ensure a continuation of the existing world order with free trade at the centre of the edifice. Europe is America's twin without the teeth, the ambition to be number one, the recklessness and the notion of manifest destiny. According to Pascal Bruckner in *La tyrannie de la pénitence*, Europe has so much fallen prey to a sense of guilt due to its colonial and imperial past that it has reached a sort of paralysis and unwillingness to confront realities.[10] Europe abdicates any role, refuses to see the world for what it really is, and leaves hard decisions to its American big brother, not forgetting, in the process, to criticize whatever big brother does. For Bruckner, Europe, refusing to act and looking for peace at any price, even a bad peace, does not commit mistakes simply because it won't attempt anything, and is turning into the Pontius Pilate of nations, washing its hands of everything. Gustav Mahler put it even more bluntly: 'Europe will die for its one principle: it does not concern me.' For Kagan, Europe fell into a state of strategic dependence on America and its blissful view of the world continues unabated:

> For Europe, the fall of the Soviet Union did not just eliminate a strategic adversary; in a sense it eliminated the need for geopolitics ... many Europeans took the end of the cold war as a holiday from strategy ... Europeans have stepped out of the Hobbesian world of anarchy into the Kantian world of perpetual peace.[11]

'The core concept of Europe after 1945', according to the former German Foreign Minister Joschka Fischer, 'was and still is a rejection of the European balance-of-power principle and the hegemonic ambitions of individual states that had emerged following the Peace of Westphalia in 1648'.[12] Why should there be any concern about this?

The EU was publicly humiliated in October 2010 when the General Assembly of the United Nations refused to upgrade its status from that of a simple 'observer' – the world's largest economic bloc, largest donor of aid, largest proponent of soft power, was given a snub by the UN. Monnet had been looking forward to the time when Europe would have one unified vote at the UN, but this is not something bound to happen soon because it is to Europe's advantage to keep its current 27 votes. One reason European cohesion could be important relates to the issue of energy supplies from Russia. Europe today imports about 25 per cent of its natural gas needs from Russia (down from an over-dependent peak of 70 per cent in the 1990s), representing less than 10 per cent of Europe's total energy needs. About 40 per cent of Russia's natural gas is sold to Europe, on the basis of long-term supply contracts linked to an ever-increasing price of oil. The next largest buyer is China, with 20 per cent of Russia's exports. In other words Europe is, by far, Russia's largest customer for natural gas, an important source of hard cash for Russia, and Europe is not even over-dependent on Russian natural gas as a whole today. One would thus expect Europe to have a strong position at the negotiating table, that is, if Europe was *Europe*. But the problem is that, when it comes to buying natural gas from Russia, Europe is a collection of countries each trying to cut the best deal for itself. If Europe spoke with one determined voice, with a coherent energy acquisition policy as part of a coherent foreign policy construct, it would have a strong hand to play. Fragmentation and competition among the club's members translate instead into weakness, with Russia only too happy to play one country against the other. The issue is not unimportant as Europe depends on energy imports for more than half of its needs, and Russia has shown, during the 2006 Ukrainian gas crisis, that it is ready to use supplies as a geostrategic weapon (Russia opposed the 'orange revolution' going on in Ukraine at the time, fearing it was a plot designed to bring Kiev into the NATO umbrella). In 2009 Europe concocted the 'third energy package' aimed at separating production and distribution from large companies in order to liberalize EU energy markets and foster competition, something that was sure to ruffle the feathers of giant Russian energy group Gazprom, which has been trying to control part of the market. A year later, having attempted to test the limits of these new rules, Gazprom found itself the target of efforts by the European Commission to block a deal that seemed to make Poland, which already imports 65 per cent of its natural gas from Russia, even more dependent on Russian supplies.[13] Europe recently seemed to wake up to the issue, and the Nabucco pipeline, a European project that is supposed to deliver gas from the Caspian region starting in 2015 and entirely bypassing Russia and Ukraine, didn't please the Russians, prompting Moscow to launch its own South Stream pipeline (with the help of Italy's Eni), running under the Black Sea, to bring their own gas to Europe. The Great Game continues, and much remains to be done to develop a common energy policy.

Greenpeace with guns

Article 5 of NATO's charter states that

> 'An armed attack against one or more of them [i.e. NATO members] in Europe or North America shall be considered an attack against them all and consequently they agree that, if such an armed attack occurs, each of them, in exercise of the right of individual or collective self-defence recognised by Article 51 of the Charter of the United Nations, will assist the Party or Parties so attacked by taking forthwith, individually and in concert with the other Parties, such action as it deems necessary, including the use of armed force, to restore and maintain the security of the North Atlantic area'.

Article 5 is the supreme insurance policy, the deterrent of solidarity. NATO has been the cornerstone of the security architecture of Western Europe for the last, peaceful, half-century, and a magnet for Eastern European countries the instant they broke free from the Soviet grip. For behind it all stands the power of the mightiest nation on earth, the one whose military budget equals the sum of the military budgets of the next five countries with the largest militaries, the one with global power projection capabilities, namely the United States of America. Formed in 1949 with the frequent references of its charter to the UN belying its fitting into America's post-Second World War global architecture, NATO is for all intents and purposes an American-led institution pooling allied military resources under

US command. Lord Ismay, NATO's first Secretary General's, cliché definition that the organization's goal was 'to keep the Russians out, the Americans in and the Germans down' was to the point.

When NATO was created, Warsaw Pact armies led by the Soviet Union represented a clear and immediate danger at Europe's door. It is too easy to forget that for most of the second half of the twentieth century the world was prey to a balance of military terror between the Soviet empire, driven by Russia and its Marxist-Leninist ideology (with its gulags) on one side, and the 'free world', driven by America and its democracy and open markets ideology on the other. Anything that happened in the world happened in the context of this planetary clash. The USSR and the US built the mightiest armies the world had ever seen, with nuclear arsenals that could vaporize most of the globe several times over. They faced each other across places such as Checkpoint Charlie and the Fulda Gap, on and under the seas, in the air, in space and on land. They came close to igniting a third world war several times, notably with the Cuba missile crisis at the time boyish John F. Kennedy was president and Nikita Khruschchev was banging shoes on the lectern at the UN. Nuclear war on European soil was a distinct possibility during the half-century period of the Cold War. But the balance of terror they had created forced them to understand the virtues of restraint. The two antagonists contented themselves with fighting their battles indirectly through proxies in faraway places – had they not done so you and I would probably have been little radioactive particles floating here and there. European countries didn't have the means, the will or the cohesion to face the Soviets by themselves; instead, many of them harboured powerful communist parties and left-wing forces that wished no better than to take power and see their countries move to the Soviet camp. As British historian Niall Ferguson put it: 'For more than forty years the outcome of the Cold War was anything but certain.'[14] Without the US at NATO's helm, Europe wouldn't have stood a chance. Today, with the Soviet empire a thing of the past, nobody really knows what the clear and immediate danger is. This new fuzziness is not conducive to Western and intra-European cohesion. As the Soviet empire was crumbling, one of its officials, Alexander Yakovlev, wisely prophesied to the Western powers that 'We are going to disappear as a threat. The glue holding your alliance together will no longer be there to keep you united.'[15] The affirmation by British Defence Minister Malcolm Rifkind in 1994 that NATO was one of the pillars sustaining the edifice of Western civilization, together with a shared belief in democracy, free economies and other 'Western' values, seems to have been forgotten.

Kabul is about 15,000 miles from the northern shores of the Atlantic Ocean. So why should an organization with 'North Atlantic' in its title and whose famous Article 5 speaks of restoring and maintaining the security of the North Atlantic area be involved in Afghanistan? After the fall of the Soviet Union, none of NATO's members knew what to do with NATO, but didn't want to see it dismantled either. So they had to find a new role for it. NATO's website gives the impression that it is a peacenik organization so many are the references to promoting peace; Bob Dylan or James Taylor would seem to be suitable background music. Since there was no longer a brief for NATO in its European neighbourhood, it had to look for business where business was or sink into oblivion. NATO was redesigned, with its scope geographically enlarged. When the Soviet empire disintegrated, together with the breakdown of Yugoslavia and Czechoslovakia, some 22 new countries were born, a decidedly complicating factor. *New York Times* columnist Thomas Friedman wrote in March 2003, at a time when the US was involved in Iraq and Afghanistan:

> At this new historical pivot point, we're still dealing with a bipolar world, only the divide this time is no longer East versus West, but the World of Order versus the World of Disorder . . . the key instrument through which the new World of Order will try to deal with threats from the World of Disorder will still be NATO.[16]

NATO nevertheless became a vector through which any kind of security challenges to the West in general almost anywhere in the world would be dealt with. For the US, to act through a multilateral institution such as NATO helps to legitimize intervention. For the reluctant Western Europeans, participating in military adventures with NATO in faraway places is something they would rather avoid, but they need to show allegiance to the cause from time to time. They would rather consider NATO as a regional peace corps, used to protect universal human rights. For the more enthusiastic Eastern Europeans, to participate in NATO activities is a way to cement security ties with the US.

EU enlargement philosophy went hand in hand with a drive to enlarge NATO. But where EU enlargement was part of the European ideology, NATO enlargement was much more of an American objective, driven by geopolitical considerations. After the Cold War was over, there was a golden occasion to attract into America's (or the West's) orbit a few countries from Russia's periphery. As we have seen, these countries were keen to be included. Overtures were made, among others, to Ukraine and Georgia. A Russia led by alpha male Vladimir Putin could not be expected to remain quiescent while its 'near abroad' was not only dismembered but turned against it. Russia's invasion of Georgia in 2009 was a stark reminder that the Russian bear had been aroused. Months before the invasion Russian Foreign Minister Sergei Lavrov had warned the West that 'We are ready to do anything to prevent Ukraine and Georgia joining Nato':[17] the West could not claim to be surprised. If Georgia had been a member of NATO when it was invaded, Tbilisi would have invoked Article 5 and Europe, the US and Turkey would have been at war with Russia. Berlin, Paris and the other members had very little wish to pick a fight with Russia over Tbilisi. The military dangers and limitations of NATO's unbridled enlargement drive had become just as obvious as the political and economic dangers of the EU's unbridled expansion drive. Once more, Europeans slammed the brakes on a process of expansion which seemed to have got out of control.

Our new best friend

In October 2010 the quiet seaside resort of Deauville, 173 kilometres north-west of Paris, hosted a meeting of two political leaders in view of the NATO summit that was to take place the following month in Lisbon to define NATO's new strategic doctrine, replacing the previous one hammered out in 1999. That Catherine Ashton, the EU's foreign minister, was not invited to join Sarkozy and Merkel in Deauville is not entirely surprising, but what is surprising is that the third guest was Dimitry Medvedev, President of the Russian Federation. The Deauville meeting was staged as a 'reset' with Russia, just like that between American Secretary of State Hillary Clinton and Russian Foreign Minister Sergei Lavrov. In 2010 it seemed that every leader in the West had been doing their best to put 'Russia' and 'Reset' in the same sentence. This stance becomes even more positive: on Christmas eve of the same year, the French announced the sale of Mistral-class assault ships to the Russians, the first time a NATO country had sold military hardware to Russia. Built for military landing operations, these 199 metre long warships carrying 450 assault troops and 16 helicopters didn't fail to attract the attention of Georgia and the Baltic countries.[18] The trend actually started earlier, with NATO reducing the number of tactical nuclear weapons it maintains in Europe by more than 80 per cent in the last 20 years, leaving only a couple of hundred spread over five countries, a pale shadow of the several thousand Russian warheads. So, 20 years after the end of the Cold War, the two antagonists, Russia and NATO, are intent on turning the page and becoming friends?

America has been keen on implementing its plans to build an antimissile shield in Central Europe, allegedly to protect the continent against missiles from rogue states such as Iran, a project that helps reassert its military leadership on the continent. Since Europe was not going to agree to this project if it ruffled Russia's feathers the wrong way (and, as expected, it did), it has been in America's interest to befriend Russia and forge some sort of partnership. As for China, its economy and technological prowess have grown by leaps and bounds in recent years. Indeed, the country has become a power in space too, having not only put a man in orbit, but also shot down one of its own satellites in 2008, showing that it has the capability to knock off satellite-based communications vital to America's long-range military operations. In parallel, China has dramatically increased its military investment in recent years, and the pace of its progress in military technology has taken everybody by surprise. US Defense Secretary Robert Gates said, during his January 2011 visit to China (during which China's first stealth fighter, the J20, was unveiled) that 'we have to respond appropriately with our own programs'.[19] Advances in anti-ship ballistic missiles are putting US aircraft carriers at risk 1500 miles away from China's shores.

China has launched its first aircraft carrier, to be followed by two more in the coming years, stepping up its power projection capabilities, at least in the South China Sea. It is admitted that America's defence budget still dwarfs China's by a factor of more than five. But the quantitative and technological gaps are fast narrowing, and while a recession-hit and debt-laden US is cutting defence budgets, China, now the world's second largest economy, unburdened by debt and enjoying gargantuan foreign reserves, may well keep increasing its own. China seems intent on robbing the US of its supremacy in the Pacific theatre or to build up military muscle in line with its economic power. Now the centre of gravity of the Big Game has moved from Europe to the Asia-Pacific region, the US will not easily tolerate a change in the balance of power in the Far East and will inevitably shift more and more military resources there to contain China.

This can only happen to the detriment of America's commitment to Europe. America will inevitably divert its attention from Europe and although Europe chose butter over guns a long time ago the US is not likely to fill the gap there as it did in the past. European defence budgets aggregated at 228 billion euros in 2009, a figure that fell to 197 billion in 2010, ringing alarm bells in Washington. In the face of such cuts Gates claimed: 'My worry is that the more our allies cut their capabilities, the more people will look to the United States to cover whatever gaps are created.'[20] America was particularly worried about the huge scale of the defence cuts introduced by David Cameron's administration: whenever the US needed to build a coalition, Britain could be automatically counted on as the first ally to join; but, assuming it maintains the will to do so, can Britain still materially count for much? Europe will not be able to increase its military expenditure (which run at about half America's 4 per cent of GDP), simply because Europe saves on the military in order to fund its welfare system (one could say the US does the opposite), and recent austerity measures following the Eurozone crisis will have exacerbated this trend. Futhermore, in all likelihood Europe will have great difficulty undertaking even Libya-style operations unless the US picks up more of the burden, which is unlikely given the austerity the Pentagon will be imposing in the coming years. Europe will thus increasingly become a sideshow for the Americans: in this context, for the US a peaceful relationship with Russia means less attention and military resources having to be devoted to Europe, thus freeing them for the Far East. For Europeans, friendship with Russia is an insurance policy against having to increase military budgets. If Russia craves respect and friends then respect and friends it will have. If Russia does not want to hear any more talk of invitations to join NATO sent to Ukraine and Georgia, then not a word will be uttered. And nobody will care to remember that in 2009 Russia conducted military exercises to practise the invasion of the Baltic States.

How to make the least of it

In Europe there effectively exist *three* militaries overlapping and competing for resources and attention, each looking for an identity and a future. First and foremost there is NATO, the American-led military alliance that has been the linchpin of European security for over half a century. This is the real force, the one with teeth because of America's commitment. It is unclear, however, how committed certain core European nations are to its future. As Berlin slowly turns away from Europe and looks eastward, it increasingly perceives NATO as an institution with limited use. Germany is tired of the travails of Project Europe and weary of being dragged into American geopolitical adventures; it has become addicted to Russian trade (expected to reach a record level of 70 billion euros in 2011) and resources, in particular natural gas (a Russo-German entente is not welcome to either Poles or Americans).

Second, every single European country keeps its own armed forces. In effect, that amounts to almost 27 different armies, ranging from minuscule contingents such as Luxembourg's, to large ones with their own full complement of army, airforce and navy and international power projection capabilities such as those of France or England. No EU country is ready to relinquish its sovereignty totally in foreign policy and defence (France, for instance, would be unwilling to hand over its permanent seat with its veto right at the UN Security Council to a Lady Ashton, or its Charles de Gaulle aircraft carrier to some international body). So, instead of maximizing efficiency and minimizing costs, with different countries specializing in different military tasks and coordinating procurement, each country acts independently, which results in overlap, duplication and maximum inefficiency. It is only in 2010, pushed into a corner by brutal budget cuts, that France and the UK decided to pool certain military resources. It was done with little conviction, a case of too little too late, and necessity made a virtue.

Third, there is the EU army, or rather, the *idea* of a EU army. Some politicians here and there (especially the French, who have never fully bought into American leadership) have been floating the idea of Europe's members pooling military resources into a structure parallel to NATO but essentially devoid of US influence and responding to EU political leadership – the old idea of separating from the US revived. The idea is viewed suspiciously by the US and does not get much support from traditional US military allies such as the UK, or from Eastern European countries.

There is also a question of capabilities. During the Balkan wars, US Secretary of State James Baker insisted that the war was a strictly European conflict and that the US didn't have 'a dog in the fight'; but the US found itself dragged in to assist foundering European efforts. The Libyan intervention in early 2011 and the cacophony around it were further evidence of the difficulty the EU and its forces would encounter in the absence of American military involvement and leadership. NATO and the EU may both be headquartered in Brussels, but there is very little dialogue between these two institutions about military affairs, mainly because of the unresolved Turkish-Greek-Cypriot question and because Turkey is in NATO but not in the EU. Examples of useless duplication of efforts abound, such as when the EU and NATO separately train police forces in Afghanistan.[21] Overall, the result is, once more, inefficiency. It is difficult to see NATO developing into an efficient military force as long as Europeans persist in duplication and fail to specialize, or at least harmonize, military equipment. They even have difficulty working together on military missions because of equipment incompatibilities. European defence markets remain fragmented and thus inefficient while national priorities prevent the creation of a cost-efficient common defence market that could benefit from economies of scale. Due mainly to duplication, in 2010 the total number of weapon programmes of European countries was 89 against 27 for the world's mightiest military power, the US, which has a defence budget more than twice as high as that of Europe (and higher than that of Europe, Russia and China lumped together). Common programmes such as the Eurofighter suffered systematic delays and cost overruns because every country wanted its say and a piece of the pie. Besides the qualitative aspect, there are also quantitative issues, given the pervasive and continuous cuts in European countries' military budgets. NATO General Secretary Anders Fogh Rasmussen sounded the alarm bell during the 47th security conference in Munich in February 2011, warning against Europe's 'disinvestment' in relation to security, and pointing out that the US share of the alliance's defence budget now stands at 75 per cent, up from 50 per cent just two years ago, which is not welcome in Washington.[22] It is well known that 23 of NATO's 28 members spend less than the agreed 2 per cent of GDP on defence, and the current Eurozone crisis is not going to improve things. Rasmussen rightly added that in an age of austerity European nations should as a minimum work on getting a bigger 'bang for the buck' by co-ordinating policies and working together on 'smart defence'. The reality is otherwise. Europe is as inefficient and incapable of much coherence in the military arena as it is in the political one, and even more so because defence matters are considered an essential part of sovereignty, something countries are not ready to give up. US Defense Secretary Robert Gates went one further, saying that NATO faced 'the very real possibility of collective military irrelevance' and pointed out that 'If Europe becomes unable to make an appropriate contribution to global security then the United States might look elsewhere for reliable defence partners... future US political leaders, those for whom the Cold War was not the formative experience... may not consider the return on America's investment in NATO worth the cost.'[23] Is NATO seeing its final years? Do Europeans fully grasp the consequences of a possible change in America's commitment to military engagement in Europe? Will the Western alliance, which was born from the Second World War and won the Cold War, disintegrate because of the absence of a common enemy?

On important matters, NATO suffers from having to obtain consensus from all its members, as happens with EU decision-making, and as a result is just as likely as the EU to make decisions based on the lowest common denominator. Once more, narrow self-interest stands in the way of what's good for Europe as a whole. On the face of it, the military pact signed by Sarkozy and Cameron seemed a step in the right direction: two foremost European military powers agreed to share aircraft carriers, set up a 5000-man strong joint rapid deployment force and cooperate on their nuclear arsenals. But the decision to work together did not come from a desire for structural reform or to lead by example in Europe, or from the conviction that it was time to integrate militarily. Both signatories acted out of the sheer necessity imposed by brutal budget cuts, The pact does not portend a real trend for increased cooperation or 'smart' defence cutting in Europe. Britain dramatically slashed a defence budget that is the fourth in the world and that it could no longer sustain, a downsizing that involved retiring famous icons such as aircraft carrier Ark Royal as well as its fleet of Harrier jets, despite the Joint Strike Fighter not coming into service for another ten years. Any ambitions these two countries might have cherished of being still able to individually play a significant strategic role on the international chessboard were illusions that had now vanished.

To the edge of the world

And then there is the big big picture. Samuel Huntington argued in *The Clash of Civilizations* that, following the collapse of the Soviet Union, the superpower rivalry which had, for half a century, defined the actions of states belonging to one of two camps, gave way to states being free to define their interests according to which of the world's current seven or eight civilizations they belong to – a civilizational paradigm as a sort of default position for states.[24] In addition, Huntington placed religion as the defining characteristic of civilization, with secular nationalism and ideology being superseded by religious nationalism. In that sense Huntington wondered if the de-Christianization of Europe and its Islamization would result in a weakening of its civilizational ties and of its relationship with a more Christian America. To explain the re-emergence of Islam, he posited, 'The revival of non-Western religions is the most powerful manifestation of anti-Westernism in non-Western societies. That revival is not a rejection of modernity; it is a rejection of the West and of the secular, relativistic, degenerate culture associated with the West.'[25] To Huntington, 'The success of NATO has resulted in large part from its being the central security organization of Western countries with common values and philosophical assumptions.'[26] If one sub-scribes to this vision, alignments and antagonisms in the twenty-first century are defined by appurtenance to a civilization and culture, the West defines itself against the 'rest', and cohesion within the West, that is, the relationship between Europe and America, is of paramount importance; if the West is to remain strong the spread of democracy throughout the world (and of EU ideals in its neigh-bourhood) has to remain a primary goal of the West because it brings 'others' closer to Western ideals and culture. To the question of where Europe ends, Huntington responded: 'Europe ends where Western Christianity ends and Islam and Orthodoxy begin',[27] with the two being separated by a line running almost vertically from the north alongside Russia's border with Finland down to the mid-dle of Romania and turning west to leave out most of the Balkans and Greece, where the Ottoman and Austro-Hungarian empires touched.

When one ponders the geographical expansion it has undergone in recent decades, Project Europe *the integrator*, the motor capable of building political and economic alliances between nations out of free will, seems to have changed into a universal ideology of good with nearly worldwide ambitions. It aims to extend its postmodern paradise everywhere. Jean Monnet hoped that it would serve as an example of how 'to create a more prosperous and peaceful world'. Recognizing the reality that expansion cannot go on forever but acts as a positive motivational force for candidate countries, Mark Leonard suggested that Europe remain unclear about where the bor-ders will lie but very clear about the criteria countries should follow for entry. In fact, the criteria to join the club are exacting and a country can really be transformed for the better by going through the process. One weakness of the system, however, is that countries bend over backwards to comply with EU requirements to get into the club, but, once in, little can be done to castigate them if they misbehave. Existing provisions such as suspending voting rights in case of persistent breach of European values are considered too dam-aging to use. The issue came to the fore when the 2010 rotating presidency of the EU went to a Hungary in which the government of Prime Minister Viktor Orban passed laws curbing freedom of the press. EU politicians, unable to enforce political standards compatible with EU ideals, were able to do little more than wring their hands. Nevertheless, the welcome sign is still by the door. Croatia is waiting in the wings and was recently told membership was likely in 2013. Serbia has been knocking at the door for a while, and now that it has surrendered the war criminal Ratko Mladic its membership depends on its goodwill on the issue of Kosovo, which the EU would like Serbia to recognize – although it is difficult to ask Serbia to do what several EU countries have refused to do. In fact most of the Balkan countries are working hard to gain entry and it is likely that the EU will include them in the not too distant future. Europe is ambivalent about letting in the poor, reckless and restless Balkans, but letting them in may be the only way to put an end to their nationalistic and warmongering tendencies and bring peace and serenity to Europe's south-eastern flank. The beauty of Project Europe's soft imperialism is that it is good at getting the moderate majority in applicant countries aroused to subdue restless minorities and institutionalize the system. A Balkans outside the EU means a restless neighbourhood at the periphery and the likelihood of more instability in the future. But a Balkans inside the EU means more and more poor countries to look after at a time when Europe is being torn apart by a debt and currency crisis featuring its weaker countries.

The dilemma of European integration remains the same today as it has been for several decades. A looser integration means less weight in world affairs and more potential for disunity. A stronger integration means more loss of sovereignty for individual states. Europe's borders have never been defined, and its lack of a clear sense of identity raises the question of where its frontiers should stop. Does the universalist philosophy inherent in Project Europe preclude the definition of a 'European heritage' (such as the notion of a 'club of Christian nations') which could set geographical limits to expansion? Will the very success of Project Europe as an integrator with no boundaries doom Europe's future by diluting the EU into a nonentity? If embracing peace and a democratic political system is a sufficient criterion to join Europe, then why not let in Azerbaijan,

Armenia or Georgia one day? Closer to hand is the issue of Turkey's membership. For centuries Turkey banged at the door of Europe with its Ottoman armies, swords in hand; it has now reinvented itself as a European state, is a member of NATO and anxious to gain entry into the club. When it comes to enlargement, Turkey dwarfs all other challenges facing Europe today, and now deserves our special attention.

FOUR

THE BOSPORUS CONUNDRUM

The question of Turkey joining Europe

Here and also there

What is most striking in the taxi journey from the airport along Istanbul's seaside avenue, with the Bosporus waters on the right, is a street sign as you approach the two bridges over the waterway, with an arrow pointing left reading 'Europe' and one pointing right reading 'Asia'. The Bosporus, the waterway connecting the Caspian sea to the Mediterranean, is about two kilometres wide at its narrowest and heavy with maritime traffic. On its western shore is Europe, on its eastern shore is Asia. What may seem like a mere river in the middle of a city represents a real division between two worlds. Turkey literally has a foot on both sides. A small portion of its landmass, including its largest city, Istanbul, lies on the European side, where Turkey shares a frontier with Greece and Bulgaria, while most of the country lies in Asia, where it shares frontiers with Iran, Georgia, Armenia, Azerbaijan, Iraq and Syria. Ankara, Turkey's modern capital, is in Asia, in the region called Anatolia, but the most important city by far is Istanbul. This city, formerly known as Byzantium (originally a Greek fishing village named Byzantion) was established by Roman Emperor Constantine in AD 330 as the capital of the eastern half of a Roman empire that had been split in two to make its vastness more manageable. The city was named Constantinople after his death. Constantine embarked on a Christianization of the entire Roman empire, with the idea that this new faith would keep it united at a time when it was fragmenting. Constantinople was thus originally undoubtedly a European and Christian city, the crown jewel of the eastern half of the Roman empire which encompassed lands in Asia, the Middle East and beyond, extending its footprint all the way to the threshold of Persia. In the West, the Rome-centred half of the empire entered a swift decline, becoming prey to barbarian Germanic invasions, and disappeared altogether in 476. The Byzantine empire, on the other hand, went on for another thousand years, enjoying periods of magnificence. Divergences in religious doctrinal views led to the Great Schism of 1054 between a Catholic Church centred in Rome and an Eastern Orthodox church centred in Byzantium.

The Turks arrived in the region in the eleventh century from central Asia. During their journey westwards they converted to Sunni Islam. The first Seljuk Turkish state, made of Turkic people from central Asia pushed westwards by invading Mongol hordes, was based in Anatolia, on the eastern and Asian side of today's Turkey, and fought many wars with Constantinople over territory in the east. After the Seljuks defeated the Byzantines at the battle of Manzikert in 1071, Turkish tribes moved in droves into the Asia Minor peninsula. The Ottoman state was initially a small emirate of Turkic people in north-west Anatolia, straddling the border separating the Byzantine and Seljuk empires. As Byzantium's power ebbed, the Ottomans increasingly pushed into Byzantine territories. In 1453, these rapidly expanding new conquerors, relentlessly pushing westwards, finally captured Constantinople, last vestige of the Roman empire. The victors went on to absorb the remnants of the huge Byzantine empire and incorporate them into their Ottoman empire. This last of the great Islamic empires came to include vast parts of North Africa, the Middle East, Central Asia, the Balkans and even parts of Western Europe. It lasted almost five centuries, up to the end of the First World War, albeit not without difficulties; there were, for example, Christian revolts in the Balkans in the nineteenth century. Islam came to dominate the former Byzantine empire now held by the Ottomans. The Ottoman empire turned into a European power in that it became, through the centuries, an integral part of Europe's balance-of-power equation, balancing the ambitions of the Habsburgs, the papacy and other powers, allying itself at one time or another with this or that European power, here siding with the French and British to fight the mid-nineteenth-century Crimean

War against Russia, there siding with the Germans and Austro-Hungarians against allied powers in the First World War, and getting involved in the affairs of Europe on the continent and abroad.

With such a tormented history, the question of whether today's Turkey is European, Asian or something else entirely is not an easy one to answer. The question would be one for scholars only to address were it not for the fact that today's Turkey considers itself part of Europe, is a member of NATO and has applied to join the EU. Historically and geographically the country is in between two worlds, a candidate to join the 'Christian club' known as the EU, but it was also head of the 57-nation Organization of the Islamic Conference. Enlargement is, as we have seen, at the core of Project Europe's philosophy and Europe has not hesitated to absorb many countries in its periphery. But the issue of whether or not to absorb a 70-million strong Islamic Turkey into the European Union is a quandary for Europeans and is not about to be resolved.

From Ataturk to Erdogan

Over the centuries Islam has spawned a number of brilliant civilizations, empires and caliphates. Most of them have been banging at the doors of Europe, from the east or the south, attempting to conquer, subjugate and convert the Christian world. The Ottomans were no different, except that ethnically they were neither Arabs nor Persians but Turkic. For most of five centuries before the end of the First World War Turkey had been a classical Muslim theocratic empire powered by the ideology of jihad and intent on bringing Europe under its rule and the banners of Islam. It is said that the delicious pastry now called a 'croissant' was invented in Vienna during a siege by the Ottoman armies of Sultan Suleiman the Magnificent who carried banners adorned with the Islamic crescent; an Austrian baker looking to boost his fellow citizens' spirit of resistance gave them crescent-shaped pastries to eat. Another present-day legacy of Ottoman rule is the traditional pleated fustanella skirt worn by Greece's Evzones presidential guard: the skirt contains 400 pleats, in memory of the four centuries of Ottoman domination. Yet immediately after the First World War (in which Turkey had sided with the Germans), Turkey found its centuries-old Ottoman empire dismembered by the victors, and it was in danger of losing its independence to the Greeks, and others, were it not for Mustafa Kemal.

An Ottoman officer who felt that Turkey had lost everything by clinging to its old Islamic ways and would have everything to gain by becoming a modern secular and Western power, Kemal, later called Ataturk ('father of Turks') by the National Assembly, won independence for Turkey and embarked on a complete and spectacular de-Islamization of Turkish state and society. This radical turnaround process labelled 'Kemalization' took inspiration from, but went much further than, the current of Westernization that swept the Ottoman state at the end of the nineteenth century. With his *inkilap* (revolutionary change), Ataturk, who firmly believed that rapid modernization was a matter of survival for Turkey, changed his country into an entity the world had never seen before: a secular Islamic country. The sultanate and caliphate institutions were abolished in 1924, and in 1937 the republic was proclaimed with a secular constitution from which all references to Islam, including the Muslim calendar, were eradicated. French President Sarkozy may be surprised to learn that his efforts to have headscarves banned from public offices and schools are nothing new, Ataturk having done the same long before, and under his rule women gained the right to vote in Turkey before French women obtained the franchise. Ataturk, still innovating, created state Islam to better keep a lid on religion. Imams became government employees. The Turkish army, the original source of Ataturk's power, became a bastion of Kemalism, the ultimate guarantor of the secularization and Westernization of the country. Turkey joined NATO in 1952, anchoring itself to Europe and balancing neighbouring Greece, in exchange for which it guarded Europe's eastern flank, blocking Russian expansion into the Mediterranean. Turkey applied for EU membership in 1987, although it was recognized as a candidate only 12 years later.

Kemalism was tantamount to the annihilation of a centuries-old Ottoman culture and its replacement with a new, Westernized one. As pointed out in earlier chapters, the disintegration of empires leads to the formation of nation-states, and Turkey was no exception. In order to produce a homogeneous nation-state Ataturk did not hesitate to get rid of minorities, such as Greeks and Armenians, often in extremely unpleasant ways. After Ataturk's death the army continued to take its role as guarantor of the Kemalist legacy very seriously, to the point of taking power in 1980, when it considered the state under threat from left-wing ideologies. It is at that time that the army, looking to feed the youth some ideology to divert their attention away from Marxist ideas, made the fateful decision to modify the constitution and introduce mandatory religious education in schools. The law of unintended consequences resulted in a proliferation of 'imam hatip' religious schools,[1] difficult to control, that started a mild re-Islamization of society. The army later recognized its mistake and intervened to dissolve the Rafah Islamic party of then Prime Minister Necmettin Erbakan, forcing him out. Ataturk's legacy had been saved, or so it seemed. But the spirit of re-Islamization had been roused.

It comes as no surprise that, as the army's powers decreased over time, the forces of Islamization made decisive inroads. These culminated in the AKP, the more moderate Islamic and free-market party that Recep Tayyip Erdogan and Abdullah Gul established when they broke ranks with Erbakan in 2001, taking power in 2002. Erdogan, a radical Islamist jailed for sedition in 1999, who correctly perceived that power was shifting from the Kemalist secular elite to the more religious central Anatolian entrepreneurial class, later moderated his rhetoric. He oversaw the country's GDP more than doubling in a decade, an economic miracle. As Turkey's new prime minister he promoted peace with the country's neighbours to the east and south, and proceeded to consolidate the power of Islamists, marginalize the army and muzzle the judiciary and the 'deep state' through a series of cunning moves.

Turkey's paramount desire to join the EU paradoxically tied the hands of the army, which knew only too well that any new undemocratic move on its part to take power in order to get rid of the Islamists would dash hopes of joining the club, because Europe does not welcome military dictatorships in its midst. This is a contradiction: the guarantor of Turkey's secularism and modernization drive, values at the core of Project Europe, was the army, but Europe could not bring itself to condone army intervention because it ran against its democratic values, even if the objective was to dampen the potentially totalitarian forces of re-Islamization. Europe made its opinion on the matter quite clear and the army could only watch from the sidelines. This constraint made the work of re-Islamization forces all the easier. It is thus that, ironically, the EU indirectly played an important role in the de-Kemalization and re-Islamization of Turkey. It remains a moot point how Islamic today's Turkey has become and how much more Islamic it can be expected to become. Is Turkey's reversal, engineered by Ataturk, irreversible, in which case the AKP's moves amount to no more than mild re-Islamization? Or will Erdogan's moves represent the start of a reversal process that will bring Turkey back to square one? The answers to these questions go to the heart of the issue of Turkey's admission to the club.

Osama's nightmare

There is no question that the majority of Turks, Islamists as well as secularists, see themselves as part of Europe, at least geographically, and would like to join the EU. And this despite the fact that, although it would still be the poorest country in Europe, Turkey's economy is doing better these days than that of most of its European neighbours. Despite the re-Islamization undertaken by their society in the last three decades, Turks perceive accession to the EU as the natural and well-deserved result of a Westernization process that was started long ago. Turkey joined the European Council in 1948, NATO a couple of years later and ratified the European Convention on Human Rights in 1954. Turkey is also a member of the quintessential European football union UEFA, where it has won prestigious European trophies. In these respects the Kemalist ideal is alive and well, and Turks feel European at heart.

Today, the biggest supporter of Turkey joining the EU might not even be Turkey itself, given its recent disappointment at Europe's ambivalence. If there is one country that would like to see accession become a reality, and today rather than tomorrow, it is America. As noted above, America tends to look at geopolitical issues primarily through the prism of security and is not particularly concerned with the possible intra-European and social impact of Turkey's joining the EU. Turkey's 600,000-strong and well-equipped army (the largest in Europe) is already a member of NATO and a bulwark guarding its southern flank, keeping Russian access to the

Mediterranean in check. Turkey can also be useful as a power in the Caucasus and one that can be an influence on the US in the Black Sea. In the eyes of America's strategists, Turkey has always been an indispensable element in the region's geopolitical chessboard. Turkey's becoming part of the EU would anchor Turkey to US-led NATO even more solidly. Moreover, the US calculates that a Turkey more firmly linked to Europe means a stronger united front against radical Islam further south, whereas a Turkey allowed to drift away from Europe may develop nostalgia for its past at the head of Islam and may even be tempted over time to join the camp of Islamist nations. The accession of this big country to the EU also makes Machiavellian sense for the US from a political point of view: it would result in further dilution of the Franco-German axis, and a more fragmented, politically weaker Europe more prone to being controlled by Washington. Often in step with their American cousins, the British favour Turkey's accession as a recipe to dilute French and German power and are not very moved by arguments concerning European ethnic and religious homogeneity. It would be wrong to accuse the Americans and British of cynicsm: all nation-states tend to make calculations and act in what they perceive are their best interests given the strategic and tactical landscape around them at the time. For Turkey as well as for the US and the UK, there is no ambivalence, no dilemma: Turkey should become a member of the EU, and sooner rather than later. Other integrationists argue that, by not letting Turkey in, Europe risks alienating the country and watching helplessly as Turkey develops closer ties to its south and east, evolving into a more radical Islamic state. The strength of this argument is limited, however, as it is tantamount to saying that Turkey should be let in not because of what it is and the benefits it brings but as an insurance policy against the damage it could do to the EU if it is not let in.

For extreme Islamic fundamentalists such as the late Osama Bin Laden, modern Turkey is the quintessential traitor to the cause of Islam. It was, after all, the first Muslim state ever to take the step of de-Islamization and turn itself into a secular state. Furthermore, secularization went hand in hand with nationalism, further anathema for Muslim fundamentalists who reject nationalism as a force which weakens the cohesion of the *ummah* (the worldwide community of

Muslims) by dividing it into secular state lines. To these radicals, Ataturk is the ultimate apostate, one who caused the de-Islamization of entire Muslim societies, who should have his legacy reversed and erased. Should Turkey join the EU, the re-Islamization process the country has recently been going through may well be diluted, if not reversed, as Western influence would increase exponentially. Turkey would probably be lost forever to the cause of Islamic jihadism. There is another, more realistic argument: this advocates rejection on the grounds that the world would benefit if Turkey became a leader of the Islamic world with a moderating influence instead of turning its attention westwards. Another argument for rejection was proposed by Samuel Huntington, who felt that Europe, as a political entity, would not survive the entry of an 'outsider' as large and different as Turkey.[2] Huntington advocated instead a role for Turkey as a strong but democratic and moderately Islamic natural leader for Islamic nations. In other words, Turkey's accession to Europe would be destructive to Project Europe, the final blow to an already fragile European political unity, whereas Turkey's role as a leader of Islam, a return to the position it held for centuries, but with a moderating influence on the *ummah*, could be useful to Western and Islamic nations alike.

The mother of all dilemmas

It was former French president Valéry Giscard d'Estaing who said in 2002 that Turkey's accession would mean the end of Europe.[3] Europe can be considered as motivated by an ideology of integration, yet rejecting applicants is nothing new: the French twice vetoed British accession to the original European Community. Accession needs the unanimous vote of all existing members of the club, which is far from a certainty in the case of Turkey. To many Europeans, asking what it is about Turkey's accession that is so alarming is like asking what bothers you about letting a buffalo into your living room. First, its sheer size: were Turkey a few million-strong moderate Islamic country the situation would be different. After all, Bosnia and Macedonia are Muslim, yet talk of their joining the club one day does not result in sleepless nights in European capitals. But, European rejectionists reason, a country of 70 million people (with a high birthrate relative to the rest of Europe), an historical foe of Europe, whose conversion to European ideals is only decades old and whose re-Islamization process is obvious is another matter. This is a dilemma for Europeans. If Turkey is allowed in, because of its sheer size there is a risk of blowing apart European political unity and the 'Big Powers' of Europe would have a new rival to contend with in their own backyard, one whose intentions and alignments are not clear in the Erdogan era.

The practical issues are these. Germany and France, the two foremost European powers, have been setting the agenda for Europe since its inception. EU enlargement to 27 members has diluted the power of the Franco-German axis. The recent economic crisis has dramatically shifted the power within this axis in favour of Germany. Yet when push comes to shove, when these two countries agree, they still call the shots; but if Turkey joins, it is so large that 100 Turks would join the European parliament: Turkey may end up with more votes than Germany. Suddenly the comfortable Franco-German *pas de deux* would turn into a much more complex three-players game where France would constantly be worried that Turkey sides with Germany against France, and vice versa. It would also make EU decision-making, already a nightmare, even more complicated. Why should France or Germany risk losing their pre-eminence by letting Turkey in? They won't, and that is the main reason why Turkey's accession to the EU is a pipe dream. It is not a question of religion, GDP or other arguments, it is a question of traditional balance-of-power politics within the EU. No wonder that 75 per cent of the French are opposed to Turkey's accession, and Germany's popular opposition is not far behind. Yet everybody is aware that if Turkey is not allowed in there is a risk of alienating it and sending it drifting east and south to become an Islamic power that could end up defining itself in opposition to Europe – or at the very least a powerful and unfriendly neighbour. Damn if you do, damn if you don't! When in doubt, prevaricate: this is exactly what Europe has been doing.

Turkey is not only big, it is also relatively poor. According to Munich's OstEuropa Institute, Turkey, if let in, would automatically find itself at the receiving end of European funds at a net cost to contributors of 14 billion euros per year. Absorbing a large, substantially poorer population is perceived by some as a potentially costly undertaking, especially in tough economic times, not unlike that of West Germany's absorbing East Germany. Furthermore, with only a few per cent of its landmass lying in Europe, and the rest in Asia, Turkey is also Muslim. At the back of every European mind lurks the religious question: is Turkey Islam's ultimate Trojan horse? Will it attempt to Islamicize Europe? Will it try to conquer from within what over the centuries it has not succeeded in conquering from the outside? However far-fetched and paranoid these worries seem, the question is made all the more acute by the convergence of several factors, including Western suspicion of all things Islamic that followed 9/11, the obvious re-Islamization of Erdogan's Turkey and the realization that the number of Muslim immigrants in Europe is becoming significant and that they are not always integrating well into European societies. Had 9/11 not happened, things may have been easier for Turkey. But 9/11 did happen, the European psyche was affected and the question of Islam is here to stay, spoken or unspoken, even if Turkey's religious fervour is light years behind that of the 9/11 extremists. Ironically, Turkey's Islam is more moderate and controlled than the Islam existing in certain European countries, and a radicalization of Turkish Islam originating in Western Europe is more to be feared than the contrary. The ultra-liberal UK has been far better at creating radical jihadists in recent times than Turkey, which has tight control over religious matters. But how many Europeans would accept this argument?

The credentials of Erdogan do nothing to calm the fears of Europeans rejecting accession because of religious fears. He was the product of a religious Islamic schooling. He went to prison for radical Islamic activism (he famously cited a poem that said 'The mosques are our barracks, the minarets our bayonets') before he moderated his instincts.[4] In 2007 the army threatened to step in to prevent his political ally Gul from becoming president, partly because his wife wore a headscarf, still today a symbol of tension between religious and secular Turks. Erdogan has, moreover, recently been accused of leading a wave of political intolerance expressed by the jailing of journalists and opponents, something that would disturb European leaders. To Arthur du Plessis, author of *Islam and the West: The Total War*,[5] for whom there is no such thing as a moderate

Muslim, the West has not woken up to the menace posed by the re-Islamization of Turkey. He maintains that the Turkish army, politically weakened in recent times, is the only element preventing Turkey from becoming an 'Islamic Republic'. He points out that the reversal of the headscarf ban in schools and government offices that Erdogan's AKP party has been calling for was already desired by two-thirds of the Turkish population as far back as 2000. For Du Plessis and others, Kemalization was but a short episode in Turkish history, now being reversed, and the real vocation of Turkey is to be what it always was, a leading Islamic power. Other arguments heard in favour of rejection include the treatment of political opposition and minorities (in particular the Kurds, whose brethren in Iraq amount to a nation without a country in a country without a nation), let alone the alleged massacre of 1.5 million Christian Armenians at the hands of the Turks in 1915, a topic Turks steadfastly avoided confronting until recently compelled to by EU accession rules. No mention is made by such rejectionists of the fact that the vast majority of Turks today are moderate, do not particularly care much about religion or the Koran, and that the AKP never gained more than a third of the votes in elections; nor do they look further back to observe that it was in Ottoman Turkey that Jews expelled from Spain found a tolerant home centuries ago.

Rejectionists, shy about the religious dimension of the debate, like to point out historical, ethnic and geographical arguments. Turks are not originally European, they come from Central Asia. Most of their country is not located in Europe but in Asia. For them, nothing in the geography, history or civilization of Turkey makes it European. So, the argument goes, Turkey is de facto not European; it is preposterous to think otherwise. And if one includes in Europe a country that is clearly non-European just because it adheres to the ideals and rules of the club, then where is the line drawn? Why not include Armenia or Azerbaijan? The process of enlargement would be endless and any remaining political cohesiveness of Europe would dilute in the process. Some, sensitive to the idealistic integrationist dimension of Project Europe, argue in favour of accession on grounds that Turkey has already proven its willingness to reform and adopt European ways and values. To these, the rejectionists offer as a counter-argument the difficulty of absorbing a country that is so poor and different from the rest of Europe. To those espousing the cause of accession on grounds that it would show the rest of Islam that Europe is tolerant and that a Turkey inside the EU would have a moderating influence on the *ummah* outside, the rejectionists argue that it is far from certain that, once they have joined the club, the Turks will become impervious to Islamic radicalization, and should the reverse happen, if Turkish youth, who by and large seem more moderate today than many European Muslims, is radicalized by their brethren from Europe or abroad, then Europe would be in for a very rough ride. This rejectionist argument posits, in other words, that young Muslims are prone to be radicalized or that there is a risk, and that it is one thing to have to deal with a small, radicalized minority such as Europe has today, and another to have to confront tens of millions in your midst. Rejectionists also point out to 'technical' difficulties such as Turkey's refusal to recognize Cyprus, itself a member of the EU; the implication here is that Turkey is not ready to espouse Project Europe's core values. Erdogan recently advocated a stepped-up presence of Turkish naval forces in the Eastern Mediterranean in concert with the exploration of gas fields in the area, a message not lost on Cyprus, Israel and rejectionists.

At least two countries do not accept the rejectionists arguments and do not even feel the ambivalence of most Europeans torn in their dilemma. To Washington and London, the issue is black and white. Rejection would be a historical mistake. For them, as we have seen a Turkey as part of Europe means cementing Turkey's relationship with US-NATO, strengthening NATO, and at the same time planting the last nail in the coffin of any idea of revival of a Franco-German axis – and better a Turkey firmly in NATO's camp than the risk, however remote, of having it join the jihadists. Accession means a stronger relationship with Turkey, as a moderate and strong Muslim country, in the global confrontation with radical Islam. Speaking at a NATO summit in Turkey in 2004, President George W. Bush was quite clear about where America stood on the issue: 'I believe you ought to be given a date by the EU for your eventual acceptance into the EU.'[6] In countering the Americans' argument, former European Commission Member Frits Bolkestein argued that Turkey was too large, poor and different to be allowed to join the EU and that 'rejecting Turkey would not be to the liking of the Americans,

but have they ever thought of letting Mexico join their union?'.
An alliance with Turkey would undeniably have positive strategic
implications for Europe, independently of what form it may take.
Geographically, the country is positioned as a bridge or a cushion
between Europe and the Middle East, depending on whether one
is an optimist or a pessimist. Turkey's stature, combined with its
moderate brand of Islam, suggests it can have a moderating influence within the *ummah*. A Turkey inside the EU would show the
ummah that the West is ready and willing to accept Muslims in its
midst, assuming this argument would have any practical usefulness.
A Turkey inside the EU would, however, have to relinquish any idea
of recovering any leading role in the Islamic world because it would
be perceived by many Muslims as having completed its journey into
apostasy.

Faced with the dilemma of letting or not letting Turkey in, some
in Europe have been suggesting that Turkey be given a special status,
a 'privileged partnership', instead of full accession, an idea originally
floated by Giscard d'Estaing and subsequently revived by Sarkozy–
Merkel. In other words, the doorman won't let you in, but he'll take
his hat off and pat you on the back. Not unsurprisingly, this idea
has not found many takers in Turkey. Symbols matter. It's one thing
if the club does not let you in, it is quite another if they actually
build a wall to keep you out. In passing it should also be noted
that, as France, Italy and Spain have been taking increasingly effective measures to stem illegal immigration from the Maghreb and
Africa to their shores, the flow of migrants has been diverted through
Greece, with an estimated 130,000 crossing from Turkey to Greece
by the Evros river in 2010.[7] Greece's announcement in early 2011
that it was going to build a wall 3 metres high along 13 kilometres
of frontier it shares with Turkey was directed at stemming North
African immigration but carried a symbolism that gave ammunition
to those, in Turkey, who feel they are being mistreated by Europe.
The issue of a 'privileged partnership' merits closer consideration.
Why not build on the reality, which is that the EU is responsible for
over 40 per cent of Turkey's foreign trade and three-quarters of its
foreign investments? Some Europeans have been encouraging a privileged partnership, and Turkey has said no. But they all seem to have
forgotten a technical detail: nobody has defined what this privileged

partnership would be. It remains as nebulous a notion as there could ever be, yet both sides react to it as if they knew exactly what it is. It would probably help if someone took the initiative to define it: after all, it may be that Turkey does not want to give up certain aspects of sovereignty that a full membership would entail. It may be that a pragmatic look at an appropriately defined privileged partnership would find acceptance in Turkey. Moreover, should Turkey embark on this path, it may be able to extract numerous concessions from a Europe only too happy to not have to make a yes/no choice. Again, what is missing in Europe is pragmatism.

Who needs Europe, anyway?

Turks today are probably asking themselves 'will my country ever be able to join Europe or are we kidding ourselves that they'll let us in one day?' They may recall that one of the well-publicized messages from the No Debacle popular referendum on the European Constitution in 2005 was that Europeans were not keen for their country to join the 'Christian Club' (an exaggerated notion, given that Pope John Paul's reference to Europe's Christian heritage was not included in the text of the European constitution in 2004). By now, Turks may well have grown disillusioned with the whole thing. For them, accession may be all or nothing: 'either we get in through the main door like everybody else or we don't get in at all. After all we are 70 million Turks, proud of our illustrious past and we don't really need your decaying Europe. We used to be called the "sick man of Europe", we may still be poor relative to the rest of Europe, but we are catching up fast, posting the highest rates of growth in the OECD (we actually grew faster than China on an annualized basis in the first quarter of 2011) and we sailed through Europe's recent economic crisis like a breeze. Europe's population is old and its economy is falling asleep. Our population is young: we could, just by ourselves, resolve Europe's upcoming population deficit problem. Our economy is rising, faster than any of your 27 economies, and the OECD says ours could become the second largest in Europe behind Germany by 2050.[8] You seem to forget that you let us in as a founding member of the European Council in 1949 and that you need us in NATO where we have the second largest armed forces after

America. We are a stable democracy, the first in the Muslim world. Our markets may still be a bit overregulated but we have, fundamentally, a free market economy with banks, deficits and debt levels healthier than most of Europe's. We are becoming a large market for goods, an important trading nation, a great low cost producer of many things which Europe needs. If Europe wants to lose the opportunity to let us join the club, so be it, let them make another historical mistake. If Europe looks down on us, the Middle East is looking up to us. And if Europeans are wondering what Turkey really is, well, we are starting to wonder what Europe really is. If you think our secular society is going to turn into some Iranian theocracy just because religion has made a bit of a comeback here and there, you are fools. You don't seem to understand that there is a lively political debate going on in our country. If you don't understand or want us, let's look east and south: we can have a bright future there too. If we access Europe, we join the club and our Kemalist dream will have come true. If we don't, then let's forget about Europe and we may regain our position at the helm of Islamic nations. Arab countries that have been through upheavals very recently have even been talking of emulating the Turkish model. By the way, you let us in NATO because it was useful to you, but not in the EU, so we'll keep on blocking any rapprochement between NATO and the EU just to make your life a bit more difficult. We may not all like our Prime Minister Recep Tayyip Erdogan nor do we like his moves to muzzle the press and reinforce his own authority; but when he said "We are not a country that would wait at the EU door like a docile supplicant ... Europe has no alternative to Turkey",[9] he was speaking for all of us. In fact we are so bored by the whole thing that the course on the EU at Istanbul's Bahcesehir University was cancelled for lack of student interest.[10] Turkey's Europe Minister Egemen Bagis put it bluntly: "The EU needs Turkey more than Turkey needs it." '[11]

The absence of a vigorous and open debate in the country today does not mean there are no dissenting voices. While all Turks are proud of their country's recent economic achievements, not all are satisfied with the political direction the country has taken under Erdogan – Turkey now holds the world record for the number of journalists in jail. The charismatic Kemal Koprulu, publisher of *Turkish Policy Quarterly*, is well informed about what's going on in

Turkey. He wrote a long open letter (later published by Europe's Robert Schumann Foundation) reflecting his misgivings about the AKP's increasingly authoritarian rule, just on the eve of elections that saw Erdogan reconfirmed at the helm of the country for a third time in a row.[12] Koprulu is one these Turks who not only decry the absence of checks and balances in their society, but are openly worried about Turkey having 'mismanaged almost all things "Western"', including the country's shift away from the West and its rapprochement with players such as Iran, and feels the AKP leadership is not really committed to entering the EU. With this in mind, where is Turkey really going?

Riding a tiger

Following Ataturk's Westernization drive, Turkey focused its attention westwards, towards Europe, to the detriment of its neighbourhood to the east and south. Partly as a reaction to finding Europe's door closed (or only half open) and as a result of the 'Erdoganization' of the country, this attitude has been reversed. Turkey recently started not only to pay more and more attention to the lands of its former Ottoman empire to the south and east, but also to embark on a much more independent and assertive foreign policy, one that happens to be less in line with Western interests. Is Turkey trying to revive the old Ottoman regional sphere of influence or is something else envisioned? Turkish President Abdullah Gul, speaking during the UN General Assembly session in September 2010, not only praised his country's status as a Muslim democracy and the dynamism of its economy. He made it quite clear that Turkey's decoupling had effectively started, that it was developing closer ties in the Middle East and intended to play an independent and pivotal role in the region. Gul didn't avoid defending his country's rapprochement with Iran, a move that is sure to bring anxiety to policy planners in Washington and Tel Aviv. Israel, a sure loser in this realignment, needs all the allies it can get in the region. It saw its previously close economic and military ties to Turkey evaporate after an ill-fated Israeli raid on a Turkish ship steaming to Gaza on an allegedly humanitarian mission; this gave Erdogan the excuse to attack Israel and ingratiate Turkey with Arab mass opinion. One certain winner in this realignment is Shia Iran, which sees trade with Sunni Turkey bound to triple in the coming five years to 6.5 billion euros per annum in the face of Western sanctions and which has allegedly gained access to Turkish banks to finance its nuclear programme.[13] Iran sells natural gas which Turkey needs, and in Turkey Iran gained a precious ally that blocked the singling out of Iran as a central danger to Europe during the November 2010 NATO summit in Lisbon and objected to a radar base being built in Turkey as part of the missile shield defence system aimed at containing Tehran. Given its newly found vocation in the region, Turkey is bound to resist Western-sponsored sanctions against Iran, such as those which forced Turkish suppliers to cancel contracts to supply refined oil to Tehran. The deterioration of Turkey's ties with Israel means that Turkey's ambition to play a central peacemaking role in the Israeli-Palestinian conflict has taken a hit: in Turkish eyes the loss of Israel's friendship is more than made up by what it stands to gain by becoming friends with Iran and Syria. The US is bound to feel uneasy about the development; but Turkey could have a calming influence on these nations and such economic and political engagement might help keep them in check. Wouldn't it be better for Palestinians to look to Turkey rather than to Iran? Here are two rising powers, Turkey and Iran, and one region: looking at the regional chessboard, could it be that Turkey will naturally replace a broken Iraq as a regional power strong enough to keep a check on Iran's ambitions in the region? However, any plans to turn Turkey into a leading power in the Middle East suffered a serious setback in the face of recent unrest and volatility in the Arab world. For Erdogan, years of political and economic investment in the region and of building ties with leaders such as Syria's Bashar Al-Assad have effectively been thrown to the air. Given such uncertainty, how realistic is it for Turkey to turn East?

Here is another scenario. Recent events in the Middle East and North Africa indicate that Muslim countries are fed up with their dictators and yearn for some form of democracy. A survey conducted by TESEV found that over three-quarters of Arabs polled considered Turkey as a successful role model when it comes to the coexistence of Islam and democracy.[14] The 'Turkish model' is making headway. The unease with which Turkey was viewed by these countries as former colonial master of the Ottoman empire may be giving way to a desire to emulate, maybe even a readiness to be *led* by, Turkey. As Turkey realizes that no matter what it does Europe will not let it in (except in NATO) and at the same time rediscovers its untapped potential in the east and south, it could decide to entirely redefine itself and completely reject the Ataturk legacy. The Cold War was the primary raison d'être of Turkey's membership of NATO and the alliance served both well. But with the collapse of the Soviet Union, Turkey's military ties to Europe and the West may one day be redefined, since Turkey may not be as enthusiastic in acting as a bulwark for Europe against eventual threats from the Muslim world in the south as it was against the Soviet threat. As a secular state with a foot in Western institutions such as NATO, Turkey has little chance to lead Islam. But if it abandons secularism, and any ambition to join Europe, Turkey could calculate that it can return to its historical role at the helm of Islamic nations (at least in the region), a role in which leaving NATO and defining itself in opposition to Europe are essential. 'Beg in the West or lead in the East' may turn out to be Turkey's calculation. Such a scenario may seem far-fetched, but it is not an impossibility, given the current trends started by Erdogan. Should it happen, the security of the entire eastern and south-eastern flank of Europe would be called in question.

FIVE

THE TINGUELY MACHINE

The shortcomings of the EU and European institutions

Home of the Eurognome

Europe's motto 'In varietate Concordia' (united in diversity) is an understatement in terms of diversity and an overstatement in terms of unity. From the time the European Community for Coal and Steel (ECCS) was established in 1952, the founding countries disagreed on which city would receive European organizations, and the situation didn't improve when the European Economic Community (EEC) was founded in 1957. Consequently, European institutions were spread among three cities, Brussels, Luxembourg, Strasbourg, with Brussels hosting most due to its good infrastructure and neutral position. There is no official capital, because the EU is not a state. But one thing the EU doesn't lack is languages. Hordes of people are employed in translating into the 23 official languages of the Union the tons of documents, papers and speeches generated daily by the EU bureaucracy. The European Commission's Directorate-General for Translation is the world's largest such service, with over 1650 linguists and almost 600 support staff, half located in Brussels and the other half in Luxembourg. The budget for this work hovers at around 1 billion euros per year since the documentation pertaining to the minutest regulation or official paper has to be translated into all 23 languages. This is little enough compared with the 180 million euros and 19,000 ton carbon footprint the EU goes through every year in 'moving expenses', since the European Parliament meets one month in Brussels and the next month in Strasbourg, 350 kilometres away.[1] All 736 parliament members from the 27 countries, with their translators, their retinue of advisors and bureaucrats, have to trek from the first city to the second in a never-ending ballet that is the epitome of inefficiency and waste. But France insisted on the parliament also meeting in Strasbourg (the place where, after all, Franco-German reconciliation started) and even managed to have this notion embedded in European treaties to ensure it would remain so.

How efficient can a meeting involving 27 leaders be, particularly when decisions are made by consensus? In all fairness, is there an alternative? In this club of 27 countries, 17 compose the Eurozone, having adopted the euro as their common currency: this means there are still many different currencies in the EU. NATO, headquartered in Brussels, includes today 28 countries: this means some, notably Turkey, are part of NATO but remain outside the EU. Some 25 European countries (notably including non-EU Switzerland but excluding the UK) subscribed to the Schengen treaty allowing a passport-free flow of people. Most of the continent's 47 countries compose the Council of Europe, a Strasbourg-based body which is concerned with human rights, including Monaco which is not a member of the EU. The list goes on. Keeping track of this plethora of organizations and of who's in or out of any of them at any given time is no mean task. Europe contains the framework for a sort of federal state, but none of the various organizations integrate *all* the nations of Europe. Working out who leads is just as difficult. There is, since 2010, a President of the EU, former Belgian Prime Minister Herman Van Rompuy (as earlier pointed out, the main criterion behind his selection for this leadership role was that he was not a leader): few people even know his name (4 per cent in Germany), and his powers are quite limited. There is also a President of the EU Commission, a position held by the colourful former Portuguese Prime Minister José Manuel Barroso, as these lines are written, of greater popular familiarity and allegedly with a little more power but still not enough to override individual countries' decisions. There is also a President of the European Council and a rotating presidency for the 27 countries; the rotating president sets the EU agenda for six months. But, with all these presidents in the EU, there is not a single leader. Finally, in addition to the 27 member countries are various countries at different stages in their application to join the EU.

Speaking about quantum mechanics, American physicist Richard Feynman famously said 'I can safely say that nobody understands quantum mechanics.' The same words could be spoken about the institutionalized confusion of Europe. The former US Secretary of State Madeleine Albright was not far from the mark when she said that to understand Europe you have to be a genius or French.

Some people have discovered how to take advantage of all this: the Eurognomes working for the EU bureaucracy in Brussels get higher pay than their national bureaucratic counterparts and enjoy preferential tax treatments and generous benefits, even by generous European standards. Eurognomes have been said at some time to have enjoyed secretarial allowances of over 150,000 euros per year and travel allowances amounting to ten times the price of an airfare ticket.[2] They even managed the rare feat of having their pay increases enshrined in EU law. It is illegal *not* to pay them more. The EU has become a faceless bureaucratic machine employing almost 40,000 people, with a budget exceeding 126 billion euros, churning out endless rules and regulations touching almost every aspect of life in EU countries. In *Rischi Fatali*,[3] the Italian Finance Minister Giulio Tremonti pointed out that Brussels has become a machine that produces a continuous stream of regulations, a super-bureaucracy that gave itself the utopian goal of creating a perfect society with a perfect market where every microscopic and perfect detail of the perfect life of a European is regulated from above, and nothing is left any more to common sense. Well-paid Eurognomes regulate on everything including important geostrategic issues such as the number of seeds to be contained in a peapod, the curvature of bananas, the colour of melons, the height of lorries (not be more than 4 metres high, which incidentally was a problem for UK lorries), and the size of condoms. More than 80,000 pages of rules seek to regulate every facet of daily life. This is red tape brought to an art form. Individual states are obliged to adopt and enshrine an endless stream of these 'Directives' emanating from Brussels in their laws, whether they like them or not. Tremonti pointed out that while Europe was busy looking inwards and codifying everything at home with zillions of rules, something very different was happening to the world: globalization. Not only did most of Europe, which never misses an opportunity to miss an opportunity, 'miss the boat' on globalization, with the disastrous results we know today, but Brussels shot itself in the foot anew by burdening European companies with quantities of regulations that it had usually forgotten to impose also on products imported from Asia.

The theory and practice of chaos

In March 2005, several months before the No Debacle, EU Commissioner Mario Monti stated during a banking meeting in Monaco that the EU was 'complete chaos'. Every time some new regulation was to be issued, he said, it became the object of endless negotiations and bickering between the then 25 countries, each one fighting for its own interests. The way it 'worked' was that one country would blackmail another into saying *yes* to this one piece of legislation in return for backing that other piece of legislation – pork-barrel politics institutionalized at the international level. Monti's concerns were well founded. In terms of decision-making, the EU functions as a minestrone, a soup in which the ingredients constituted by the national interests of all members are thrown in, and the whole thing is stirred to try to achieve consensus at the right dilution and temperature. It can't be expected that any clear and strong decisions come out of the pot. The end product will taste like a bit of everything, with compromise after compromise, mostly leading to adopting the lowest common denominator. Rachida Dati, Member of the European Parliament and former French justice minister, diplomatically said decisions are the outcome of 'balance-of-power' discussions. The EU is a supranational entity: in each member country there exists a plethora of political parties and specific national political dynamics based on national agendas defining each country's national interest. Where the US, with comparable landmass and population, has two political parties, one currency and one language (one language and a half today including Spanish), Europe taken in aggregate has hundreds of political parties and a wide variety of languages and currencies. If this smorgasbord is not a recipe for fragmentation, inefficiency and un-governability, what is it? The disconnect between the bureaucratic monstrosity the EU has morphed into and the EU's populations, laid out in the open in 2005, has turned into a chasm five years later. The EU now works too often in *opposition* to its member states, even the most powerful ones, and in complete disregard for the European peoples, like an alien being that gets its power from the knowledge that it has so much become part of their bodies and lives that they won't be able to shake it off no matter what. No wonder that an increasingly large number of Europeans have come to see the EU itself as part of the problem.

According to Jeremy Rifkin, the EU is the 'rule-maker and gate-keeper. It establishes the directives that govern the play, brings together the players, and helps facilitate the process among parties. The EU is the first purely regulatory state whose function is to serve as an arbiter among contending forces.'[4] To its credit, Europe is conscious of its shortcomings, accepts that it will never be a geopolitical leader, will let someone else be the hare and contents itself with its role as the turtle and with Galileo's saying 'Eppur si muove'. In 1988 British Prime Minister Margaret Thatcher famously warned of a 'European super-state exercising a new dominance from Brussels'.[5] But again, what is the alternative? If decision-making efficiency is inversely proportional to the number of participants around the table, to the divergence of their individual self-interests and to the degrees of freedom and power they enjoy in advancing such disparate interests, and if any country can effectively veto a decision of the EU, what else can be done? The EU is an easy target and has been vilified everywhere as a bloated white elephant; yet, in all fairness, the 55,000 employees of the EU represent only a third of the total number of employees of the 'fisc', the French tax department, for example, and their total cost is only 6 per cent of the EU budget. The EU is not less efficient than any of the big bureaucracies anywhere in the world. The only way to turn the EU into an entity that speaks with one voice would be to achieve total political integration in Europe – today as much in the realm of the possible as achieving teleportation. The EU is thus likely to continue its way, unable to decisively articulate a common policy on most issues.

The EU is supposed to be the mother of all common markets and free trade zones, but this is too often only an appearance. Here is a taste of European reality:

French retailer Carrefour, Europe's biggest . . . wants to buy its own-brand cheese from the Netherlands, but is prevented from doing so by France. Why? Because Dutch Emmenthal is produced in 15kg moulds, and France insists that it be made in 40kg ones. When Carrefour ships French-made chairs to its stores in Italy, the French safety certificates must be countersigned by an Italian laboratory. Absurdly Carrefour says it has to confirm that the chairs will not be used for the purpose of torture.[6]

American columnist Charley Reese probably had the EU in mind when he said 'Government is inherently incompetent, and no matter what task it is assigned, it will do it in the most expensive and inefficient way possible.'

The happy cow

The good thing about the EU budget (the budget of the supranational entity called the European Union, approved by the European Parliament) is that it is naturally balanced. In a nutshell, individual countries contribute money, mostly in proportion to the size of their respective economies, and funds are also raised from EU customs tariffs and a share of member countries' VAT. The aggregate pie is then split among the same countries. As noted above, there are necessarily winners and losers in this game of redistribution, and Germany, Britain and France are usually net contributors to the pie. Since the EU itself does not borrow (no EU bonds have been issued so far, for instance, and none will ever be if Germany has its way, as later chapters show), it only spends what it gets, and there is no risk of overspending. This may be a good thing, but how is the money actually spent? Is it allocated efficiently and used to stimulate growth and promising sectors?

The answer is no. We saw earlier how competing national interests shape the cutting of the cake. The most obvious example of the inefficient use of this money is, again, agriculture. In 2011 more than 40 per cent of the EU's 126.5 billion euro budget went, as usual, to agricultural and regional subsidies – not to technology, R&D (research and development), SMEs (small and medium size enterprises) and the like, not to industries that can innovate or create new jobs. It's all about making cows and farmers happy. Someone made a calculation showing that each cow in Europe gets the equivalent of

2 euros per day in subsidies. If the figure is correct, that's more than people earn in some very poor countries. Europe wants to make its cows happy (and its farmers too), so 40 per cent of EU funds are allocated to a sector that represents only about 6 per cent of the EU's workforce and less than 2 per cent of its economy. A large part of the EU's agricultural budget finds itself distributed as subsidies to French farmers, which is why, as pointed out earlier, Thatcher's Britain forced its way to obtain a 'budget rebate' concession in 1984 to correct the imbalance. And while European agriculture is subsidised, the EU indirectly makes it really difficult for poor countries outside Europe, especially sub-Saharan African countries, to export their agricultural products to Europe and develop the one sector that may have a chance of lifting them out of poverty. To them the EU prefers to send crisp euro notes, which end up to a great extent in the pocket of corrupt and inefficient dictators and governments. The EU sends poor countries lots of money as foreign aid, but forgets to open its agricultural markets to them and give them a chance to earn a living for good instead of begging year after year. But Europeans' consciences are clean and the cows are happy.

EU budget controls are notoriously lax. The gold medal for laxism goes to the so-called Regional Aid Programmes, which account for more than a third of the budget. More than 50 billion euros per year go to these poorly designed and supervised, often useless programmes mainly intended, in theory at least, to assist the development of weaker economies and pay for environmental clean-ups, roads and various projects. The European Commission (the EU's executive arm) itself recognized that over 700 million euros were misspent from the 2009 regional aid budget alone. That national and regional governments can freely decide how to spend money on projects under 50 million euros is a sure recipe for waste, and everybody knows it. Examples of profligacy and waste are myriad; let's cite just a few for 'fun': Money was allocated to help Tyrolean farmers increase their emotional connection with the mountainous landscape of their region.[7] Over 400,000 euros were spent on a dog fitness and rehabilitation centre in Hungary that was never built.[8] Almost a million euros from an EU regional aid programme directed at the Campania region of southern Italy paid for an Elton John concert held at the Pedigrotta Festival in Naples (the European

Commission did order it to be repaid a year later). Farm funds for the UK have been known to end up in hunting lodges and golf clubs. Adding insult to injury, the EU pushed for a 5.9 per cent increase in its 2011 budget just as countries were implementing draconian austerity measures, attesting to the disconnect between Brussels and European reality. Not content with ensuring the happiness of European cows, the EU asked for 8 million euros to *promote* its agricultural policy to the European public; it wanted to make sure the European public was happy about making the cows happy.[9] In foreign affairs, the few Europeans who heard that an obscure and inexperienced baroness, Catherine Ashton, had become head of the newly created EU Foreign Service were expected to be thrilled and proud to know that this new (and mostly useless) department would cost 476 million euros in its first year of existence, 2011. As if this were not enough, the EU, as an institution, was asking for an increase in its *administrative* budget to 8.4 billion euros to pay for the Eurognomes and their work; so the Eurognomes get their own benefit, with 240 million euros earmarked for a new administrative home for them in Brussels, more than 5 million euros spent on a fleet of limousines for members of parliament and a similar sum spent on a culture club for Eurognomes in Luxembourg. So far these instances are subject to voluntary controls, which is not a recipe for moderation. What of illegal acts? Maarten Engwirda, who worked at the European Court of Auditors, which is supposed to keep an eye on how budget funds are spent, publicly denounced in an interview in Amsterdam's *De Volksrant* the way representatives (in particular from Italy and France) have been cooking reports.[10] It is enlightening reading.

At just over 1 per cent of Europe's GDP, the EU's budget is, however, relatively small. As a result Brussels' clout rests with regulatory powers rather than money. But it would be a huge disappointment to expect the EU to use its budgetary, regulatory and other powers to stimulate European economies to become better and bigger. For instance, roughly 70 per cent of the EU's economy consists of services, but most EU politicians steadfastly refuse to modernize this sector. So money is continuously poured into a tiny agricultural sector with no future while no attention is given to structuring the EU to be a world-class competitor in the large and promising services sector which could create jobs and act as a force multiplier in the EU economy. And yet the so-called Lisbon Agenda, hammered out by the EU to great fanfare in 2000 with words such as 'the most competitive and dynamic knowledge-based economy in the world', saw an unflappable and proud Romano Prodi, then President of the European Commission, declare to the whole world that within ten years the EU would become the most competitive economy in the world. To his credit he was speaking from Brussels, a place divorced from reality. It took him a good four years to publicly recognize the emptiness of his promise. A decade has passed since then and the very similar rankings of the World Economic Forum and Switzerland's IMD World Competitiveness Yearbook[11] show that the only EU country ahead of the US is Sweden, which ranks number 2 (after Switzerland), Germany remaining steady at number 5; after that it's an obvious decline, with France moving from 12 to 15 during this decade, the UK from 7 to 12, and then a dramatic decline, with Italy moving from 24th to 48th position, Portugal from 30 to 46, Spain from 23 to 42 and Greece from 43 to a disastrous 83, and Eastern Europe doing badly. This is no joke: in an open world economy, if you are not competitive, it is like treading water by yourself in the middle of the ocean: you won't go very far and might be food for the sharks – as the Greeks, the Spaniards and a few others have learned. So, as former Harvard Business School Professor Michael Porter turned superstar would have said, 'you better know what competitive environment you are in, what your competitive strengths are or should be, pick the segment in which you want to compete, and focus'.

This unbearable lightness of being the euro

They say one should beware of wishing for something too much, because it may actually happen. When the euro was introduced in 1999 (first in electronic trading, then made legal tender in 2002) every European, even citizens of European countries not belonging to the Eurozone, felt a sense of pride. The single currency was a powerful symbol, representing the apex of a century-long process of integration that brought peace and prosperity. The Eurozone covered a large geographical area in which trade was expected to be boosted as companies would not have to worry anymore about currency fluctuations and would see their dealings simplified. People would no longer have to change money every time they crossed into a neighbouring country. The European Central Bundesbank, officially known as the European Central Bank (ECB), was established, underpinning the currency with a strong mandate to fight inflation, to maintain price stability, reflecting the philosophy of the German central bank, the Bundesbank, its most powerful constituent (German inflation-phobia became embedded in Germany's consciousness after 1923 when Weimar Germany was rocked by hyperinflation, with prices up trillions of times compared with pre-war prices). The Bundesbank ensured that the ECB was located in the same city, Frankfurt, to keep a close eye on it. The central banks of the various Eurozone countries effectively became the shareholders of the ECB, providing it with capital reserves that, in 2010, totalled almost 6 billion euros.

One may rightly wonder why, in the first place, Germany, the leading economy in Europe, the one with the strongest and most stable national currency, agreed to give up its beloved Deutschmark (DM) for a new and unproven currency. Germans were decidedly unenthusiastic about the prospect of abandoning the DM. But in 1989 the Soviet Union collapsed and the reunification of West Germany with East Germany, to render the motherland whole once again, was around the corner. The French President François Mitterrand was only too aware that unification of Germany meant France would once again have to face a big, strong, united Germany. The famous 'German question' that had haunted Europe since Bismarck united Germany in the nineteenth century was back on the table. To keep Germany under control, Mitterrand decided to entangle its destiny even more with that of Project Europe, and the common currency would be the ultimate glue and the ultimate insurance policy rolled into one. Since West Germany was part of the European Community, it needed France's green light to absorb East Germany, so Mitterrand, the 'Sphinx' as his fellow-citizens called him, made German acceptance of the euro a precondition for unification. The Germans couldn't resist the temptation to see the motherland whole again. So, if on one side the euro was the natural end-product of continued European integration, on the other side it was the child of traditional European balance-of-power political considerations, and essentially a French project. Germans, however, agreed to let go of their DM on the condition that they were in charge of the euro. They wanted the euro to look like the DM, not like the Italian lira. The Stability and Growth Pact set the 'magic numbers' (the so-called 'convergence criteria') at 60 per cent and 3 per cent. That is to say, a country belonging to the Eurozone (adopting the euro) could not let its external debt go over 60 per cent of its GDP or its budget deficit go over 3 per cent of its GDP. This was necessary to ensure the fiscal and financial discipline needed to keep the currency strong and stable. Mechanisms were devised to punish countries that flouted these rules; but these mechanisms had no teeth and the consequences, as later chapters show, would be dire for Europe as a whole. In the period immediately following introduction of the new currency, people found out that their old currency bills, carrying pictures of national heroes or poets, had been replaced with insipid Euronotes depicting bridges. Retailers, taking advantage of the public's confusion with their newly priced goods, generated a sharp bout of inflation by rounding prices up. But, on the whole, the public welcomed the new order.

That Europe's monetary union with the euro as its crown jewel would not be easy was, however, known from the beginning to those more knowledgeable. A freely tradable currency is supposed to reflect the underlying country's economic health, competitiveness and financial or fiscal discipline. How could a single currency be expected to reflect the disparate economies of different countries with substantially different competitiveness, growth rates, fiscal policies, societies and ambitions? And the 12 initial countries were expected to more than double over the coming years, compounding the complexity of monetary management. A single currency also means a single interest rate imposed by a single central bank. The interest rate is one of the most powerful instruments a central bank has at its disposal to influence the economy of its country. How could there be a single interest rate when some slow-growing countries in the Eurozone may need a low rate to boost growth but higher growth countries may favour a higher rate to fight inflation and asset bubbles? For example, in March 2011 ECB head Jean-Claude Trichet was faced with a dilemma: Europe's incipient recovery was uneven, with Germany growing well, France at just 1 per cent, but Italy, Greece and Portugal in negative growth territory. Moreover, inflation, which was supposed to be under 2 per cent, was close to 2.4 per cent due to raising commodity prices. Was he to raise rates to fight inflation, or keep them low to help weaker economies recover? More fundamentally, how could there be a single monetary policy but 12 different fiscal policies and national budgets? How could there be a central bank but no central treasury? What if some countries spent recklessly while others led a thrifty and disciplined life?

The euro was a flawed project from the beginning, something economists such as Milton Friedman predicted as far back as 1999 when he said it wouldn't survive its first major crisis. Friedman was not alone in harbouring major doubts: the German central bank, at the outset, warned that monetary union was not viable without fiscal and political union. In other words, today's crisis of the euro was not unexpected. The euro had been known by many to be a bomb waiting to explode when exposed to severe stress. Moved by a mix of Europhoria and recklessness, the promoters of the Maastricht Treaty, which paved the way for the single currency, chose to ignore these warnings or simply took the gamble that the magic numbers would be adhered to and would somehow miraculously make disparate Eurozone economies converge. This they failed to do.

Monetary union came with a sharp reduction in the power national governments had over their national economies and thus the well-being and stability of their societies. This encroachment over sovereignty was something totally new and unproven, and nation-states were increasingly turning into empty shells. Former European Commission president Jacques Delors' 1989 'Report on economic and monetary union' paved the way for the euro but warned that without more integration in the political and macroeconomic spheres it wouldn't work. Convergence among the disparate economies of the countries that joined the euro was necessary for monetary union to work, and the euro was supposed to force structural reforms and bring about this convergence. The painful structural reforms many countries had avoided taking for a very long time would now be expected to magically happen and their disparate economies would look more and more like clones of each other. This incredible assumption was supposed to hold together the entire con-struct. There was, however, no Plan B in case such convergence was not achieved. The Maastricht Treaty specifically prohibited bailouts: its founders thought that no bailouts would thus be needed and that fiscal discipline would be the natural outcome of having assigned theoretical limits to budgetary deficits and debt levels.

In addition, the advent of the euro meant inefficient countries would have to forget competitive devaluations and would be com-pelled to resolve their problems through structural reforms instead. A competitive devaluation is what used to happen for example when Spain, in periods of slow growth, would devalue its own currency, the peseta, thus making the price of its products cheaper in the international markets, and artificially boost exports and economic growth. Now the peseta would be dead, buried, and the euro was, for all intents and purposes, managed by strangers in Frankfurt. So this colossal assumption implied that countries such as Spain would be content to let go of the easy solution of competitive devaluation and not only embrace naturally the measures needed to reinvent or redesign their economy but also succeed in doing this. One of the implications of imposing fiscal discipline to profligate coun-tries was that they would need to cut social security and welfare, among other options. But this was not autocratic China: this was Europe where politicians facing elections at home would stand little chance if they campaigned on the idea of selling such cuts. Struc-tural reforms imply hard political choices: was the political will really there?

The seeds of sour grapes

But, everybody wanted to join the party. On the road to the euro in the early 1990s, individual countries were straining to put their houses in order, tame inflation and budget deficits and clean up their acts to qualify and join the club. Some eager beavers, like the Greeks, added some so-called creative accounting to the hard work in order to meet entry criteria. Enthusiasm was the norm, although a few countries, including the Eurosceptical UK and the independ-ent Swedes, opted out. This new bout of Europhoric convergence didn't last long though, and it soon was back to each one for himself, with diverging national economic and political imperatives in the driving seat again. In the watershed year of 2005, just a couple of years after the euro had become legal tender in the Eurozone, Stephen Nickell of the Bank of England Monetary Policy Committee was already depressingly pointing out the paradox according to which 'one of the effects of economic and monetary union is to weaken the incentives for structural reform in the larger member countries'.[12] In the same year Mario Monti worried about the impossible task of fiscal convergence, as the newcomers needed low taxes to kick-start their economies while the initial members needed high taxes to pay for their high social costs. Italy, used to the panacea of frequent competitive devaluations of the lira to boost the price competitiveness of its export-driven SME-based economy (always easier than going through structural reforms) was already having second thoughts about the euro that same year, as the then Labour Minister Roberto Maroni started voicing his nostalgia for the lira, a feeling shared by many of his fellow citizens.

Monetary union around a single currency requires discipline and rules for the credibility of the currency. The rules of the euro required every country to abide by the magic numbers. Indeed, Italy, Greece and even France and Germany soon breached the rules they had themselves imposed despite German Chancellor Gerhard Schröder having proudly said that 'Germany has a habit . . . to stick to agreements concluded and contracts signed'.[13] How ironic to see Germany posturing in 2011 as champion of fiscal discipline and rules when in 2003, together with France, it refused to be fined for going over the 3 per cent limit on budget deficit! This is very significant because once rules had been breached by the leading countries nobody took them seriously anymore, a fact that contributed to a culture of unbridled profligacy within the Eurozone. In any case, nobody lost any sleep in 2003 over the rules having been so brazenly flouted. There was simply no mechanism to enforce penalties. No objections were raised when Greece joined the Eurozone in 2001, while everybody knew it had been manipulating the figures to meet the entry criteria. The whole fiction exploded in 2010, but many had chosen to ignore the warning signs: it was a case of the captain choosing to linger on the dance floor while the *Titanic* headed for the iceberg.

In any such misadventure there needs to be a scapegoat. During the past decade, whenever Eurozone countries had difficulty finding common ground on any given issue regarding the euro, they had no difficulty at all in agreeing on a scapegoat, the ECB. European economies suffer from high taxes, rigid labour markets and overregulation, but the heavy constraints imposed by the Maastricht Treaty that ushered in the single currency have not helped European economies. When growth was low in the Eurozone, European politicians habitually blamed the ECB for imposing high interest rates (even at times when these rates were, in trade-weighed terms, no higher than when the euro was originally launched). The task of the ECB was made more difficult by the bleak performance of European economies. It is easier to blame the ECB than to undertake the painful but necessary structural reforms aimed at controlling runaway budgets and over-rigid labour markets. What central banks can and cannot do depends on the power of their mandates. In the case of the US, for instance, the Federal Reserve (the Fed), the American central bank, watches out lest inflation gets too high or economic growth becomes too low or too high (its mandate includes promoting employment), and frequently intervenes with instruments, including the base interest rate, to choke off or ease the supply of money in the system. In Europe, the Maastricht Treaty, which set the basis for the monetary union and the ECB, limited the ECB's mandate to one of watching over inflation (Germany's *bête noire*). The ECB values its independence and does not take kindly to interference from politicians. The ECB is therefore very cautious about responding to needs to stimulate or constrict economic growth in any particular country, even if pushed by that country. So when a country's economy is growing slowly and needs to be stimulated, its government no longer has the means to lower interest rates by itself within its borders. The instrument that country's government has left to stimulate growth is domestic budget deficits: spend to boost, and borrow to cover the cost. But here again, the so-called Stability and Growth Pact requires the country to keep its deficit under 3 per cent of GDP. The country's political leaders therefore had three options: to flout the rules (as everybody did), to suffer from endemic growth and thus high unemployment (as most did), or to enact structural reforms (which few apart from the disciplined Germans cared to contemplate, being tantamount to political *seppuku*). One can also pray for convergence and the stronger political integration that would allow for common fiscal and labour policies, among others, something of a fantasy. Or take the easy road and flout the rules. European monetary authorities have no teeth: the law says they can impose fines and other punishment, but the reality is this has never happened. Nobody wanted to slap the bad student on the hand, because next time it could be their turn to get slapped.

The emperor had no clothes and everybody knew it from day one; but everybody felt things would somehow work out. The crisis of 2010 laid bare the problems of the European model and the fallacy behind the creation of the euro (described in later chapters), threatening to destroy Project Europe in the process.

SIX

THE CIVILIZATION OF ENTITLEMENTS

How the welfare state got out of hand

'Please, fire me!'

Here are three typical stories. Adrian was a good employee, one with a future, doing a good job. Young, dynamic, mid-twenties, with good mental and physical health, apart from a nasty smoking habit and a bit of a paunch. There was nothing unusual when he walked into my office. His request, though, was as unusual as it was simple: 'Boss, can you please fire me?' Non-plussed, I asked whether there was any problem at work or with his colleagues. Not at all, he said. Finally, he spilled the beans: he had researched the way the system worked, checked with friends and found that if the company fired him, the government would pay him virtually 70 per cent of his current salary for a couple of years. Whether his figures were exact or not, he felt the unemployment stipend would enable him to enjoy a comfortable two-year holiday, at the end of which he would start looking for a job. Another employee had a similar request a couple of months later. These were surely not isolated cases: *The Economist* decried France's rigid labour laws, saying 'bosses believe some workers try to get fired in order to win generous tax-free redundancy'.[1] In this system, long-serving employees have an incentive to get themselves fired.

The sister of my friend Marie is another shrewd one, because at 31 she's never had to work a single day in her life. She didn't inherit, she didn't find herself a wealthy husband, she didn't collect life insurance, she's not handicapped or afflicted by some chronic sickness. She lives in France and simply found the way to collect a pension of 450 euros per month from the 'system' for the past six years, which would have increased to 600 had she been living in her own place. She is on a lifelong holiday trip paid by other citizens who actually work, something which doesn't prevent her from complaining about everything. Giuse was a friend of my mother and is probably in her late seventies by now, living somewhere in Italy. One would not expect someone that age to be still working in Europe. But one may be surprised to hear that this charming woman has actually *never* worked a single day in her life: she didn't have to. She married, then separated, with no children to keep her busy. And, just like Marie's sister, she played the system, and has been collecting not one but *two* different pensions since she was in her late twenties – that's almost 40 years of pensions collected without putting anything into the system. Every month a couple of cheques come in. They won't make her rich, but they are enough to get by and do the occasional tourist trip. You don't even have to collect the money, they send the cheque to your home. You just have to *spend* the money. These stories would be amusing were it not that they are real (the names have been changed). These are among the many 'professional' European scammers, the legions of people who have worked out how to make a living from the system without ever putting something into it. In some areas of southern Italy, it is said that absenteeism reaches 70 per cent when the hunting season starts or close to holiday time, and numerous people collect benefits for being blind although they have driving licences and drive cars around. Some regions in Italy were strangely reported as seeing sudden jumps of up to 75 per cent in the number of pension-collecting disabled as soon as their governments changed from centre right to centre left. There is a huge number of such cases, especially in southern Europe where the concept of social responsibility is not part of the culture as it is in northern Europe.

There are also legions of citizens who have managed to wrest out of the system benefits entirely disproportionate to what they have put in. For example, the dockers of the port of Marseilles, in France, who work 18-hour weeks can retire at the tender age of 55 with a very comfortable 4,000 euros monthly pension. They priced port services out of the market in the process, but, they did not care: the government pays. It was reported that recent pension reform would not even affect people such as Didier Le Reste, head of Cheminots de France, the railway union, able to retire at a young 50 with a lifelong pension of 2300 euros per month.[2] France, by the way, has had the dubious honour of producing the youngest pensioners in the entire OECD (no wonder the last time it balanced a budget was more than three decades ago) and French pensions can reach 75 per cent of a wage compared with 40 per cent in Britain. In Europe babies can replace a job to create income: in the UK women with children out of wedlock obtain preferential treatment for social housing and their benefits have almost doubled during the past decade, with the result that Britain has one of the developed world's highest teenage pregnancy rates.

These examples are just a microscopic few among the thousands, hundreds of thousands, maybe millions, of Europeans who take advantage of the system one way or another on a daily basis, particularly in southern Europe, completely disinterested about the consequences. You think they are freaks, outlaws? Not at all: European society and systems seem to condone, if not encourage, this behaviour. More than 1.2 million well-to-do British families have been receiving, among other government-sponsored freebies, child benefits for years and years: how do the parents spend the money? They spend it on consumer goods for themselves, as if it were a Christmas bonus. In the UK 13 per cent of the total population, or 5 million people, has been subsisting on benefits;[3] that is, they are paid to do nothing and collect benefits without putting anything into the system (the size of these benefits is not unreasonable by European standards, but the sheer number of recipients in the UK is unreasonable – in France the total is 3 million). No wonder the UK budget deficit had ballooned to 11 per cent of GDP, making it one of the largest in the world (draconian budget cuts have been enacted by David Cameron's Tory government at the end of 2010). When a law was introduced in France by the left in 2000 prohibiting people from working more than 35 hours per week (the law actually increased the hourly cost of labour working beyond the 35-hour limit, while EU regulations put a cap of 48 hours on the working week), some newspapers reported that government inspectors were going around Paris to check on offices with lights on in the evening to catch and fine transgressors who would be fined for working. It may have been a myth, but it is a very real fact that in many places in Europe, if you have a shop you are not allowed to open it on Sundays (the one day people would have most time to go shopping: this European logic makes the very pragmatic Asians laugh). This is because those who don't want to work on Sunday have the upper hand in the system and can actually prevent you from opening your shop to make more money to send your child to a better school, buy yourself a new car or go to Thailand for a holiday. More often than not, in Europe the lowest common denominator sets the benchmark. It can be argued that nonsense like this exists everywhere in the world. But one would be at a loss to find any place in the world where this happens on such a systematic scale and is considered by society to be a normal state of affairs. Europe, especially the Europe with left-leaning political tendencies, seems to love people who take advantage of the system this way: they feel they are taking something away from the rich, that they are righting some wrong. And such people vote to perpetrate the system.

When the young, instead of being the dynamic ones, the risk-takers, those dreaming to take on the world, decide that they should instead take advantage of the system and do nothing; when the system rewards parasites and is stacked against those who work hard or take risks; when the lowest common denominator becomes the benchmark; when mediocrity is not only tolerated but people feel comfortable with it and come to worship it; when initiative, drive, new ideas, entrepreneurs are treated suspiciously or with contempt and have to fight against an entire system to survive; when political parties send 15-year-old children to the barricades to demonstrate against raising the retirement age to prevent the pension system from going bankrupt; when social responsibility does not even come into consideration in the national psyche; when the growth of benefits has taken on a life of its own and dwarfs the growth in national wealth, it is finished. This disease has been affecting Europe, especially its southern half, and changing this mentality is by now impossible.

A perfect crime

One thing is sure: Europeans are doubtless very clever, always one step ahead of everyone else. Not only did they figure out the largest collective scam in the history of mankind, but one where the risk of being caught is nil. Stealing from future generations means that you can safely enjoy the fruit of your pillage today in the knowledge that you won't be around when your victims demand retribution. Europeans have mortgaged their children and grand-children's future for the sake of enjoying their high-quality lifestyle and privileges today. The perpetrators have got away with it and, what is more, they don't even see it as a scam. They would feel offended should one dare insinuate that they are taking advantage of the system, damaging future generations or driving their coun-tries to bankruptcy. You would be shouted at, accused of being a dirty capitalist, a fascist, a Nazi, a racist and what else. Benefits are an entitlement, a birthright, not to be questioned. The atti-tude has become embedded in the culture of the continent, the new European philosophy of 'I am therefore I am entitled to'. Why waste your time and energy on duties if you are entitled to happiness by virtue of being born in Wonderland? Duty is old-fashioned, social consciousness a thing of the past. Europeans have, in their collective psyche, invented the perpetual motion machine, the one that automatically creates wealth; why not take advantage of it?

Not everybody acts like this. For this system to work, some people actually have to work to produce so that governments can tax their work and transfer some of that tax money to the others so that they can enjoy life. That's called division of labour. Everybody specializes in what they do best: some in enjoying a free ride, others in working to pay for that free ride. But even those who actually end up doing the work are not stupid: they grasped the idea and wanted to benefit, too. So they decided to work less, and retire earlier in order to enjoy life. In France they even managed to have the law say they can't work more than 35 hours in a week. But nobody will compensate for the imbalance – at least nobody alive today. The bill, it was thought, wouldn't be due for a while, so nobody cared. But the severity of the post-2008 recession has accelerated the timescale, though even this is insignificant compared with what is to come when the bills become due. Future generations won't even worry about working harder to compensate for this profligacy after the fact: they have been educated into thinking that they don't really need to work too hard, provided they find jobs that is. The coffers will, however, be empty at some point; so their living standards will plunge compared with those of their parents, and their own children's standards of living will inevitably be lower than their own. But why worry about the unborn, while we can enjoy the party, month-long holidays, early retirement and generous medical, welfare and pension benefits?

Let's go back to our usual example of France since, unfortunately, it is one of the most intractable pupils in the class. In September 2010, several million Frenchmen took to the streets in protest against French President Nicolas Sarkozy's plan to raise the retirement age from 60 to 62. These mobs were oblivious of the fact that if there was one thing that made France stand out it was the young age at which the French stop working. At 60, their retirement age has been the lowest in the developed world, standing at more than four years below the European average and six years below the American, resulting in the French spending on the average six more years in retirement than their peers in other OECD countries. Because of a substantial rise in life expectancy, the average Frenchman works for 41 years and enjoys retirement benefits for 35 years, double the time his parents enjoyed. Fewer than 40 per cent of people aged 55 to 64 work in France, compared with 56 per cent in Germany. Only one Frenchman in five between the ages of 60 and 64 is still in the workforce, against 50 per cent of the subset in Germany, 61 per cent in America and 75 per cent in Japan.[4] And let us not forget that when a French civil servant retires, his monthly pension amounts to no less than 75 per cent of his *final* six months' salary average. In more general terms, baby-boomers are reaching retirement age and life expectancy in France is rising, which means less people working (thus contributing less tax) and more people collecting pensions (and for a longer time). In other words, less and less money flows into the pension system just as more and more is needed. So something had to be done. In trying to find a justification for the protests, the then French Interior Minister Brice Hortefeux pointed out that 'for the last century and a half the sense of history has been the reduction of working hours. The reform is an incredible break with this history. It is normal that the French feel upset.'

The government did the maths: the end result was simply that the French state pension fund faced a shortage of 42 billion euros by 2018 and the pension deficit, standing today at over 32 billion euros, could have ballooned to over 100 billion euros a year by 2050 if left unchecked. So something had to be done to prevent the country from rapidly going broke. Armed with their calculators, government experts realized that for the pension system to stop losing money and gobbling up more and more of the national budget, and in order for it to break even by 2018 (so that the money collected from taxes to pay for it equals the money actually spent on pensions), the maths said you had to increase the retirement age from 60 to 62 and from 65 to 67 for those claiming full retirement benefits.[5] With a shrinking ratio of active workers paying into the system, the deficit would bankrupt the country. And despite the fact that the French government accounts for 56 per cent of the GDP (a higher proportion of government in the economy than that of any other Eurozone country) unemployment has consistently historically remained above the zone's average, an unsustainable and inefficient system: with two additional years of work the patient won't be cured, but at least the extra bleeding will be stopped. Yet even at 62 the retirement age in France would still remain one of the lowest in Europe (the more disciplined Germans did the maths too and raised it from 65 to 67). Nevertheless, a good 63 per cent of the French decided that this was too much sacrifice to ask for; so they took to the streets. The French are not alone in this. Actually, in some sectors of some countries in Europe, retirement age is as low as 50. Greece was even worse than France in this respect. And trying to change that is a supreme uphill battle. It brings mobs to the streets. In Italy it took about 15 years of political fighting to raise the minimum retirement age to 60 by 2009 and to 62 by 2014 – 15 years to implement something that the maths showed was necessary to avoid going broke.

In the meantime, to sustain the high costs of such collective folly, government spending has ballooned everywhere and debt has piled up to dangerous levels, recently leading some governments to take reckless measures to cover short-term needs. France, for instance, pillaged the coffers of its 'Fonds de Reserve Pour les Retraites' (its retirement fund) in 2010 to the tune of 20 billion euros to provide cash for a fund that will pay for some of today's social benefits. Ireland used its own National Pensions Reserve Fund to inject 10 billion euros in support of its bank rescue package, to take the pain away from bankers and debt-holders and transfer it to the people. Some European governments have, in other words, raided the long-term assets of existing retirees to fund their short-term follies. Anything seems permitted when it comes to funding profligacy.

The young and restless

Newspaper pictures from the September 2010 demonstrations in France show that some of the demonstrators were young people in their early twenties, some even 15 and below. Perhaps one can understand why a man approaching retirement age would selfishly want to see it come sooner. But that a 15-year-old child who hasn't even yet taken up his first job takes to the streets to demonstrate against the plan to raise retirement age is sickening. True, the French have been used to striking and demonstrating as a way of life, a blend between a birthright and a festive carnival, and without the slightest consideration for the disturbances caused to the rest of society or to the economy (the total cost of the eight-day September strike has been estimated at over 3 billion euros, with the SMEs being the first to suffer). The September strike was a reminder that the weapon of strike has been used in cavalier fashion throughout Europe, resulting at times in the population and economy of a country becoming hostage to a group of selfish people ready to use violence and undemocratic means to achieve their objectives. What is even more surprising is that the right to protest, destroy property, use violence and bring a country to a standstill is so embedded in the European way of life that it is not even contested. On the contrary, polls showed 70 per cent of the French as approving the protests (and the same percentage said that raising the retirement age was the right thing to do!).[6] Nobody seems to question whether the right to freedom of expression comes together with the right to wreck things. In other words, the message from the French is: 'we hate the status quo, except for the alternative'.

Yet behind the truculence of young Europeans today hides a fear of the future. French youth demonstrated in 1968 because they wanted to shape the future. French youth demonstrated in 2010 because they were *afraid* of the future and they were shouting this fear out loud. In fact the young have turned into the conservative force in society. Some of them carried placards saying 'No to reform!'[7] Nothing can be more conservative than that. The signs were already there after all: the young were already involved in demonstrations against pension and labour liberalization reforms (such as Sarkozy's 'Contrat de première Embauche', or CPE) in 2003 and 2006. Surveys showed that the young wanted to start their professional lives with the sort of lifelong guaranteed employment only a government job could give them. One can certainly sympathize with the plight of young Europeans (especially in the south) today, as more and more of them are starting to realize how uncertain their futures will be. What opportunities do they have to build a future for themselves? Surely less than their parents had. The number of French men and women under 25 years old looking for a job went up by 72 per cent in the past few years, pointing to the growing scarcity of entry-level jobs. In Spain this number has reached 40 per cent. Four out of ten young Spaniards you meet today in the streets of Madrid, Bilbao or Barcelona have no chance of finding a job. In France they have to wait, on the average, till they are 27 years old in order to get their first job. French youth have a bad deal because high minimum wages (labour costs in France are about 10 per cent higher than in Germany today, mainly due to high payroll taxes) and rigid labour rules take away incentives for companies to hire them. One can't blame them for feeling that the job market is a zero-sum game, that if you extend retirement age it means less entry-level jobs available, even if their assumption is totally wrong: it is the *rigidity* in labour laws and the high employment costs that induce companies to stop hiring. A two-tier labour market has in effect been created, with a privileged class holding overprotected long-term contracts to the detriment of the rest, mostly younger, who will have to become used to a life of short-term contracts with very little protection.

This general anxiety among the young population throughout Europe translates into their being scared of any reform that touches the education system. This was demonstrated by the huge student protests that took place all over Italy in 2010 when Education Minister Mariastella Gelmini produced a bill aimed at allocating scarce funding to the most deserving schools, promoting meritocracy and streamlining the education sector. Being young in southern Europe today is no joy, as you are facing an uphill battle to find a job and you will be stuck with having to pay the bill for the previous generations' follies. Governments have been piling up so much debt to pay for the collective folly that you are likely to have to work until your eighties to pay it off. Youths are, moreover, used by unscrupulous politicians to advance their own agendas. In fact, governments load more and more costs onto the young, because there are more and more old people in the population who represent a larger pool of voters, and more of the old people, in proportion, go to vote than the young ones. Politicians tend to care only about votes; so they'll cater to the needs of the old before those of the young. This translates, for instance, into cuts in education budgets more drastic than those for retirement and health. That politicians incite young children to join demonstrations in some countries is proof of the moral bankruptcy of the political class and of society in general. Very young children join because they'd join any demonstration about anything; it's more fun than studying or working, the system lets you do it, studying is free and your peers might even praise you for taking to the streets. However, if there is one thing they should be worrying it is not whether they'll retire at 62 instead of 60, but whether there will be a pension system for them at all when they retire. An intergenerational war is inevitable in Europe; the question is, what form it will take. Expect at the very least to see more and more burned cars and smashed windows in the future.

With Marx and Jesus

In nineteenth-century England the destruction of a machine could get the perpetrator the death penalty. This was just one of the many excesses that were by-products of the Industrial Revolution in Europe at the time. The age of machines and industrial production had arrived. Until then the European economy had been one of guilds that regulated their own industries and where members actually owned their own tools and means of production. A new class of capitalists and merchants was now emerging which owned the new machines and means of production and hired external labour to man the machines. The Industrial Revolution transformed these European societies of peasants, guilds and craftsmen into societies of people who either owned machines or worked with them for someone. It enabled rapid economic development but also wreaked havoc in European societies, as machines were literally taking the place of men and the few who owned these means of production could dictate their terms to the many who only had their labour to offer. Power, which in the past had been in the hands of the nobility, was now in the hands of a new class of industrial capitalists who could rapidly amass wealth at the expense of the rest and thrived on free-market, unregulated economies. It is interesting to note that at about the same time, a Europe hitherto fragmented into a myriad small communities, principalities and city-states saw the nation-state come of age, a new and efficient political construct that aggregated communities under a banner and provided a framework enshrining and protecting property rights and fostering national market economies in which this new industrial drive could fully flourish. The new capitalists could freely bid down the price of labour. In too many cases they were free to exploit or mistreat powerless workers in ways that often were even worse than those the lower classes had suffered at the hands of the nobility. Social protection for workers was unthinkable at the time; workers were at the mercy of capitalist masters only intent in maximizing profits, whose excesses were not even curbed by the state. Entire swathes of the population found themselves working in harsh conditions, living lives of misery and destitution, earning near-starvation wages, with little hope for improvement. Life in the cities in the second half of the nineteenth century was brutally harsh for the have-nots. Social inequalities between rich and poor were sharpening, increasingly obvious to all as populations were urbanizing and masses were confined to the cities where everybody was living side by side, rich and poor alike.

It was inevitable that people would become impatient of this injustice. Sharp inequalities, obvious to all due to city life promiscuity, generated an irresistible call for egalitarian reforms that spread throughout Europe. Protest movements took place in the cities (1848 saw many revolutions) and spawned the egalitarian and positivist philosophies that would define the left. Thinkers such as Karl Marx, a German Jew, developed the idea that the class of 'proletarians' (the workers) was in effect involved in a state of war against the class of capitalists who exploited them, and it was inevitable that proletarians would eventually unite and take over the means of production. They would get rid of capitalism just as capitalism had got rid of feudalism. His emphasis was on union and action by the workers to obtain equality. Recognizing that 'The whole history of mankind... has been a history of class struggles, contests between exploiting and exploited, ruling and oppressed classes',[8] he emphasized equality and predicted that the new industrial age would rapidly produce enormous wealth and an unjust widening gulf between haves and have-nots unless something radical was done. Marx and his associate Friedrich Engels wrote the *Manifest der Kommunistichen Partei* (the *Communist Manifesto*) in 1847. This small book, which remains today in the curriculum only in North Korea and Cuba, became the philosophical basis for the political programmes of communists worldwide, stating that 'society as a whole is more and more splitting into two great hostile camps, Bourgeoisie and Proletariat', denouncing the fact that 'labourers are a commodity... and are consequently exposed to all the vicissitudes of competition', the workman 'becomes an appendage of the machine... enslaved by the individual bourgeois manufacturer', and calling for the 'organization of the proletarians into a class, and, consequently, into a political party... compelling recognition of particular interests of the workers'.[9]

For them, bourgeois capitalism had succeeded feudalism, and capital was tantamount to a type of property which exploited wage labour. They protested the 'crying inequalities in the distribution of wealth' that were the consequence of a few owning the means of production that many derived their subsistence from, concluding that 'the theory of Communists may be summed up in the single sentence: abolition of private property', in order to 'centralize all instruments of production in the hands of the state'. To such thinkers the violent overthrow of the bourgeoisie was inevitable. Their creed became a religion that inspired working-class people all over the world. It can be said with hindsight that the rise of such philosophies was itself inevitable, given the circumstances and the cultural and historical heritage of the continent. Articulated by these and many other thinkers, the ideology of the left would forever change the face of Europe and the world. Calls for equality spread throughout Europe, and the step to the beginning of the welfare state was short. It is interesting to note that it was Bismarck, by no means a communist, who set up the first national insurance scheme in a Germany he had unified in the 1880s. Moved by new ideals of justice and equality, states started delivering public goods such as minimum wage regulations, retirement pensions, mandatory education and voting rights for women. But all this came at a cost and governments, in need of income to fund the novelty of welfare, started to shift more and more of the burden of taxation onto the richer people. Once the idea of the welfare state had caught on, European nations never looked back.

Communism emphasized the redistribution of wealth, the abolition of child labour, free education, graduated income taxes and so on; in that sense it can arguably be said to have inherited and incorporated some of Europe's Christian philosophical heritage. Marx may have argued that 'religion is the opium of the masses' and advocated the eradication of religion from society. Yet the marriage of positivism, Europe's new materialistic philosophy, with the egalitarian ideals of Christianity, the old defining religion of Europe, resulted in the ideology of the left. Religion reinvented or morphed into ideology. Modern Europe may think it has freed itself from religion, but in reality its influence is pervasive, not only in the ideology of equality, social justice and redistribution of wealth, but also in areas such as soft power and foreign aid. Socialism was not born as an ideology of wealth creation but one of wealth *redistribution*. When it came to the implementation of Marxist ideas, Leninism later developed extreme methods and instruments to take over and control the state. It is interesting to note that nowhere in the world has communism arisen from gradual reforms or free choice; in Leninist tradition it always came as a result of the violent takeover of the state from the inside or imposition from the outside, a notion that has never particularly bothered communist sympathizers anywhere in the free world. For the creation of wealth, socialism advocated a positivist mechanism based on faith in industry, science and central planning by governments, and abhorred decision-making by individuals and free markets. In keeping with the original ideas expressed in the *Communist Manifesto*, companies, businesses and the means of production and of creation of wealth should belong to the state, since the state was neutral and the best arbiter of social justice and in the best position to justly allocate wealth and jobs. For the left, the state should be in charge of the well-being of its citizens for life and should impose fewer working hours, more worker protection. Their paradigm was a

black-and-white one, with rich capitalists intent on exploiting workers on one side and poor and oppressed people on the other, and the
socialists' mission was to right that wrong by whatever means. The
left was firmly on the side of the communist USSR during the Cold
War despite its totalitarian character and remained fundamentally
anti-American. Many of the recommendations of socialism have
become an integral part of today's modern capitalist societies worldwide. The socialist narrative is, at its core, fundamentally unchanged
today, even though the red colour has faded to pink.

Capitalism's raison d'être, on the other hand, is the creation of
wealth. More than an ideology, capitalism is an age-old mechanism,
one that relies on the individual to take risks with his capital in
order to make a profit. Capitalism reveres free markets and their
self-regulating nature and free enterprise, assuming that enterprising
people will inevitably produce wealth when left to their own devices,
as if guided by Adam Smith's image of a benign 'invisible hand'.
Whereas capitalism is based on trusting the individual to thrive in an
open system for the good of all, socialism mistrusts the individual as
being flawed and prone to injustice; thus it promotes a closed, controlled society with centralized decision making for the 'good' of all.
Both ideologies may have their usefulness in shaping a social framework; but, for the creation of national wealth, history has proven all
over the world time and again that liberal economies and capitalism
have been the best motors and that centrally controlled societies and
economies (whether politically at the left or at the right) have been
unsuccessful at generating collective wealth and personal happiness.
The case of China may be the best example, a unique case of transi-
tion from one system to another (if I may venture to say so) which
took place right before our eyes and which I had the privilege to
witness first hand in the eighties and nineties: it was only after Deng
Xiaoping launched free-enterprise-minded reforms in the late 1970s
that China rose from the destitution it had been subjected to during its (few) truly communist years and unleashed economic forces
that turned it into the world's second economy, having overtaken
Japan in 2010. As my late father used to say, a dose of leftist ideology may be necessary and useful to curb the excesses of the right, but
left to its own devices this ideology stifles the creation of wealth and
results in centralized, oppressive societies. While extreme capitalism

risks making a few happy rich and many unhappy poor, extreme socialism risks making everybody poor and unhappy.

Ying versus yang

British statesman Benjamin Disraeli said that 'power has only one duty, to secure the social welfare of the people'. Yet with two strong and opposed ideologies having each conquered the hearts and minds of large portions of European populations, the result could only be the profound cleavage that the internal politics of European states have been subjected to, in particular since the end of the Second World War. Political life in European countries has been largely defined by the constant fight for power between the representatives of the two political ideologies of socialism and free enterprise capitalism (under the guise of Christian Democrats or other such parties). During the Cold War, most Western European countries had in their midst Communist parties with strong ties to Moscow and who would have wished for nothing better than to overthrow the existing order in democratic societies. In any particular European country, the left, given its ideological origins, is naturally pro-welfare, pro-state involvement, suspicious of free enterprise and big business, suspicious of America (as the champion of capitalism). It advocates high taxes for corporations and wealthier classes, and it is generally pro-immigration because of its egalitarian streak. The part of the political system and of the population that subscribes to the ideals of the left fundamentally feels that capitalism is evil, that the drive towards redistribution of riches still has a long way to go and should not abate, and that the cradle-to-grave privileges and entitlements obtained so far have come as the result of righting injustices and should be defended at any cost. The left does not concern itself too much with mundane issues such as the creation of wealth. The tragedy of the left is that it is mostly unable to comprehend that the creation of wealth is not a given. For the left, wealth is there already; it is something you merely redistribute, and not something you need to worry about producing. The right sits on the opposite side of the fence on all issues.

Each of these two political movements commands a large swathe of polarized followers in the population, resulting in a continuous struggle between them. Modern democratic mechanisms mean that swings of the electoral pendulum can bring one or the other side to power, with widely differing ideologies, giving rise to political zigzag and inconsistencies, both at home and in foreign policy. This is a gross oversimplification of political life inside individual European countries, which is far more complex and nuanced than described here, but it suffices for our purposes. The political landscape in the US, for instance, has historically been relatively simpler, made up of only two parties (which in Europe could be considered centre and centre right) with ideological differences that are far less marked than in Europe and which alternate in clear fashion (although American society is becoming increasingly polarized, a worrying trend).

As for where European political parties stand with regard to the Civilization of Entitlements, things are not as clear-cut as one would expect. Following the No Debacle in 2005, French President Jacques Chirac, who ran a centre right government, was quick to reaffirm the sanctity of the 'French model'; that the government would do all it could to protect the welfare state and the benefits associated with it against any 'foreign' encroachments. That such a populist politician would play on popular fears is not a big surprise. What is surprising is that he was defending the sort of leftist ideals that you would not normally expect to be defended by a centre right politician. A new 2011 law from Sarkozy's administration to the effect that companies with more than 50 employees have to grant bonuses to employees if dividends are increased was a clear indication that this tradition continues to be followed. This goes to the core of a European model more concerned with redistributing wealth than creating it. These ideals, despite their leftist origins, have so much become embedded into the European psyche that they have by and large been espoused by the entire population and political spectrum, left and right alike. Paradoxically, after the Second World War centre right governments enthusiastically embraced the welfare state to hinder the advances of communism: they assumed that the more benefits they showered onto the masses, the less people would fall prey to the siren song of the left. As surprising as it may sound, the welfare state played a role in the struggle against communism. It is thus not entirely surprising that in the case of social benefits the ideological chasm between left and right becomes a mere crack and no politician from any camp would survive for long if he or she advocated a dramatic rollback of the social benefits piled up over the decades that people have come to consider as their birthright. The ideological abdication of the right in checking the excesses of the welfare state and the whole construct that goes with it has made it easier for the Civilization of Entitlements, free of constraints, to thrive and prosper throughout the continent. The result is that layer upon layer of benefits accumulated year after year, until too large for the system to bear. The ideals of the left may have started as a good and just idea, but it is one that has got out of hand. These ideals, having outlived their usefulness as a check on the excesses of the right and overstepped their mandate to improve the dismal conditions of the working class, went into excess mode, turning into a drag on the entire system and planting the seeds for their bankruptcy and demise.

'Private property must be abolished.' One would have expected to hear these words from a Karl Marx or a Lenin about a century ago. This sentence was instead spoken loud and clear in early 2005 by Fausto Bertinotti, head of Italy's far left political alliance that still represented 10 per cent of voters in Italy. Europe may be the only place left in the world where leftist ideology still captures the hearts and minds of a great many people. Russia got rid of it, Eastern Europe never bought it in the first place, and in today's China the foreign-born ideology of communism is a mere façade used by government to keep society under control. It is true that today's right is still able to produce from time to time its own spectacular and monstrous excesses, as recently witnessed during the banking crisis when too much laissez-faire in the financial system resulted in the destruction of wealth on a gigantic scale, like a supernova explosion. The deregulation drive started under US President Ronald Reagan meant that nothing was left to check the excesses, greed and recklessness of Wall Street capitalists: it made it possible for them to bring down the financial system and hit America and most of the world with the Great Recession. To exacerbate matters, the same Wall Street capitalists and other perpetrators managed to shift the bill for their folly onto the average American. A left that had lost its bearings failed to latch on to the challenge posed by this injustice and reassert itself.

The left feels that corporate profits have been allowed to rise at the expense of wages, another way of saying capital is being rewarded disproportionately well compared with labour. In the 15 richest OCDE countries, the share of total salaries to GDP declined from an average of 67 per cent at the end of 1970 to 57 per cent today. The left says the difference amounts to 35 billion euros that went to shareholders and that should have gone to workers instead. In a sense they may have a point, because, for instance, since the start of the 2010 recovery, in Germany aggregate corporate profits have increased by 113 billion euros while employee income went up by only 36 billion euros,[10] and in the UK profits went up by nearly 14 billion euros while employee income actually fell by a couple of million. Yet employees are not shareholders, and they don't share in the losses of the companies that employ them. It is equally true that today's European left remains mired in the past, nostalgic for the barricades and ready to take to the streets or go on strike at the slightest occasion, an old ideology unable to face the realities of today's world or propose any concrete and workable solution to today's new challenges and crises. Its dialectic and narrative cannot shed the old ideas of a struggle between classes, opposing rich capitalists to the working masses. It still sees companies and businesses as instruments that should serve the social purpose of creating jobs and securing them for life.

The left still insists that reducing working hours is a panacea for resolving the unemployment problem. In France, it was socialist President François Mitterrand who lowered the retirement age from 65 to 60 in the early 1980s and socialist Prime Minister Lionel Jospin who introduced in 2000 the 35-hour week invented by socialist Martine Aubry. The left's egalitarian ideology sometimes borders on the utopian or the bizarre, as when socialist Zapatero's Spain created a 'Ministry of Equality' which was abolished in 2010 in recognition of its uselessness;[11] or in Sweden, when the left suppressed grades in schools as relics of outdated authoritarianism only to reinstate them when it was found that the school results of Swedish students had taken a nosedive.[12] The lack of credible strategies from the left to turn European economies around and create jobs has resulted in its decline in recent years, as the electorate have become more concerned with practical economic matters and less with ideology.

Born in opposition to the established order as a force for change, the European left has effected a 180 degree turnaround and become today *the* conservative force in European politics, one whose new role is now to guard and defend, at all costs, the layers upon layers of social and other benefits it wrested from the system over decades. This conservatism sometimes takes absurd dimensions, as when the left establishment took up arms in France to block Sarkozy's launch of the CPE, a more flexible employment contract aimed at encouraging enterprises to hire young first-time jobseekers, on grounds that it could open the door to reducing the privileges of those who *already* had a job. Needless to say, the CPE was rejected, and there are as many young unemployed people as there were previously. The left didn't miss this one additional chance to miss an opportunity. The left is, by and large, in decline across Europe today, it has become passé, having little to offer in terms of new ideas.

I am, therefore I am owed

In the 1950s and 1960s, Europe was doubly blessed by full employment and high growth, and tax revenues were flowing in to finance a fast growing welfare state. The European model was working. But the early 1970s saw growth abate throughout the continent in part because of the oil shocks. Full employment rapidly gave way to chronic mass unemployment. Yet the tragedy of Europe is that the welfare state kept growing as if nothing had changed. Layer upon layer of additional benefits continued to be added, in full disregard of the fact that states no longer had the means to pay due to substantially lower growth rates. The presence of a strong welfare-state ideology hard-wired into the psyche of a large part of the European population makes it extremely difficult to undertake meaningful structural reforms, particularly when it comes to labour market rigidity, entitlements, pensions and the like. This is especially true in Europe's socially undisciplined south. If capitalism is concerned with the creation of wealth and socialism with its redistribution, then in theory both have their usefulness. The excesses of both should be curbed and a balance should be sought in any modern state. An excess of capitalism can exacerbate inequalities, breed social discontent and create bubbles the bursting of which is painful to all of society. But no substitute has been found for capitalism and free enterprise as engines to fuel economic growth and development, as pointed out earlier. The ideology of redistribution ushered in the welfare state that, left unchecked, evolved into the unsustainable Civilization of Entitlements. Europe seems to have suffered from an excess of leftist ideology. Deep reforms are not feasible; only tinkering at the fringe is allowed, unless a catastrophic crisis such as the one in 2008–2010 forces such reform on the system. Even then, Europeans, especially in Europe's southern half, will resist structural reforms tooth and nail. Sarkozy managed to ram through his pension reform but had to abandon a large chunk of the reform agenda he was elected to implement, including in the service sector that related to pharmacies and taxis: French *immobilisme* would have none of that. Europe's ideological make-up condemns it to structural rigidity, contributing to its inevitable economic decline.

There is nothing in the failings of the modern European mentality that is as damaging as the philosophy of entitlements it invented. The concept of 'Civilization of Entitlements' deserves to be approached from a wide perspective, one that recognizes its historical, political and philosophical roots, grounded in the fertile soil of European ideas; yet we shall focus only on its practical aspects. The former European Commission President Jacques Delors recognized the problem when he said that 'if each person thinks he has an inalienable right to welfare, no matter what happens to the world, that's not equity, it's just creating a society where you can't ask anything of people.'[13] What started as the welfare state has evolved into a so-called European model based on the collective illusion that the layers upon layers of benefits piled on for the past couple of generations are birthrights, that their sustainability is not even to be questioned, that the natural order of things in the universe is that people will work less and less and enjoy life more and more, that prerogatives rank ahead of duties, and that the state's primary role is to ensure the perpetuation of social benefits forever – I am born, therefore the state and society have a duty to take care of me, they owe me. Once this philosophy has become hard-wired into the brain of the average European it is virtually impossible to dislodge it. Particularly in southern Europe, the idea of collective responsibility, of social discipline has been replaced by selfishness and hedonism. Traditional values, civility and responsibility have faded away. It is not just about pensions and retirement age. It also has to do with the

attitude towards work, towards social duties, towards the companies that are supposed to create jobs. Europeans have created a new
hedonistic paradigm that does not work. The complex equation that
relates the high cost of welfare and pensions, labour market rigidity,
the disincentivization of businesses, and other perverse specifics of
the European ecosystem has only one solution: decline and gradual
impoverishment.

I recall a Hong Kong businessman sharing his amazement with
me at the fact that, during the recession in Europe, his company had
tried to contact their Italian supplier several times in the summer
to place a rush emergency order, but the only person answering the
phone at the factory was a janitor who, of course, didn't know a word
of English. So the supplier didn't get the order: bosses and employees were all at the beach. Even when business is bad, Europeans will
put their vacation time ahead of work whatever the consequences.
It starts with children. European children generally have a couple
of months off during summer: few of them work during the summer school break, and they too just play. Contrast this with the
US, for instance, where the social norm is that children not only
work during most of summer, they also get jobs in the evening or at
weekends after school during the school year. During their professional lives, Europeans get far more vacation time than anybody else
in the world, with six weeks average against two weeks in America
and many other places. It is not unusual to see people taking close
to a month off during the summer to go to the beach, a full week
off, or two, during Christmas and another one or two during Easter
to go skiing, as well as countless long weekends. Taking Friday off
when there is a holiday on the following Monday, 'the bridge', has
become socially accepted. Fifteen-year-old children demonstrating
in Paris against the government's reform of the retirement age conveniently did so just before the autumn break. In southern Europe
where social discipline and consciousness are quite underdeveloped
compared to northern Europe and Germany, selfishness is the natural by-product of this state of affairs. Many Europeans have been
complaining loudly for years that the American model is inhuman,
with no social net and a selfish culture. Certainly, the OECD says
that over 26 per cent of EU GDP is redistributed as social benefits, more than double the figure in the US. But they forget that

during the abnormally hot summer of 2003, over 15,000 people died in France (almost five times as many as the number of people who perished during 9/11), mostly elderly people who had been left without help by their families and society. Politicians throughout Europe have sustained for a long time the illusion that the cost of the Civilization of Entitlements was affordable, all the while letting the bills pile up to be picked up by future generations. The problem is that the young have been educated to think that this social protection and the generous benefits that go with it, are forever and that they too have the right to them.

European attitudes differ substantially between the north and the south, with the north more disciplined, less inclined to profligacy and selfishness. Northern European countries do well despite social costs as high, if not higher, than in the south because they compensate with greater dynamism and innovation in their economies (higher growth), more women integrating into the workforce (more contribution to tax receipts), more social discipline (less freeloading) and far less dishonesty. So the argument with the shortcomings of the Civilization of Entitlements is by and large directed at Europe's southern belt. Second, the sorry state of affairs described here has little to do with Project Europe or the EU. Project Europe has other flaws and may have latched on to some of the bad habits stemming from this new European philosophy. It may, through its normalization process, have even helped spread inefficiencies, and may be guilty of having succumbed to political pressure and of allowing the wages and social welfare in poorer regions to climb up closer to those in richer regions, with the results witnessed in the recent crisis, instead of allowing industries to relocate production to lower wage areas as would have been the case in a real free market. But Project Europe is not part of the origin of the folly. This utopian social model is one that developed in the European collective psyche, one that individual European countries and their leaders and citizens chose to adopt and embed in their countries' systems, with various degrees of extremism, in the course of a few generations. This model seemed to work for sometime because of the phenomenal wave of growth and prosperity that set in after the Second World War. Prosperity, growth and full employment seemed to be the default setting, they just had to be shared by everybody. But, as growth abated, social costs kept rising, globalization set in and the world changed. Yet Europeans refused to recognize the reality that the model was no longer sustainable. It is not that they would not believe the maths. It is that they didn't *care* for the maths. It was their governments' duty to find ways to keep delivering these benefits to them. Otherwise, they would take to the streets.

The old man and the sea (of debt)

The world is aging, and fast. About half of the planet's population is under 28 today. But in Europe, the median age, at about 40, is much higher than the world average, with Germany and Italy leading the elderly league tables. In 2050 half of the world's population will be over 40 and half of Europe's will be over 50 (35 in America). By virtue of having on aggregate the lowest fertility rate of any region on the planet, Europe's population is expected to decline by over 13 per cent by mid-century. The average age of the remaining population will increase. The UN forecast that by mid-century in rich countries one out of three persons will be a pensioner. This pensioner needs to be taken care of: this has a cost. Europe is going to become one big retirement home, like Japan. Most of Europe, reflecting what is happening in the world in general but in a more acute manner, is going through a demographic transformation which will increasingly impact on societies and economies and bankrupt the system. The OECD estimates that half the public debt accumulated by OECD countries in the past two decades has been generated by expenses related to the population aging. Aging significantly contributed to the sovereign debt crisis.

Standard & Poor's Rating Services (S&P) has been analysing the implications of government spending for the elderly around the world, including pensions and health-related costs since 2002. Their 2010 report states:

'population aging will lead to profound changes in economic growth prospects for countries around the world, alongside

heightened budgetary pressures from greater age-related spending needs...the financial crisis has interrupted government
efforts to manage the burden of aging-related spending...the
challenges ahead are daunting...particularly in cases where
market pressures are pushing policy makers to embrace budgetary consolidation simultaneously with structural reforms of
pension and health-care systems. For some sovereigns, this may
put the relationship between the state and electorate under
strain and severely test social cohesion...the fiscal pressures
will become increasingly unsustainable...the aging demographic profile of their electorates could well make the political
climate for reforming pension and health-care programs even
more difficult than it is currently.' For Europe S&P pointed
out that 'The projected deterioration in public finances over
the period 2010-2050 is particularly significant in advanced
economies and emerging market economies in Europe. The
relevant characteristics of this group of countries, in our view,
are a relatively high level of existing social security.'[14]

In most of Europe the total yearly amount of pensions paid is
more than the total cost of wages paid. In Britain for instance
total pensions amount to 64 per cent of GDP.

If spending policies, population patterns and growth remain
the same as they have recently been, if this madness continues, by mid-century the government debt and budget deficit of
countries like Germany, France, the UK, Belgium and Greece
will have reached astronomic levels that exceed respectively
four times GDP and 25 per cent of GDP. Italy would surprisingly fare a little better with 'only' 2.5 times GDP for debt.
Other European countries wouldn't fare much better. No country can survive when taking care of the elderly accounts for a
third of its GDP, or the national debt amounts to four or five
times the GDP, or its budget deficit is a quarter or a third of
its GDP. The system would implode well *before* numbers even
get close to these figures. The cost of caring for the elderly
is going to overwhelm the budgets of many countries (not
just in Europe, but in Europe more than elsewhere) unless

extremely drastic and unpopular measures are taken. Due to the deteriorating financial health of these countries, sovereign ratings are going to take a beating, which means financing all this debt will become impossible anyway. Granted, these figures reflect trends existing before the series of drastic budget cuts recently undertaken throughout Europe; yet even allowing for these cuts the gaps remain too high. The *current* system is clearly unsustainable and a catastrophe looms somewhere soon. America is not immune to this disease: the country spends four times as much on people over 65 years old as it does on those under 18.[15] In Britain, the head of the public service trade union warned of a 'huge benefits time bomb' as,[16] due to a combination of rising unemployment and tighter household budgets, fewer and fewer people can afford to put money aside for their pensions just at a time when people are living longer and longer. We are talking about a time-bomb, one home-made by developed economies, that will explode in slow motion.

The mature industrial economies of Europe, with their unfavourable demographics, are the most vulnerable, although Japan and the US, with their huge levels of debt (over twice GDP for Japan, although most Japanese debt is held by Japanese, and thus is less vulnerable to the international markets), may also be heading towards their own moment of truth. Degradation of sovereign European ratings, already under way with the Eurozone crisis, may push borrowing costs to unaffordable levels, and, if governments can't borrow, they can't function. The US and the UK, although not in the Eurozone, are not faring much better, a consideration which has implications in the larger context of the decline of the West in general in the world. In comparing the American and European models, it could be argued that a large part of American debt and deficits comes as a result of its insistence on being the world's policeman, an endeavour unsustainable at current levels, but which could undergo substantial cuts if the US decided to retrench, and it could arguably do so without overly affecting the American way of life. More importantly, despite its shortcomings, America is a country that has a knack for creating growth in its economy, something generally lacking in Europe. Yet the trend in US age-related spending mirrors that of Europe, albeit at lower levels, and is a contributes to the likelihood of a shrinkage in American security commitments around the world in the coming decades, or at the very least a refocus towards the Pacific at the expense of the European theatre. But our concern here is Europe, and the unravelling of the European model, the Civilization of Entitlements, with its unsustainable costs, is inevitable. Either the welfare state is very brutally redimensioned, or taxes are dramatically raised (not good for the economy), or growth miraculously returns to the levels of the 1950s and 1960s, or the doors must be opened to immigration to counterbalance declining population trends. The alternative is bankruptcy: game over.

Ali Baba calling Sesame

We've been talking about budgets, deficits, sovereign borrowings and ratings: what do these mean, how do they work, and why should we worry about them? The expert reader can skip this section, but for a novice, although what follows is an oversimplification, knowing a bit more will provide the basis for a better understanding of the following chapters dealing with the Eurozone crisis. The principles governing the finances of a country are not unlike those governing your own household's finances or those of your company. You have expenses, such as sending the children to school, paying rent, buying food or a new car; the government has expenses in delivering 'public goods' such as public transport, defence, welfare. You have income from your salary, and maybe also from things such as the dividends from some stocks you bought in the past; the government also gets income from various sources, but mainly from taxing people like you or the company you work for on what you make (so the more an economy grows, the more taxes can be collected, *therefore* growth is indispensable). Many people live beyond their means; they spend more than they earn, running a budget deficit, so they borrow from their bank or their uncle or they lean on their credit card to fill the gap. Countries, especially developed economies, by and large like to live way beyond their means, so they have chronic budget deficits that they need to finance, just like a private person, from various sources, and just as in the case of an individual, the result is that debt (in this case 'sovereign or national debt') is accumulated. A country repays its debt from money raised from taxes; so if expenses grow faster than tax receipts the debt keeps piling up. The difference between a private person and the government when it comes to getting money to fund a deficit or repay debts is, first, that the government can print money. But money is like everything else; the more there is of it around, the more its value goes down. So, if governments let the printing presses loose, the price of goods and services keeps climbing as the value of the money goes down and inflation sets in. Second, the government can increase taxes but beyond a certain point that's going to make voters unhappy and poorer and they're likely to reject that particular government. Third, the size of the debts a country piles up can be gargantuan, in the hundreds of billions and even trillions: in 2010 Greece's public debt was in excess of 500 billion euros, France's triple that amount, and Germany's a huge 1.9 trillion euros. Fourth, to finance their deficits countries can tap the pockets of a large number of lenders at home or abroad by convincing them to lend the government some of their money in exchange for a piece of paper, an IOU (such as bonds) that says the country is going to give them back their money in, say, ten years, and in the meantime pay them a yearly interest.

For example, you decide to invest in a new ten-year Belgian bond with 100,000 euros face value and carrying a fixed 3 per cent coupon to fund your child's future studies at university. You'll get 3000 euros per year for ten years from the Belgian government, and at the end of the tenth year it will give you back your 100,000 euros. Germany may, by the way, also be selling ten-year bonds to raise money, and being perceived as more solid than Belgium (lower risk that it might default, that is, not make good on its promise to repay you in ten years), the German bond will, like any product of higher quality, command a higher price, which translates into enabling Germany to pay you a lower interest than Belgium, say 2 per cent instead of 3 per cent. During the ten-year life of such a bond, it may actually be bought and sold (traded) many times by different investors and change hands at prices that reflect how good an investment it seems to be at the time of the transaction, once many factors have been considered, and its purchase price variations results in an *actual* yield different from the original coupon. In our example, if, a year after, the outlook for Belgium turns bleak, the quality of your bond will be perceived as lower. If you suddenly need to resell your bond because the new house you wanted to buy is finally available, you have to find a buyer in the market and the buyer of your bond will give you only, say, 90,000 euros. From the standpoint of the buyer, he is paying 90,000 euros to buy the bond from you but he will still receive 3,000 euros per year and 100,000 euros from the Belgian government at maturity, so the yield he actually gets on the bond is higher than the original 3 per cent you were getting (reflecting market deterioration). The international market for bonds is huge and yields fluctuate on a daily basis, reflecting not only changes in the risk perception of a bond but many other factors as well. Governments can't ignore the mood of the markets and will keep an eye on these current market yields to price their new bond issues. If the market demands today a 4 per cent yield for Belgian ten-year bonds, the Belgian government cannot issue bonds at 3 per cent: too few people would buy them.

So, at the end of the day, the markets (which have the cash) dictate the price at which a government can borrow at any point in time. Markets are interested to know if a country is going to be able to repay its debts, and the higher the level of accumulated debt, the higher the natural profligacy of the country, the lower its growth, the more the question of capacity to repay will stick out like a sore thumb. How do you know a country is more or less risky than another? There are experts in rating agencies such as Standard & Poor's, Moody's or Fitch, spending their lives analysing every nook and cranny of these countries' finances, and the safest countries get a gold medal called an AAA rating, and the riskier ones AA+, down to B and so on (it stops almost there, as Z ratings don't exist, although some countries nowadays seem to do everything they can to obtain it). Countries are graded, just like pupils at school.

What does this all mean in practical terms? During 2010, the year of the European sovereign debt crisis, Germany, considered as Europe's benchmark with its gold medal AAA rating, could borrow money for ten years at under 3 per cent, whereas Portugal, which was considered an increasingly risky country and saw its rating downgraded from AA− to A+ (and then lower) was burdened with bond yields as high as 6.67 per cent by the end of 2010 and went on to reach 8.59 per cent in April 2011. On a 50 billion euro borrowing, each additional 1 per cent in coupon means 500 million euros of additional 'interest' to pay every year. This large difference of almost 6 per cent between the two countries' borrowing costs in 2010 meant an extra 3 billion euros per year to pay, and by the end of 2020 Portugal would have had to produce an aggregate 80 billion euros to repay the 50 billion it had borrowed. Similarly, a 1 per cent increase in interest on France's 1.7 trillion euro debt would mean an additional 17 billion euros to repay each year. These are all rough approximations, but we can see why a country would want to preserve a good sovereign bond rating and why European governments were scared that the markets could be affected to the point where interest rates keep rising across the board: since governments need to borrow all the time, it would be a cataclysmic disaster.

A country with high debt and high borrowing costs has a problem; or let's say *you*, as its citizen, have a problem because the one saddled with the debt is you. Centuries ago, the sovereign was the ruler, and the ruler, king or prince, borrowed, say, to finance his wars. With today's nation-states, the sovereign is the country, with its resources and people. Government debt is an indirect debt of a country's taxpayers. This means every man, woman and child in your country is responsible for your country's sovereign debt. You can take the entire amount of outstanding sovereign debt of your country, divide it by the number of its citizens and the result is how much debt each of you have on your shoulders. From the day you are born, whether you like it or not, you share this burden, and you are going to work all your life and pay taxes to your government to reimburse it. Not all debt is bad, of course: debt which a country incurs for such things as building factories or funding R&D that will generate future returns, enabling it not only to repay the debt but also to grow further, is, in a sense 'good debt'. Debt incurred to finance the running costs of a country's living beyond its means is 'bad debt' that can lead to ruin if it continues to pile up to levels that the country cannot repay.

Bad debt has been piling up all over Europe as current generations have been borrowing heavily (and continue to do so) to fund the Civilization of Entitlements and, through the bond markets, shift the bill to their sons and grandsons. We also need to keep in mind Murphy's Law: unexpected things can happen that brutally and suddenly add a big amount to an already big pile of debt, as when the governments of most developed countries, especially in the US and Europe, had to spend vast amounts of money to save the banks and the financial system during the recent crisis, something they had surely not planned or budgeted for. The fact that many governments largely left ownership and management of the institutions they were saving to the same people who had been running them into the ground speaks volumes, but that's another story. In Europe, sovereign debt exploded also because of the crisis: the additional debt governments had to raise to fund the rescue of the financial system has been estimated to aggregate at 14.5 per cent of the region's GDP.

If a country can't repay its debt the road can get rough and lead to default, the nightmare of investors who'd be left holding mostly worthless pieces of paper. Government debt default is not uncommon, although it is a phenomenon more associated with developing economies. Among others, Mexico defaulted in 1982, Boris Yeltsin's Russia in 1998, and Argentina in 2002. Even France defaulted eight times a long long time ago. The Harvard economist Kenneth Rogoff pointed out that Greece holds the world record in debt defaults, followed by Spain and Portugal. Interestingly, Rogoff found out that a country close to default doesn't solve its predicament through exports or growth, but through debt rescheduling. So risky countries can default, even in Europe, leaving those who bought their bonds high and dry. This is why, when you heard that the bond market was getting the jitters about Greece, Portugal or Ireland, you knew these markets could quickly raise their cost of borrowing (to compensate for added risk) to unsustainable levels or even completely shut these countries out of the debt markets for a long time. A country that can't borrow is a country that can't function, because virtually no developed country balances its budget anymore. So a country will do everything in its power to find money somewhere before throwing in the towel and defaulting.

The question arises as to what threshold, what amount of debt (usually these figures are measured as percentages of GDP) is sustainable, and what amount triggers a sovereign debt crisis that can lead to default: 50 per cent of GDP? 100 per cent? Economists don't know. The Maastricht Treaty came up with the magic numbers of 60 per cent of GDP (as upper limit of a country's debt) and 3 per cent of GDP (for its budget deficits). But they don't rest on anything concrete – you could say it's all subjective. These numbers made Eurozone regulators comfortable because they thought the markets would feel comfortable with them. In fact there are no magic numbers. Mexico went into default with a 20 per cent debt level, while Japan survives well at more than 200 per cent. But many economists agree upon one thing: that once yearly payments to service the debt reach 50 per cent of the money the government receives from taxes (fiscal receipts), disaster is unavoidable. Similarly, it is widely considered that when market yields reach 6 per cent, the cost of new borrowings becomes unsustainable. This is why the ECB intervened by buying Italian bonds in the markets in 2011 to bring their yields down from 6 to 5 per cent, although they later went way over 6 per cent. When a country is said to be 'under attack' by the market it means the market is so concerned about that country that it demands higher and higher yields for its paper because there are lots of sellers and few buyers. Who holds the debt is also important: if a government borrows heavily but mostly from its own citizens, then most of the debt is held at home and the government has more control over it and a debt crisis is less likely. This is the case in Japan, which carries on with a debt of over twice its GDP. But in cases such as Greece where total debt stands at 135 per cent of GDP, with two-thirds of it held by foreigners, the government has much less control of what these bondholders will do (they could dump the bonds); so the country is at the mercy of the fickleness of international bond markets which, when they get nervous, can rapidly increase borrowing costs to unsustainable levels, as we observed above. Other than that, there is no particular reason why suddenly a sovereign debt crisis happens, except that the markets become so subjective when they lose confidence in a country.

The Great Gatsby

'We have created a leisure society … but our model does not work anymore',[17] lamented Klaus Zimmermann, President of the German Institute for Economic Research. One thing is sure: developed countries have been living way beyond their means, and lately they have been getting the money to finance this rich lifestyle from developing countries. This is the poor financing the rich or Robin Hood in reverse. First, developed countries have dramatically increased their borrowings in recent times. For instance, the debt of the richer countries has shot up to an average 70 per cent of GDP today, up about 50 per cent from 2007 levels, and this 70 per cent is almost double today's average of 40 per cent for developing economies. China, whose per capita income is only 5183 euros (it ranks just below that of Macedonia, in nominal terms), compared with an average 20,954 (on a PPP or purchasing power parity basis) in Europe, has been financing richer countries' debt, in particular the US. China has basically no debt (it has the world's largest foreign reserves, the opposite of debt if you will, which exceeded 2.6 trillion dollars in 2010), and the sovereign debt levels of countries such as India and Brazil have gone down in recent years. We spend (on non-productive items), they save and invest (on productive items). The outcome is obvious.

Things have got out of hand. The debt of the most important countries has never been so high (aside from periods of war). It is ready to threaten their well-being and viability. The former French politician and philosopher Jacques Attali wrote a book with the ominous title of *All Ruined in Ten Years?* The book was published in 2009, which does not leave much time to enjoy the last rays of sunshine, given his imposed deadline, although the question mark Attali mercifully added in the title leaves a glimmer of hope. For Attali,[18] the situation is as clear as it is horrifying: 'The ruin of the West is a credible scenario.' He took care to describe how the scenario could unfold. From our own observations we could say that Europe is the most exposed when compared with the US because total European sovereign debt and government spending averages respectively 80 per cent and 51 per cent of GDP, against 54 per cent and 40 per cent respectively in America; because Europe is growing older than America; and because of its slower growth. Attali pointed out that in today's France, government income is about 45 per cent of GDP while its expenses are about 55 per cent (social welfare represents almost half this total expense), which means that each year there is a shortfall roughly equal to 10 per cent of the country's GDP which needs to be financed by adding new debt (or increasing taxes, in the absence of solid growth). It is thus not surprising that from 1980 to today, in the space of one generation only, the country's public debt has multiplied by five. This entails suffering for each person in the country because taxes will need to go higher, and/or the quality of life and purchasing power will decrease. People will inevitably become poorer.

How inevitably? Most European countries will have no choice, in the coming future, but to drastically tighten their belts, that is, reduce expenses; in many cases the process has already started. This translates into lowering the amount of public goods delivered, with drastic cuts to the money government allocates to everything, including schools, pensions, defence (Americans must get used to the idea that they'll need to fight by themselves in the next Afghanistan), government employees' salaries, slashing investment in innovation (which also means less productivity in the future, thus less growth) and so on. The entire social model will be put in question, something bound to create social tensions. Attali pointed out that in order to bring Europe's average deficit to the 60 per cent required by Maastricht, European countries would need, on average, to cut their budgets by 20 to 25 per cent for several decades, something their populations won't tolerate. But enough won't be enough, and these governments will do everything they can to increase income, that is tax income. So they'll try to close all loopholes to collect every little cent they should be collecting from everybody and relentlessly increase the taxes people and businesses pay (a further constraint on growth). And since this won't be enough they'll pray for economic growth. The end game has, in fact, already started. The recent Great Recession followed by the sovereign debt and currency crisis laid bare the system's shortcomings. But before looking into this let us briefly touch upon the issue of immigration and multicultural European societies, something which could have dire implications for the continent's social stability.

SEVEN

THE 28TH COUNTRY

The problems of demography and immigration

Ellis Island it is not

America was made of wave after wave of immigrants, most of them from poor European countries. It may be a unique case, but this country, actually defined by its immigrants, became 'number one' in less than two centuries. Immigrants pouring in were not attracted by America's social welfare system; essentially there was none. What they wanted was to find work and become part of a system that gave them the chance to succeed independently of origin, creed or social status – the American Dream. They naturally integrated into American society because they had subscribed to its system and values even *before* reaching its shores. It was a society, by and large, made up of people just like them. If not achieved by often illiterate first-generation immigrants, full integration was generally achieved by an educated second generation. Imported people provided a ready-made pool of low-cost and eager labour and contributed to the country's dynamism and rich cultural diversity. Among these immigrants no group represented a challenge to the existing system or population. The case of Europe is, unfortunately, radically different.

We need to briefly dip our toes again in the currents of history, which offer an understanding of issues surrounding immigration in Europe today. The present narrative centres around the plea and integration of Muslim communities, minorities originating from outside Europe. It is easy to forget that these are recent arrivals and that, before them, Europe had already had problems with nationalism and the issue of non-Muslim intra-European minorities. The frontiers of empires were external and vast; inside them empires had amalgamated nationalities and ethnicities. As empires fell, like a tide retiring they left in their wake a patchwork of nation-states which defined themselves through a particular nation or ethnicity, by definition excluding 'others' from their narrower frontiers. Populations coalesced into nation-states comprising a majority of people who shared a common language, culture and history, as well as some ethnic homogeneity, despite the important population movements and mixings the entire continent had been subjected to over time. These people submitted themselves to the laws and authority of the nation-states, which proved to be efficient machines in their ability to marshal and organize economic, military and other resources for the collective benefit. The nationalism inherent in the nation-state didn't, however, always look with sympathy on minorities remaining inside its borders, even if these nation-states were democratic. Following the First World War, the victors at the Treaty of Versailles tried keeping minorities where they were and conferring international legal protection on them, an endeavour that didn't work properly. For instance, Turkey and Greece had their own population exchanges: entire minorities of Greeks living in what had, after the First World War, become the new nation-state of Turkey, had to move out and go to Greece, just as entire communities of Turks living in Greece were deported to Turkey. More recently, between 1939 and 1948 90 million people were either killed or displaced across Europe; these were not Muslims or Arabs. Intra-European minorities have been the object of much suffering and of mass transfers of population through the ages. They were only too often mistreated, deported or worse. This hostile European attitude to foreigners, even to fellow Christian Europeans, however useful to the local economy they may be, has not gone. It comes as no surprise that Dutch political parties, worried that East European immigrants provide most of the labour for its greenhouse agricultural industry, have recently been protesting strongly against a 'tsunami' of Eastern European immigrants.

Following the Second World War, in the 1950s and '60s Europe underwent a period of spectacular economic growth and full employment. Manpower was sorely needed to fuel this unprecedented development, and migration was regarded as a welcome and indispensable ingredient of continued growth. Almost 20 million people were criss-crossing Europe, mostly temporary workers from Italy and other places coming for seasonal contract work. At the time, governments did not concern themselves too much with regulating immigration since these workers were considered a necessity and were naturally assumed to be a temporary phenomenon. Yet even then, when it came to migrant labour from fellow European countries, segregation, discrimination and racism were simmering. Some restaurants in Switzerland famously hung up signs saying 'No entry for dogs and Italians' attesting to a problem, already at that time, with accepting fellow Europeans. European societies were not liberal at the time, either in regard to minorities or in the treatment of women, who only gained the right to vote in Switzerland in the 1970s. The needs of business and capitalism for migrant labour were at odds with the idea of an ethnically homogeneous nation-state, yet, as intra-European migration didn't suffice, employers started looking abroad. The closest, most natural and less socially disruptive source of cheap manpower would have been Eastern Europe. The problem was that Eastern European countries were stuck on the wrong side of the iron curtain. This pool of nearby talented and cheap labour could not be used, because of the Soviet Union. Europe was compelled to look elsewhere, and that meant mainly the Muslim countries of the Maghreb to the south and Turkey to the east, as well as former colonies in Africa and elsewhere. This was assumed to be a temporary phenomenon, yet European countries, with their open door policy, let vast numbers of migrants permanently settle, import their families as well, and become citizens.

These immigrants, for the most part from poor backgrounds, were readily used as a pool of low cost manpower in times of labour shortages. But their relatively low skill sets resulted in low job security vis-à-vis employers; they were the first to be laid off in times of labour surplus, as marginal manpower. As a result, when economies started slowing down in the 1970s, attitudes towards immigration started to change for the worse. As early as 1977 West Germany's Federal Commission stated: 'The Federal republic is not an immigrant country', little differently from what some politicians are saying in Germany today. German academics even petitioned

at the time for the deportation of all immigrants in order to preserve the 'Christian values of Europe'. Issues of race and immigration
were taking front stage in European politics, and it started to dawn
on mainstream Europeans that the continent would soon have to
deal with multiracial societies. To compound the problem, instead
of shutting the door when its economies slowed down, generous
Europe continued to keep its doors open to immigration. The stage
was set for the severe problems we see today. Immigrant minorities who, because of their conspicuously different ethnicities and
cultures, had never really been considered 'real' citizens in the first
place, suffered disproportionately high unemployment rates compared with the rest of the population, adding to their feelings of
injustice and alienation.

Immigration into Europe is a very recent phenomenon, having
mostly taken place in the last 50 or 60 years. Immigrants reaching
Europe came to countries that had been in existence for a long time,
made up, generally, of homogeneous nations and mature societies.
They were not reaching a work-in-progress nation as had been the
case with America. Most of them originated from former colonies
or societies with substantial ethnic and cultural differences from
the new host societies, which often had been their previous masters. Europe had never erected a Statue of Liberty that said 'Give me
your tired, your poor, your huddled masses yearning to breathe free'.
When they arrived in America, immigrants *joined* a nation in the
making and would be part of its making, without being questioned.
When they arrived in Europe immigrants joined the lowest classes
in existing, mature societies and were *tolerated* because they were
needed to do work that Europeans no longer wanted to do. Because
of this, contrary to America's melting-pot philosophy which acted as
a motor for integration, immigration into Europe created from the
outset two separate classes of people: the native population, generally richer and more educated, and the barely tolerated immigrants,
poor, conspicuously different, and with little chance to make it into
the first class. True, European countries had invaded each other
time and again. Yet no country on the continent has ever defined
itself through wilful immigration as America did. European nation-
states had been busy most of the time defending their frontiers
from invaders; so letting outsiders in was not part of their natural

inclination. American culture was naturally integrative: European culture was naturally not.

With such premises immigration was bound to become a problem in any country of Europe once the newcomers evolved into a conspicuously large and permanent population subset. The issue would inevitably be exacerbated in times of economic crisis and by the growing perception that these immigrant populations remained alien. The absence of a social safety net in the US meant immigrants knew they wouldn't be able to live from handouts and needed to quickly find a job and integrate with the system. The modern European system, by contrast, made it often too easy for immigrants to survive on government handouts and take advantage of the situation. In America, the sons and daughters of first-generation immigrants were, by and large, integrated into the American system. In the case of Europe, the sons and daughters of first-generation immigrants found themselves born in a country that was supposed to be 'theirs' but in which they were conspicuously different and regarded as such by natives. Social, cultural and religious alienation was the natural and unfortunate outcome of this state of affairs. These new generations, searching for an identity which they could neither find in the country where they were born nor in the countries their parents had come from, started looking elsewhere for an identity or defining themselves in opposition to the system. Paradoxically with Muslim immigrants, the first-generation immigrant parents have generally been secular: it is the new generation that uses religion to gain an identity of sorts. From there to some falling prey to manipulation, crime and radicalization, religious Islamic or otherwise, the distance is short.

Who am I?

Because immigration has the potential to alter forever the human fabric of a nation, it represents an issue that strikes at the heart of the notion of sovereignty and national identity, one that can impact on and transform the soul of a country, its ethnic homogeneity, its self-respect, its particular culture and history. Economic policies, wrong or right, and other political decisions have a relatively temporary impact; there is always the possibility of change.

Immigration is another matter altogether because of the long-term irreversible implications – barring mass deportations unacceptable to mainstream public opinion today.

What does it really mean to be Dutch, Danish or Spanish today? If you live in a country that was not originally your own, do you have a duty to blend in, accept its historical heritage and submit to its laws and cultural customs? Must you adapt to your surroundings like a chameleon? Or are you entitled, while being there, to keep living in your own separate world and submitting to alien laws? Does it make any sense for a country to import, on a permanent basis, people who actually do not share its values, let alone who may openly advocate its demise? Does it make sense to let people in when there is virtual certainty that they will not find decent jobs and are likely to turn to crime to survive? Once people have been imported, has the host country the duty to do everything in its power to integrate them or should this duty belong to the newcomers? Is a country, a society, entitled to take action to curb immigration if it becomes necessary in order to keep its own specific ethnic-cultural character, or does it have to yield and open its frontiers in the name of international human solidarity or other imperatives and accept a dilution of its national character? Who is to make decisions on these matters? Are they too important to be left to governments and should the people have their say by means of referenda? Can citizens of a given country be expected to accept that strangers be involved in decisions on this all-important issue? How do you decide that enough is enough, that your country 'risks' too much in terms of dilution of national character or of social instability by continuing to import foreigners? What to do with immigrants who happen to come from very alien cultures? What if *they* want to remain different? Is the marker of identity religion or language/culture? In terms of loyalty, a concept still important in nation-states, are today's immigrants Muslims first and, say, German after, or the opposite? Is the traditional nation-state model based on a relatively homogeneous nation still valid or should it give way to something else ? Should a passport just be like a credit card, something easily acquired for convenience, or should it remain the privilege of those who, at the very least, pledge allegiance to and accept conforming to and espousing the values of the society they join?

Citizenship occupies a central part in today's world, and these very complex issues go to the core of a country's national character. It would only seem fair that the citizens of a country that calls itself democratic, being rightly or wrongly worried about the competition from immigrants for increasingly scarce jobs and for the resources provided by an already strained welfare system, and worried about the deterioration in public security, be given the chance to have their say on these issues, given the direct and lasting impact they have on the social environment they, their children, and future generations will be living in, and given that such issues directly concern the historical and cultural heritage of the country and society they and their forebears have been living in. Political correctness has meant that public debate of these issues has been conspicuous by its absence, another case of European democratic deficit.

Take the example of France. The immigration of the past few decades has changed forever the make-up of its society, creating a new minority of almost 10 million Muslims, most of whom fit in while others, albeit a minority, are ready to take to the streets at anytime, even over issues related to Muslims abroad, a force that can also impact French foreign policy. It is already difficult enough that within individual European countries there has been no national debate, no democratic political process involving citizens in decisions concerning such issues. The fact that an alien, supranational entity such as the EU, by making decisions on its own and imposing them on member nations, effectively appears to rob citizens of this debate cannot be expected to be to the liking of Europeans for very long. True, EU policies originally said that immigration policy throughout the EU was to be subject to the unanimous consent of all of its members, thus effectively giving any single country veto rights over EU-wide immigration policies. But this modus operandi changed: unanimity ended by being watered down to majority vote. This means a country that does not like a new immigration regulation about to be imposed throughout the EU but finds itself outvoted is going to have to live with the consequences. It is expected to willingly give away control of the direction of its human and ethnic fabric.

The dislike citizens throughout Europe feel for this situation is naturally exacerbated by intra-communal tensions. In the absence of a frank public debate, if citizens are unhappy, their only solution is to start voting for populist anti-immigrant parties at home, as became obvious in 2010. This sea change was not lost on mainstream politicians, who adjusted their messages accordingly. One-third of Germans surveyed felt their country was overrun by foreigners, oblivious to the fact that recently more Turks are leaving Germany than have been coming in and despite Christian Wulff, President of the German Republic, saying 'Islam is part of Germany'.[1] The danger from too much dilution of the 'nation' component of the nation-state is the opposite reaction, a rebirth of the ethnic purity concept in the idea of nation-state, with all the dangers it poses to minorities in general, Muslim, Jewish or other. Extreme nationalist Serbian leader Slobodan Milosevic made that clear when he stated that 'The loss of national identity is the greatest defeat a nation can know, and it is inevitable under the contemporary form of colonization.'[2] Nationalism tore Europe apart in the nineteenth century and right up until the First World War. The creeping erosion of sovereignty of the nation-states inherent in Project Europe generates confusion. Yet nations have always mixed, immigration always existed and in some cases, as we shall now see, immigration can even be a necessity.

The strange case of the disappearing Italian

Italy is running out of Italians: the birthrate has fallen dramatically. Perhaps the burden of caring for children is not to their liking anymore, or they are too busy simply trying to make ends meet to risk having children. Yet welfare benefits for young mothers are generous, coming close to half a year at full salary. The aging of Italy's population has become visible wherever you travel in the peninsula: this applliles also to the country's political class – carbon dating may soon be necessary to determine their median age. Gone is the image of large Italian families with children running around, particularly in the more affluent north and centre of the country. In the 1990s Italy's fertility rate fell below 1.2, one of the lowest in the world, recovering later to 1.41 but still well below the 2.1 minimum necessary to keep the population stable (two offspring per woman to replace the parents and 0.1 to compensate for sterile mothers and other contingencies). Most of the increase in fertility was due to immigrants; more foreign babies are born in Italy today than Italian. The mathematics are simple: if current trends continue (and there is no reason to believe Italians will start making babies again), Italy's population, which is 60 million today, will, according to some estimates, have dwindled to less than 50 million by mid-century[3] and continue its decline thereafter to 10 million by the end of the century:[4] the total population of Italy will be less than the population of Shanghai. A threshold of doom has already been crossed with this implosion, mathematically ensuring that the number of teenagers will forever remain below the number of people over 60.

Instead of babies, Italians have taken to producing *pensionati*, retirees on a state pension. And here comes the economic side of the coin, which, combined with the population meltdown, points to a catastrophe. Almost one person out of four you meet in the streets of Milan, Rome or Verona is a *pensionato* (the actual figure comes to about 22 per cent, one of the highest percentages in the world), compelling Italy to spend over 15 per cent of its GDP to fund their retirement cost, the worst state of affairs in all of Europe, a dubious honour, and a situation expected to worsen as the 22 per cent is likely to jump to 33 per cent within a couple of decades. As the population shrinks, ages and retires, more and more old people will need to collect pensions but less and less young people will be there to work and pay the taxes the government needs to collect to fund these pensions. In 2001 the UN produced a study showing that to maintain today's Italian population unchanged by mid-century, you'd need to import almost 20 million people.[5] Virtually one Italian in three would, by that time, be an import. If not there would be about 20 million fewer people in the country than today – unless Italians change their habits very rapidly and take up again the joys of making babies (and it may even be too late for that) or the government boosts taxes (hammering the last nail in businesses coffins), or drastically cuts down pensions and sends people onto the streets, or imports huge numbers of people.

The Italian ethnic landscape is already profoundly changing: the most frequent first name of owners of new businesses established in Milan in 2010 was Maria, followed by Mohammed, for bars and restaurants it was Hu and Mohammed, and for new construction companies Domenico ranks equal to, again, Mohammed.[6] Foreigners now represent 7 per cent of the country's population, up to 12 per cent in some regions. Like America a century ago, Italy may soon need to welcome increasing numbers of immigrants to fuel its work engine; but in the case of America they were reaching a vast new country where everything needed to be done, whereas in the case of Italy they'd be reaching an exhausted country way beyond maturity. If Italy chooses the solution of opening its doors, the questions will be to find the immigrants, and how to integrate them and avoid social instability.

The problem of aging and its implications for immigration is Europe-wide. Spain's population, 39.9 million strong today, could shrink to 31.3 million by mid-century.[7] Germany is almost as bad as Italy, with a disastrous 1.35 fertility rate today. In the absence of immigration it has been estimated that the German workforce, today numbering 44 million, could dwindle to 26 million within a few decades with dire consequences for its GDP. With several sectors of its economy facing acute labour shortages following the 2010 growth spike, Germany is forecasted to be short by 400,000 skilled workers for its growing economy, just at a time when the net inflow of immigrants is only about 200,000 per year,[8] a shortage costing an estimated 15 billion euros per year to its economy. In the longer term, McKinsey forecasted that by 2020, in just under a decade, the shortfall of qualified people would jump to 2 million.[9] From 16 million today, the number of Germans aged over 65 will reach about 24 million by 2030, causing a shortfall of 1 million workers, and the current low fertility rate is not going to help. What the maths show is that Germany, for one, needs immigrants not today, but yesterday. Even Turkey, not yet European, is affected, with its 6.18 children per woman in 1960 having dwindled to 2.43 in 2003. One of the few exceptions is France with a 2.01 fertility rate not seen since the early 1970s:[10] yet it is said that already more people are leaving France's workforce than entering it.

Looking at the overall picture, the total population of Europe, standing today at about 800 million, could by mid-century have shrunk to 632 million, and to a mere 480 million, or a loss of 40 per cent, by the end of the century. The number of people of working age is set to fall from 305 million today to 255 million by mid-century.[11] In the 1990s, European women gave birth to an average 1.8 children, already short of the 2.1 mark, a number that fell to 1.5 in 2003. As a consequence, by mid-century a good third of Europe's population will consist of people over 65, against 15 per cent today. From an economic standpoint, aside from losing competitiveness because of an aging population, the European Commission predicted a few years ago that Europe's share of world GDP could fall from 30 per cent to under 10 per cent by the second half of the century. Qualitatively and quantitatively, disaster is looming. Europe will become a cross between a sort of new Africa and a continent-wide retirement home. From an economic standpoint, as Europe's population shrinks and becomes older, who will support the retirees? Either Europeans become breeders or Europe will have to dramatically increase retirement age and brutally cut pensions (from today's average of 60 per cent of median wages): the alternative is massive immigration, or a combination of the above.

Pension schemes can be funded, which means the money to pay for pensions comes from the income generated by pension funds, which is the case in Holland, Britain and the US for example, or they can be unfunded, which is the case in the rest of Europe, meaning the money to pay for pensions primarily comes from taxes (it also means that the real cost of labour is substantially higher than just the sum of current wages, because part of it needs to be paid later). In the unfunded case the tax base shrinks because the working and contributing population shrinks. In essence, the problem in Europe is that there are fewer and fewer people contributing with taxes and people live longer and retire earlier, which means the time they spend in retirement is longer. Consider Finland, which has the fastest aging population of all of Europe. Statistically there are currently about four 'young' Finns supporting every single Finn *pensioner* (four people working and funding the retiree's pension with their taxes), a number that is expected to dwindle to three by 2015. Unless the Finnish government finds ways to stimulate growth, Finland will be broke. It is even worse elsewhere in Europe: forecasts show that between today and mid-century the number of working people supporting each Italian *pensionato* will shrink from 3.0 to 1.5, in the case of France from 3.5 to 1.9, for Germany 3 to 1.6, Britain 3.6 to 2.4 and Greece 3.4 to 1.6.[12] There is a dramatic reduction in contributing people across the board in Europe, averaging 3.5 today to 1.8 by mid-century. Some experts calculated that in order to maintain a constant proportion between the number of actively working people and the number of pensioned people they support, Europe's deficiency would need to be made up with up to 25 million immigrants per year, merely to ensure the pension system doesn't go broke. The 2004 total of 2 million actual immigrants looks very small.

The maths tell us that this situation is unsustainable: given such population trends, the welfare state, pride and joy of modern Europe, is bound to fail in the coming decades. A thorough reform of the system is needed in any case, involving dramatic streamlining, governments turning a lot of this business over to the private sector, programmes providing incentives to make babies, retirement age increases and so on, but it is more likely not to be enough. Either Europe sees its generous welfare and pensions system shrink to an unrecognizable level and rejects the Civilization of Entitlements, or it will need to import people, in huge numbers. A 2002 UN report entitled 'Replacement Migration' made the case that immigration could be a solution. But massive immigration carries its own problems as the implications for cultural identity and social stability are dire.

Integrate or disintegrate

It has been estimated that almost a third of all people on the streets of London belong to an ethnic minority and that by 2015 about 80 per cent of the increase in working population of this city will be made up of such minorities. In France it is said that close to 10 per cent of the population consists of minorities. In Germany it has been estimated that there are almost 2.5 million Turks, of which more than 700,000 have become German citizens. Some 20 million Muslims are said to live in Europe on aggregate, equivalent to the population of a mid-sized country, a 28th country, a Muslim archipelago within Europe, made up of immigrants spread among 27 countries. In 1991, when Europe was only 12 countries, French intellectual Jean-Marie Domenach already spoke of 'a fear growing all across Europe of a Muslim community that cuts across European lines, a sort of thirteenth nation of the European Community'.[13] These numbers will keep growing as immigration continues and the birthrates of these minorities far outstrip those of the natives. As these minorities grow in size, they naturally become more self-confident and assertive. Few will argue with Graham E. Fuller, who reminds us in *A World without Islam* that Islam is today the world's most politically self-conscious and assertive culture.[14] They have demands and their gaining voting rights means they become courted by politicians: their voices will increasingly be heard. The sheer size of the numbers means that the issue of integration of these minorities cannot be ignored. How this diaspora integrates with European societies, and how much of a rallying cry Islam can be for this diaspora, is bound to have a huge impact on the social stability of the continent and may very well be the defining factor for many European societies in the twenty-first century. The problem is that the cleavage between mainstream and minorities is widening to alarming proportions. Religion has turned into a convenient marker of identity for both sides, and amalgamation becomes the easy solution for the mainstream. Minorities feel increasingly humiliated, alienated by their second-class status and their lack of a real identity, and the mainstream increasingly sees them as parasites and thinks that no matter what the host country does, they simply won't blend in. Oil is thrown on the fire by the well publicized actions of 'rejectionists', a minority within the minority, who actively reject European values. If integration is such an important issue, can a model of integration be found? Can the majority and the minority live happily side by side? Is the issue being properly debated?

Different countries have tried different models, so far with dubious results. At the liberal end of the spectrum was the politically correct laissez-faire model of 'multiculturalism', championed by the UK, by which minorities could live any way they wanted to and retain as much of their cultural heritage and value systems as they wished to, with no obligation other than paying taxes and abiding by the law of the land. Within the context of such cultural relativism, there was no pressure pushing them to assimilate, and they were allowed to keep their own totally separate identity from the mainstream. The problem with this model is that it lacked by definition a motor for integration: the end product was, below the surface, a mosaic of self-contained, segregated communities and cultural diasporas that remain alienated from each other and that share little more than the subway. In a fit of malignant neglect, the state abdicated its requisite that its citizens abide by a common system of society and values and its role was relegated to administering a geographic area made up of separate ethnicities. The nation-state becomes the 'nations'-state'. Minorities have not even been required to try to integrate, and the easy solution for many of them is to cling to their own communities, in a sort of voluntary apartheid. Polls carried out in 2005 showed that only 28 per cent of immigrants felt they should espouse British culture and values, a clear sign that the vast majority was not there for the love of the British or Britain. Not only that: some groups opposing equality for women and Muslim schools preaching intolerance were actually given financial aid from the government. The London Underground attacks, leaving 56 dead and 700 injured in the summer of 2005, were perpetrated by Pakistanis born in the UK who seemed to have perfectly integrated with British society on the surface but were really living in a different world. In the name of generosity, tolerance and universal freedom of choice for the newcomers the British renounced the primacy of their own values or cultural heritage in their own home and ended up promoting fragmentation instead.

The by-product of this ideology was an immigration system where laxity knew no bounds. Any immigrant arriving in the UK and asking for political asylum was not only let in, but also provided with financial support, inviting abuse. Britain became an ideal entry point, a source of funds and a breeding ground for radicals. Among the perpetrators of the failed July 2005 underground bombings in London was Osman Hussein, who had arrived in the UK with fake Somali documents, claimed and obtained political asylum (and handouts) as well as British nationality. The August 2011 riots that turned several cities of the UK into war zones, with their multiracial dimension, were a sign that malignant neglect had not been confined to immigration issues alone, but to society as a whole, where laxness and permissiveness on hooliganism and petty crime has known few bounds for too long. The marginalized children of the welfare state of this most economically unequal European nation, second- or third-generation misfits with no jobs, no hopes in a stagnating economy hit by harsh austerity measures including closure of youth centres, having been raised in a culture of entitlements had decided to try their luck with 'aggressive shopping'. David Cameron condemned his country's 'Moral neutrality, relativism' leading to a 'slow-motion moral collapse'[15] – too late.

The final nail on the coffin of the multiculturalist idea (*multikulti* in Germany) was hammered in October 2010 by none other than Angela Merkel with her 'Multiculturalism . . . absolutely failed', adding, in defence of *Leitkultur* (dominant culture): 'We feel attached to Christian values and those who do not accept this have no place here'.[16] From Horst Seehofer, head of the CSU Christian Social Union: '(Germany is) not an immigration country . . . (it) does not need more immigrants from different cultures . . . multiculturalism is dead'.[17] The social experiment started by Gerhard Schröder in 2000 when he ended blood rights and permitted double nationality,[18] the old debate between those in favour of the *multikulti* approach and those defending *Leitkultur,* is essentially over today. Just when Germans discovered that 16 million people, or 20 per cent of their population, originated from immigration. Germany is still looking for a way to integrate its immigrants of which a third are of Turkish origin, dating from the arrival of wave after wave of *Gastarbeiters* half a century ago when nobody was thinking about the issue of integration. Having now decided that a basic knowledge of the German language is a minimum prerequisite for integration, Germany is taking steps to make German language courses mandatory. Turkish Prime Minister Erdogan's attempt to throw a monkey wrench in such plans, when, during a visit to Dusseldorf in 2010, he called on the Turkish community living in Germany to teach their children Turkish *first* and German second and said 'We are against assimilation',[19] is not going to endear these immigrants more to Germans nor is it going to improve the chances of swaying a German government unfavourable to the accession of Turkey to the EU. The British finally became aware of the shortcomings of their half-a-century-old policies when David Cameron declared

Under the doctrine of state multiculturalism, we have encouraged different cultures to live separate lives, apart from each other and the mainstream ... we have failed to provide a vision of society to which they feel they want to belong ... we've even tolerated these segregated communities behaving in ways that run completely counter to our values.[20]

With this indictment of the British policy that started in the 1960s he decided that 'passive tolerance' was over and that it was time for 'muscular liberalism'.[21] The Labour opposition swiftly accused him of catering to far right racist groups, and British Muslim organizations complained that Muslims were once more victimized. Britain will sooner or later pay the price for its avoiding an open and frank national debate on the future integration of a British Muslim population that will rise from today's 2.4 million or so to an estimated 5.6 million by 2030. The same applies to Europe in general, where the Muslim population will aggregate 10 per cent of the total by 2030 (according to Pew statistics).

Possibly moved by Gallic pride, the French took a different route, with their model of 'assimilation' requiring immigrants to make an effort to integrate. The notion of the religious identity of a community, Muslim or otherwise, clashed with French state ideals. In exchange for immigrants adopting French as their language and sticking to the *valeurs de la République*, and in particular its *laïcité* (secularity), they would be given French citizenship and be considered as French as Jeanne d'Arc. The government wouldn't recognize that there were minorities in the country, religious, ethnic or otherwise. This model, which didn't recognize religion as a key marker of belonging, didn't work either because the state may have considered the newcomers as fully French but, by and large, the French native population did not buy it. If England let radical Islam flourish on its soil, the french government intervened to limit its spread, creating a state-sanctioned Islam (as Ataturk did in Turkey) and establishing limits on wearing the veil (very much as Ataturk did). When it comes to the intractable problem of the suburbs, the *banlieues* (some of which have become virtual states within the state, like so many Gaza strips), integration is just a façade. The French government, like many others in Europe, often shies away from applying certain laws to the country's vocal minorities, because they are quick to mobilize, turn violent and take to vandalism, burning cars and even taking to ambushing and shooting at police cars. The isolation and Islamization of the *banlieues* is a fact. It has been estimated that in the *banlieues* illegal business (traffic of cars and parts, weapons, drugs and so on) amounts to 90 billion euros per year (needless to say, the state does not collect any taxes on this). Some 45,000 cars are burned every year on average and violence within immigrant communities has been steadily on the rise. Such abdication of the state's authority contributes to the majority's perception that these minorities are taking advantage of the system, are beyond the law: it further promotes national cleavage.

If the many models that have been tried throughout Europe don't really work, what is the right way to integrate immigrants into a society? Is there a right way after all? There is no tested recipe on how a modern, mature, democratic society is to deal with a massive influx of people from different cultures. The problem is not just European, and it goes without saying that a minority can be more readily tolerated or absorbed if its numbers remain limited, and ethnic and cultural differences with the host population are minimal and jobs plentiful. There probably does not exist a right way to make a conspicuously different population subset blend perfectly into an established host country's population. Look at the case of minority schools: what may at first have seemed a good idea ended up furthering self-segregation and ghettoization of youth. Yet the social stability of countries such as the UK, France or Germany, with millions of immigrants in their midst, can be greatly affected by the issue of integration.

One question, which at first seems pernicious, has been recently asked with increasing frequency: what if immigrants *don't* actually want to integrate? What if they feel it is their right to refuse to integrate? What if their values are so far from those of the host countries and so dear to them that they are the ones who, in the first place, do not wish to or cannot in any circumstances become part of modern European societies?

Of veils, minarets and purple cows

Bernard Lewis is famous not for his opinions on fashion but as a scholar, a world renowned expert on Islam and the Middle East. Yet he recognizes that the 'headscarf and the veil have become powerful emotive symbols of cultural choice'.[22] They have also become loaded political symbols. The case of the veil, this little piece of cloth that weighs a few grammes and is said to be worn by fewer than 2000 women in the whole of France (someone pointed out that many more Muslim women in France wear bikinis than burkas), has taken a life of its own and turned into a high profile and divisive issue that, in the eyes of European majorities, brings into question the growing assertiveness by minorities of their separate identity and their willingness to integrate in European society. The more extreme burka is now prohibited in public in France, Belgium and the Netherlands. More generally, in the debate over the integration of Islamic minorities in Europe, few issues arouse as much passion as that of the treatment of women. In Europe women fought hard for equality and obtained it; it is now a crucial part of the European psyche and culture, and European society does not view kindly aliens living in its midst trampling this equality.

How justified is the growing anxiety of the European public with regard to the assimilation of Muslims in their societies? Looking at the idea of an Islam-Christian conflict from a very broad historical perspective,[23] Fuller posits that religion is not in itself the cause of conflicts but a convenient vehicle, a vector by which worldly interests and rivalries, local or geopolitical, are confronted and that conflicts among Muslims, or among Christians themselves, have been far more common than so-called 'civilizational conflicts' pitting Islam against Christianity. Coming back to today's world, the total number of mosques throughout the EU has increased to more than 6000, a conspicuous addition to Europe's physical landscape, a symbol of the growing presence of Muslim immigrants and the permanent establishment of an Islamic cultural subset. It doesn't help when, as occasionally happens in Paris and other places, Muslims block city streets to worship in groups numbering hundreds: to mainstream Europeans it smacks of defiance. Modern Europe's secular ideals meant it didn't pay too much attention to the religious dimension of its immigrant populations until recently, with the exception of Greece, whose Orthodox Church has always fought against the establishment of mosques. Otherwise tolerant Europe now feels under siege. Mainstream Europeans ask themselves: didn't

Saudi Arabia build Europe's largest mosque not in France, which would have been a more natural place since it hosts the largest Muslim population, but in Rome, the capital of Christendom, home of the Vatican and the papacy? Didn't the Saudis specifically request the Roman minaret to be higher than the Vatican's highest building (request refused)? Didn't Muslims request visible minarets to be built on top of their mosques throughout Switzerland, the country of the purple cow (request refused)? Examples abound, such as that of Abdelkader Bouziane, Imam of the Venissieux Mosque in France, who trumpeted that the Koran authorizes a man to beat his wife and that the entire world should become Muslim. London's Finsbury Park mosque and Berlin's Al Nur mosque have been known for years to be sanctuaries for Islamic militants. Europeans may be less and less religious but they have difficulty accepting the presence of increasingly religious communities and the fact that mosques, in some of which hatred is openly preached, proliferate throughout the lands of Christendom, whereas few churches are allowed in Muslim lands. Christians living in the Islamic world have recently often been the subject of collective mistreatment. The network of mosques is often perceived to have been used as a conduit for the radicalization of Muslim youth, compelling governments throughout Europe to impose controls.

What if they don't want to integrate? On the radical fringe, the number of Salafists has been steadily increasing across Europe, and their ideology, rooted in the old ultra-conservative Islam of Ibn Tamiya and Abd al-Wahhab, opposes any idea of integration. Closer to the mainstream, some Muslim families have subjected themselves to Islamicized codes of life, to the extent of parents refusing to send their daughters to co-educational schools or mixed gender swimming pools, and parents sending their children to Islamic schools to be taught in Arabic. Fathers and brothers have been reported to turn violent when their daughters or sisters dress immodestly, let alone when they date Westerners, to the extent of a few lunatics committing heinous crimes in the name of Islamic rectitude. Germany has seen its share of such crimes perpetrated by Turks in the name of Islam: in 2005 Hatun Surucu, a young girl of Turkish origin, was murdered by her own brothers because she had divorced her husband and was wearing T-shirts. Such occurrences are extremely rare, but the high level of publicity gives them a different dimension. In recent years, some Muslim immigrants have turned increasingly vocal about rejecting the secular laws of their host countries and requiring instead to be subject to Sharia law, which they feel is their cultural right. A 2006 ICM Research poll showed for instance 40 per cent of Muslims in the UK liked the idea of Sharia law applied in parts of Britain.[24] European governments that at first rejected such requests outright have started giving in, introducing Islamic law in piecemeal fashion, oblivious to the fact that they may conflict with the secular laws of the land. It's not only in Europe: the Ontario province of Canada, for one, has been studying ways of having its Muslim communities judged according to Islamic laws instead of Canadian laws. The end result of such a process, still embryonic today, is bound to be two communities subjected to two different sets of laws within a country, institutionalizing cleavage and further diluting the essence of the nation-state. Moreover, if Europe accommodates such requests, natives will ask where does it stop? What about Islamic laws demanding corporal or capital punishment? What about polygamy, divorce laws and other regulations incompatible with today's European values?

To Italian essayist Oriana Fallaci, Europe has become 'Eurabia',[25] a colony of Islam. Wearing the veil, demanding Sharia law, building more and more mosques, advocating the subjugation of women, requiring segregated swimming pools and gymnastic classes in schools, asking for more Koranic schools and more: some Muslims feel this is their cultural right. A very few even feel that honour killings (generally performed by the husbands or brothers of female victims), polygamy and forced marriages are their cultural rights, and there have been cases in which European judges have seemed to side with their views. But these are, in truth, the demands of a very small minority of immigrants, and the immigrant majority in general does not care much for religion or this sort of attitude. But to mainstream Europeans this minority is amalgamated with the majority, they see it as one and the same, and it all increasingly smacks of defiance, of provocation. They fear that instead of Islam becoming Europeanized, it is Europe that risks becoming Islamized and that it has already gone too far in trying to accommodate immigrants.

It is easy for the majority to fall into the trap of viewing the entire minority as a monolith that is increasingly alien. The result is inevitably that the mainstream decries the importation of systems and values that are proven to be dysfunctional abroad and perceives a political show of force implying that the minority's allegiance is not really to their host country but to some alien cultures and ideologies often incompatible with Europe's secular and democratic values and way of life. This was one of the main themes of the former German central banker Thilo Sarrazin's bestseller *Germany Does Away with Itself*, which sold over half a million copies in just one month in 2010, attesting to how 'hot' the issue had become in Germany. Because of the actions of a minority of rejectionists and fundamentalists, Islam in general becomes increasingly identified as a scary, militant and uncompromising ideology that promotes backwardness and radicalism. Europeans fear the gradual emergence not only of a nation within the nation, but also of a state within the state, communities turning into Bantustans with their own laws and their own de facto frontiers.

Most Europeans can't understand why such minorities would insist on visibly asserting separate identities when they seemingly have everything to gain by blending in. After all, there is a subset of immigrants from whom you rarely hear about problems of integration, and their small number is not the only reason. These immigrants from Asian countries such as Vietnam, China and Laos, where culture puts a premium on education, hard work and respect of state authority, are unencumbered by any religious baggage. Statistics from INED (Institut National d'Etudes Démographiques) in France show that the children of these Asian immigrants outperform those of native families at school. Half of French women of Asian descent have degrees, against 37 per cent of mainstream women. Chinese and Indian immigrants came to the UK just as poor as their Muslim counterparts, but have been out performing them in jobs and education. Why is it so? More directly, Europeans ask why do Islamic rejectionists stay in a Europe where they clearly don't have a place. Why don't they go back to regions of the world where they could find societies with systems closer to their ideals? Why would a Pakistani emigrate from Pakistan to an England he actually hates? Does he want England to become like the Pakistan he was fleeing?

Europeans increasingly wonder to what extent Europe is supposed to compromise in the name of tolerance. To mainstream Europeans, these rejectionists obtain a passport of convenience, latch on to social benefits and take advantage of the rule of law while importing their backward ways and becoming parasites of society.

In truth the vast majority of the immigrant minority in any given country remains moderate, pays limited interest to religion and wants nothing more than to make a living in peace and blend in. The problem is that assertive, radical and rejectionist elements represent an increasingly visible subgroup, a minority of the minority, yet one whose actions are well publicized, and one that cannot be ignored. This subgroup poses a real threat to societies not only by reason of its radicalism, but, more importantly, because an exasperated mainstream comes to associate *all* immigrants with the radicals, threatening the future cohesiveness of Europe's new multiethnic societies. That is exactly what the most radical of the radicals want.

Guerillas in the midst

If there is one society that has historically been open-minded, progressive and tolerant it is Dutch society. Centuries ago, the Netherlands built a trading empire that reached places as far away as today's Indonesia, on the way inventing modern finance. The Dutch are as internationally minded as they come, used to mingling with and accepting foreign cultures, and take their freedom and tolerance ideals quite seriously. It would be difficult to shake their beliefs. It was during the watershed year of 2005 that the Dutch got their wake-up call. As they were preparing to vote for the EU Constitution in a referendum, Theo Van Gogh, a popular local film director who was working on a film that criticized the way Muslim men treat their women, had his throat slit by Mohammed Bouyeri, a Muslim fanatic, an immigrant who, like thousands of other immigrants, was supposed to have integrated into Dutch society and espoused its ideals of tolerance. Not only did the assassin express no regret, but he also declared to the court loud and clear that he was proud of what he had done in the name of his faith and that he did not recognize Dutch laws.

In that moment the Dutch were brought face to face with two crises. First came the painful realization that no matter how welcoming their society was to foreigners, no matter how universally appealing the Dutch deemed their social ideals to be, some of the immigrants who had been imported and were assumed to have become part of the fabric of Dutch society did not necessarily share these ideals and even rejected them and were responding instead to alien imperatives incompatible with the essence of Dutch society. Immigration had suddenly revealed a hidden dark side. Second, it dawned on the Dutch that their country was no longer in full control of its destiny, since more and more decisions impacting on Dutch immigration policies were no longer made by Dutch people but by faceless 'foreign' Eurognomes in Brussels. The timing could not have been worse for the EU, and the issue of immigration certainly had a lot to do with the Dutch 'No' vote for the EU Constitution. Instead of Dutch society changing these immigrants for the better, it was the immigrants that had changed Dutch society for the worse, causing it to shed its tolerance.

The British got their own wake-up call in July of the same year, when terrorists blew themselves up in the London Underground, leaving 70 dead and hundreds wounded. These attacks, and those which had taken place in Madrid in 2004 that left 200 dead, were a general wake-up call, forcing Europeans for the first time to lift the taboo on openly discussing the issue of the Euromuslims living in their midst and of their allegiance. Until then conventional wisdom had been that the struggle was between the West and medieval jihadists from the Middle East. This was wrong. These terrorists had not infiltrated from Saudi Arabia or Pakistan. They were British citizens of Pakistani origin, born and brought up in England (except for one in Jamaica). They followed cricket. One of them worked in his father's fish and chips shop in northern England. Britons killing Britons for religious reasons was, sadly, nothing new given the horrors witnessed in Northern Ireland. But what was new, just as in the Theo van Gogh case, was that the perpetrators as well as their faith were recent imports into British society whom the country had welcomed and who were assumed to have come because they wanted to be part of England, not blow it to smithereens. The nation was shocked to learn that there existed a fifth column of

British passport-holders who could blend in as anyone's neighbour but were actually out to kill them in the name of a foreign creed. Giving immigrants an education and a decent job suddenly didn't seem enough to integrate them: what else could be done? Jihadism had been able to infiltrate the Euromuslim community, where it could easily blend in, stay beyond the radar screen, and develop terror cells which lay dormant until they struck. To extreme jihadists mired in medieval ideologies, there is no country or neighbourhood. There is just Dar al-Islam (the House of Islam, areas under Islam domination) and Dar al-Harb (the House of War, areas not yet submitted to Islam).

The 16 July 2005 issue of *The Economist*, entitled 'In Europe's midst', featured a study of the new phenomenon of European-born jihadists. It pointed out that the terrorists were 'seen smiling and laughing in closed circuit-television pictures at King's Cross station, then blew themselves up on three Underground trains and a bus'. The implication is that they had fallen prey to an ideology that completely perverted their minds and turned them into total alien psychopaths. *The Economist* spoke of 'internal colonies', 'ghettos cut off from the culture of their new homeland' and added that 'the London bombings were not simply the act of isolated malcontents but a sign of the continued existence of a transnational terror network'. Well, wake up England: having allowed radicals, a known terrorist organization and hate preachers to flourish freely in your midst for years in the foolish hope that this Faustian pact would shield you from their acts, why were you now surprised to find a terror network in your midst? The article concluded that 'Europeans need to stiffen their campaign against indigenous jihad ... tighten the law at home ... take a harsher line on the firebrands who preach violence and murder'. Yet the same magazine voiced its opposition to Tony Blair's proposed measures against terrorism and the spreading of radical ideas, writing one month later that such measures would 'serve the terrorists ends by undermining the civilisation they attack' and that by threatening naturalized citizens with deportation one would 'create two classes of citizens, the British born and the rest', and that 'laws are not created in order that indesirables be put away' (say again?). So does England know what it really wants? Jihadists have had no better ally in Europe than political correctness and this inbuilt respect of civil rights and freedom of expression that some Europeans are loath to damage, even when it could kill them and their children. A year earlier, German Interior Minister Otto Schily had lamented 'is there not a right of self-defence against terrorists who plan mass murders?'[26] German courts have been known to let a terrorist suspect walk free and strike down his arrest warrant issued by Spain on grounds that evidence obtained from eavesdropping was unconstitutional. It took almost a decade for the UK to decide to expel Abu Qatada, widely known to be Al-Qaeda's spiritual ambassador in Europe and wanted in Jordan for bombings, who had settled in Acton from where he had been encouraging British Muslims to become *shaheen* (martyrs) and inspired terrorists such as Richard Reid. Omar Bakri Mohammad, expelled from Saudi Arabia for his radicalism, landed in the UK, asked for political asylum and obtained it, settled in the UK where he and his seven children obtained government money and British nationality, and for the next 20 years openly preached radicalism to British Muslims, going as far as to say that the life of a non-believer was not sacred and that the flag of Islam should fly on 10 Downing Street. When interviewed by the BBC after the London bombings, Abu Izzaddeen, born in England and a leading figure in the group Al Ghurabaa, refused to condemn the bombings and made a comment to the effect that the bombings would make Britons 'wake up and smell the coffee'. But the most astonishing comments came from Ajnam Choudry, former head of the now banned Al-Mujahiroun extremist organization that Bakri headed for a while. In a nutshell, he complained that on the one hand the government said you had freedom of expression, but on the other hand the government didn't let you blow people up or allow a good jihadist to do his job in peace.

The re-Islamization current going through the *ummah* (the worldwide community of Muslim faithfuls), while not threatening in itself, reached the shores of Europe where it mixed with the simmering discontent and frustration of minority populations due to social and economic issues, and provided an ideological framework. This ideology found in Europe a tolerance, a liberty of expression, a freedom of networking and recruiting it could not even dream to find in repressive Islamic countries such as Egypt or the Maghreb, enabling radicalism to flourish. This powerful ideological cocktail

resulted in the radicalization of many young Euromuslims, spawn-
ing the small but deadly subset of Eurojihadists, the radical army
of the 28th country. Eurojihadists are to Euromuslims what the
Brigate Rosse or Baader Meinhof was to the European left decades
ago: a group of violent radicals that had found justification for their
acts in an ideology they interpreted as requiring them to kill. Some
Eurojihadist soldiers go to Pakistan, Afghanistan and other places
for training. Out of 1.6 million British Muslims today, or about
3 per cent of the population, 15,000 were labelled al-Qaeda followers by a British government report. This may be a lot in absolute
terms, like a small army, but it represents about 1 out of 100,000
British Muslims. It would be a tragedy to stigmatize 99,999 people for the despicable actions of one (or one out of 60,000 in the
case of France, since French security services estimated that over
10,000 French Muslims, out of a total of more than 6 million, can
be considered dangerous); it would result in irreversible alienation
and cleavage, hardly a desirable outcome for two populations that
have to live side by side forever. Following the London bombings,
President Pervez Musharraf of Pakistan made the (correct) comment
that the bombers, having spent over 20 years each in Britain, had
not been indoctrinated in Pakistan but in England. Of the 1600 or
so mosques in France, over 50 have been known for a while to be in
the hands of radicals. Undoubtedly, the tolerant societies of Europe
have been perfect incubators for Eurojihadists.

It reminds me of a brief conversation I had years ago with the
very moderate Dalil Boubakeur, a Muslim leader in France: as we
discussed the radicalization of Islamic communities in Europe, he
said his main concern was that Europe was *too soft* on radicals. This
tells you that the vast majority of Euromuslims would be quite happy
to see radicals eradicated from their midst, a very important point
that Europeans fail to keep in mind. But the problem is that neither Europe nor the majority of the minority has the political will
to do this and both parties are worse off because of this abdication. A TV comment from then Scotland Yard head Sir Ian Blair
after the London bombings speaks volumes: 'The fact that these are
British-born Muslims changes the paradigm of terror...can (the
Muslim community in Britain) move from being fairly close to
denial about this into a situation where they really engage with us.'

For one, implicit in this statement is an 'us' (the non-Muslim main-stream British) as opposed to a 'them' (the Muslim British). More importantly, the implication is that the mainstream Muslim popu-lation is partly responsible or at the very least guilty of not doing anything, a notion made all the more realistic by the absence of any widespread demonstrations against the bombings after 7 July 2005 by mainstream British Muslims. Blair was reflecting the mood of the majority British population. This means that the terrorists have achieved their goals, a complete cleavage between the 'us' and the 'them'. In the absence of Euromuslims cleaning out their own house, or at least speaking out, the actions of the small subset of Eurojihadists in their midst are probably enough to cause profound changes in the tolerance attitudes of the European mainstream. The beginning of a reversal was felt in 2005 in Britain with a brutal surge in religion-motivated crimes against individuals and mosques following the bombings; it continued with a visible trend towards tightening of the judicial and police systems; and it appeared in 2010 with the coming to power of rightist political parties and politicians campaigning on anti-immigrant platforms. Yet the British don't seem to understand and, under pressure from human rights activists and civil libertarians, David Cameron's Tory government moved in early 2011 to relax Britain's 'control orders' regulations on suspected terrorists.

La Reconquista

Having had the privilege of spending my life on various continents, I firmly believe that the vast majority of people from any ethnicity, culture and faith anywhere in the world are simply looking to make a living, bring up children, ensure their future, and live a peaceful life. If you think this observation does not apply to Muslims, take the plane to Jakarta, capital of Indonesia, which happens to be the largest Muslim nation on earth. Apart from visiting a country that will astonish you with its natural and cultural treasures you will see some of the most welcoming and peaceful people you could meet anywhere. You don't even need to go that far: go to Turkey or visit Marrakesh in Morocco. The danger lies in sweeping generalizations that promote fragmentation and hostility. To say that Muslims are naturally prone to violence by virtue of their creed makes as little sense as saying that Germans are Nazis by virtue of being Germans. Those convinced that Christians are immune from violence conveniently forget that until very recently Catholics and Protestants were still blowing each other to pieces in Ireland and that Christians slaughtered Muslim women and children in Srebrenica in the Balkans a mere few hundred kilometres from vacationing Europeans in the 1990s. It was a blond, blue-eyed Anders Behring Breivik, a Norwegian and a Christian, who killed almost 80 people in July 2011 in Norway (his gesture was supposed to be a protest against the perceived Islamization of his country). Just as immigrants, legal or not, are, before all else, trying to improve their lot – a natural aspiration for any human being – a country tries to balance its need for tolerance of imported alien communities with its desire to maintain its identity and lifestyle – a natural aspiration for any country. Relationships between different communities sharing a country are always delicate, and, as we saw, European history is rife with mistreatment of *native* European minorities. Serious problems arise when the majority feels that a minority which has become permanent has not only outlived its usefulness but starts to become a parasite and a threat to jobs or security.

That Europeans are scared of Islam is not in doubt. Bernard Lewis wrote: 'For almost a thousand years, from the first Moorish landing in Spain to the second Turkish siege of Vienna, Europe was under constant threat from Islam. Islam is the only civilization which has put the survival of the West in doubt.'[27] In France 68 per cent of people feel Muslims are not integrated,[28] the number climbs to 75 per cent in Germany, and in both cases 40 per cent feel Islam is a menace to Europe. There is no denying this perception. The question is what Europe will do about it. Whether or not natives like it, today's Europe, by virtue of its immigration policies of the past half-century, has de facto become a multiethnic continent. Its minorities are now an integral part of its social fabric, and barring a process of mass deportations, which is unthinkable today, this situation is not only irreversible but likely to become even more acute as minorities' birthrates outstrip those of declining native populations. If minorities have become a permanent feature, logic would have it that everything should be done so that they integrate and live peacefully side by side with the majority. Moreover, if, as was pointed out, certain European countries are going to need *more* not *less* immigration to make up for dwindling native populations, everything should be done to turn immigration into an orderly and useful process, that is, 'intelligent' immigration. Logic would have it that if it is established that, due to demographic trends, Europe cannot survive without substantial immigration, then Europe should decide very pragmatically what it needs in terms of people, quantitatively and qualitatively, and where it makes most sense to get them from, and should devise ways to properly integrate immigrants since they are bound to become part of society anyway. To avoid compounding today's problems, Europe may end up having to close its doors to further immigration from parts of the world too ethnically and culturally different from its majority, and instead open its doors to cheap labour markets such as those previously closed by the Cold War. Yet unless there is full deregulation of the labour markets *inside* the Union, Europe will never be able to take full advantage of this opportunity.

Missing: the vital debate

The eradication of criminal elements and political and religious radicals from within minorities, to the extent of stripping troublemakers of the host country nationality and deportations, as unpalatable as it may seem, may soon come to be perceived as necessary to prevent a stigmatization of the *entire* minority by the majority, potentially leading to social strife. Majorities will have to accept once and for all the fact that established minorities are there to stay, and make room for them. Minorities will have to shed any desire to assert their different identity in opposition to the host country's, which does not mean forgetting their identity but toning it down, and adapting. Minorities should instead assert their being part of the mainstream by espousing host country values whenever possible and assisting the majority in eradicating radical and criminal elements in their midst. These are some of the things logic would dictate should be done. Will the mainstream and the minorities be able to rise to the challenge? In Switzerland immigrants represent just a few per cent of the total population. Yet, to the eyes of the native Swiss majority, their relatively small number is responsible for a disproportionately high share of criminality; almost 60 per cent of homicides are carried out by immigrants, and about 60 per cent of prison inmates are immigrants. This disproportion feeds the idea among the mainstream that immigration has gone too far and that importing people who won't have a job when they settle in is tantamount to importing criminality. Who can blame them? As 2010 was drawing to a close, the far-right Swiss People's Party (SVP), the same populist party that engineered a political ban on the construction of minarets in 2009, got 53 per cent of Swiss voters to endorse new regulations to deport foreigners guilty of crimes such as murder or fraud involving social benefits. Needless to say, Switzerland was attacked by its EU neighbours for its tough new stance, to the extent of being labelled the 'black sheep' of Europe. Germany's left-leaning *Suddeutsche Zeitung* ran headlines clamouring that Switzerland was violating international law.

Political correctness may still be de rigueur throughout Europe, but cracks are happening in the edifice as more and more Europeans demand change. Tough measures aimed at getting rid of the visible radical and criminal subset of the minority would reduce sources of inter-communal friction. But will Europe have the political will to follow that route – and follow it without excess? When, in mid-December 2010 in North Rhine, Westphalia, and Lower Saxony, German security forces raided radical networks seeking the imposition of Islamic states in Europe, all the authorities could do to try to stop them was to invoke laws against Nazism.[29] For too long there has been an absence of a legal framework within the EU to deal with radicals who endanger society. There have been laws against prostitution, drugs, paedophilia or rape, but few laws against the spreading of hatred and lots of tolerance of domestic violence and polygamy throughout Europe. Have liberals really been doing a favour to everybody by advocating absurd and unsustainable levels of tolerance? Similarly, is it in the interest of the moderate majority of Euromuslims to remain silent, and risk being labelled accomplices or at the very least sympathetic to the cause of the radicals? Some Europeans have said that if the moderates want to show they are really moderate and intent on becoming an integral and permanent fixture of Europe without creating social dislocations, they need to mobilize, to organize themselves, and make their position known loud and clear to the mainstream, to actively police themselves and work with the state to get rid of the political/religious radicals and criminals that give their community a bad name. Will the moderates take the step? To date nothing in their actions shows that they will, and, on the contrary, a current of demarcation appears to be making inroads.

Political correctness and denial has meant that in Europe to talk about minorities was taboo. Bringing up the subject used immediately to elicit accusations of political or racist intent, preventing meaningful dialogue. As long as the debate is not brought into the open in clear and pragmatic terms, as long as the native populations and the moderate majority of the minorities refuse to confront the issues face to face and within their own camp, the situation is bound to worsen and with it the cleavage between communities. As Europe declines, as living standards and job opportunities fall, native populations are bound to increasingly perceive minorities as alien and parasitic subsets paradoxically starting to obtain privileges which the majorities don't get. Minorities are bound to grow increasingly resentful, alienated and restless. This is a vicious circle. Social strife is a distinct possibility in some areas. Political parties based on xenophobia have already started their ascent. With the coming of populist politicians playing on the majority's fears, in particular in times of economic difficulties, today's political correctness could rapidly give way to intolerance, leading to dangerous changes.

It happened before in Europe's modern history and it can happen again. True, the far right's ascent throughout Europe these days is also due to Euroscepticism, leading to nationalism, and, in the case of richer countries, also to popular dislike of bailing out Europe's weaker countries. But immigration is also at the forefront – as shown by the rise of the True Finn party in Finland and of the Danish People's Party in 2011; by the September 2010 election to the Swedish Riksdag (parliament) of an anti-immigration party whose leader Jimmie Akesson described Muslim population growth as the biggest threat Sweden has known since the Second World War;[30] by the doubling of the Dutch Freedom Party's parliamentary seats, an anti-immigrant party whose leader Geert Wilders professed that there is no such thing as moderate Islam and that he wouldn't let one more Muslim immigrate. Campaigning on an anti-Islam plat-form, Austria's Freedom Party (FPO) got over 25 per cent of the votes in October 2010 for Vienna and polls show that, should elec-tions have been held at the national level, they were likely to confirm this proportion, putting the party ahead of the ruling Christian Democrats. Polls suggested at the time that if an anti-immigrant party was formed in Germany, it would get 20 per cent of the votes (the possibility of a nationalist party campaigning on a platform to restore the DM would also have to be taken seriously). In France, the UMP ruling party was losing scores of voters to the far right Front National (FN) led by Marine Le Pen in early 2011, to the extent of polls putting her in the lead for presidential elections. Unem-ployment and dire economic times historically favour the rise of the nationalist right in Europe, and a left in disarray is not going to count for much. Mainstream politicians across Europe are going to have to take into account the rise of a right riding on a wave of discontent with immigration, globalization, the EU and perceived loss of national identity, and will inevitably incorporate some of the right's arguments in their narratives to satisfy electorates. The rise of the right across Europe can't be dismissed as a marginal or tempo-rary phenomenon. It is happening and, while Europe's commitment to democracy is not in doubt, Europe may be turning its back on half a century of liberal and tolerant politics. In the coming years, its politics are likely to increasingly be concerned with nationalism, anti-immigration and protectionism.

When talking to European mainstream voters, one does not get a feeling that they actually hate immigrants, Muslim or others. Reli-gion has little to do with perceptions except as a marker of identity as we have said. But mainstream Europeans feel less and less at home, feel invaded by people from alien and incompatible cultures who are becoming a problem; they decry the increase in crime and violence; and with their votes they are saying 'Enough!'. We are witnessing the first stirrings of a 'reaction'. The writing is on the wall. The anti-immigration and anti-Islamic ideas of the far right are becom-ing more and more mainstream throughout the continent. It is too easy to assume that the ghosts of the past are forever buried and that Europe, which seems quite tolerant and pacific today, won't one day concoct some new extreme xenophobic ideology. In the not too distant past, Europe produced communist, fascist and Nazi ideologies that were not based on ideals of tolerance. If history teaches us anything, it is that Europe the tame can turn into a monster, Dr Jekyll becomes Mr Hyde. It is not impossible to envisage a scenario in which relations between communities worsen dramatically against a backdrop of sharply rising unemployment, declining economic fortunes and provocations from radicals on both sides. Who is to say that the most extreme scenario wouldn't result in a complete rejection of minorities, causing social strife, mass deportations and more. Indeed, ethnic cleansing reared its ugly head again at the doorstep of Europe in the Balkans in the 1990s.

EIGHT
THE END OF GROWTH
The roots of European economic decline

Airport

Singapore Airlines flight SQ333 from Paris lands at dawn at Changi Airport, on the southern tip of the island city-state of Singapore. Impeccable service on board, possibly the world's best airline, the industry's youngest fleet of planes, a spotless safety record – and the airline actually turns a profit. Upon touching the tarmac the plane swiftly taxies to the sprawling and beautiful new Terminal 3, a marvel of modern architecture and efficiency. Changi is for all intents and purposes a remarkable shopping centre with an airport built around it, one of the very few airports in the world where one actually would make it a point to arrive early to enjoy shopping, eating and maybe even a film or a live band. After a short taxi on the runway it takes no more than a few minutes of walking through immaculate carpeted walkways and designer lounges to reach immigration counters. The waiting line is short: your passport is checked and stamped in a few seconds by one of the many smiling inspectors who rarely fail to offer a sweet. A minute's walk takes you to the luggage belt where your bags are *already* waiting for you. Another minute or two takes you to the efficiently managed and short taxi line. You are on your way to your hotel in under thirty minutes from the time your plane touched down. Welcome to 'Singapore Inc.', officially known as the Republic of Singapore, epitome of efficiency, where the future started yesterday, the skyline will amaze you, and everything smells of excellence and efficiency. As soon as you land the government wants you to know that it means business.

Now brace yourself for the return journey. You land in the early morning at Paris's sprawling Charles de Gaulle (CDG) airport. It takes almost half an hour for your plane to taxi to its arrival gate. When passengers are finally allowed to disembark, which can take up to a few dozen minutes depending on how alert ground personnel are that morning and if the mobile gangway is ready, they all end up squeezed into a narrow, decrepit corridor. Two policemen are blocking the way for a first perfunctory passport check, causing the jam to back up to the inside of the plane. You then continue your journey through more poorly indicated and run-down corridors leading to the formal passport control area where a single inspector ensconced in his kiosk is handling the several hundred frustrated passengers, just arrived after a 13-hour flight and now packed like sardines in front of him. You've been waiting for over half an hour like everybody else in this run-down area when a second inspector finally shows up and opens his booth for business – no smile or sweet. Finally out of passport control you wonder where you should go to get your luggage because it is not properly indicated. The travellator that is supposed to get you there may or may not be working. Receiving your luggage can take from half an hour to one hour or more, assuming the handlers haven't brought it to the wrong area of the terminal or haven't taken a coffee break. You finally come out of your terminal one and a half to two hours after you touched down, that is, if everything goes well and there are none of the frequent airport personnel strikes. If you have not missed your connecting flight by now, you must rejoice in knowing that, after decades during which going from one terminal to another was a fully fledged safari, CDG launched an automatic shuttle train connecting them. CDG is everything Changi is not: inefficient, run-down, a maze of roads, terminals and corridors, bad service, endemic strikes, and certainly no exciting shopping or eating experiences. Welcome to Old Europe, where the notion of mediocrity has been elevated to that of a cult. This is no exaggeration: in the summer of 2009 a survey of airports in major cities placed Changi airport as the best in the world and CDG as the worst.[1] And it's not just the airport: Singapore was ranked again by the World Bank in 2010 as the world's number one country in terms of ease of doing business, with France a distant 26th.

Let me clarify one point. There is nothing anywhere in this book against France per se, and nobody will deny this great nation's beauty, its rich historical and cultural heritage. Moreover, today's France is still capable of remarkable feats and certainly has no monopoly on mediocrity or decline. Writing on Christmas Eve 2010 on the catastrophic performance of European airports hit by snow, British columnist Roger Cohen said 'a few inches of snow have cast Europe into chaos. Britain has joined the third world with France in hot pursuit' and noted that eight out of ten Eurostar and Eurotunnel trains connecting London to Paris had broken down, attesting to the general dysfunctionality of transport systems in Europe.[2] But France is a special case that deserves particular attention because the country has become the incarnation and leading voice of Old Europe and the so-called European model. It is the country that 'invented' the 35-hour week, where the retirement age was lowest, where political leaders have no qualms in sending 15-year-old children to demonstrate against increasing retirement age, where millionaire football players went on strike (the real national sport) during the South Africa World Cup with the entire world watching, where government tax revenues stand at 17 per cent of GDP or six points higher than the Eurozone average (almost double Germany's), and so on. France is certainly not the worst off in Europe, but here is what former French Prime Minister Raymond Barre had to say about his country: 'France . . . has simply got used to mediocrity.'

But I forgot one little detail: on the Singapore Airlines flight the airplane was the roomy Airbus A380, the huge double-decker marvel of aerospace technology that dwarfs a jumbo jet and takes up to 853 passengers in one go. It is 'made in Old Europe', and mainly assembled in Airbus's factory in Toulouse, in the south of France. On one hand, here is this frustrating inefficiency, this decaying system, this tolerance of mediocrity that has become the hallmark of Old Europe. On the other hand, Old Europe is still capable of some amazing achievements unmatched in the world. Is Europe the Europe of the A380 or the Europe of CDG? Can the two live together? What is their future? And what about the fabled quality of life of Old Europe?

Airports and the transport industry in general are part of the service sector. This sector represents about 70 per cent of the EU's economy. Wouldn't it make sense to unleash its full potential? But this sector is stuck in a time warp, saddled with protectionism and overregulation. There is no such thing as a European-wide service economy, as this sector remains largely fragmented along national lines. One of the companies I started in Europe was involved in the franchising business, and despite everything that is said about EU-wide regulations, when it came to contracts we were confronted with having to hire different lawyers in each country to ensure compliance with each country's laws and translate documents in a multitude of languages – in theory up to 27 times the cost and headaches of doing the same thing in a truly homogeneous market like the US. A reformed and liberalized service sector could do miracles for the European economy, enhance its global competitiveness, spur growth and the creation of enterprises and jobs across the continent. CDG could become more like Changi. In the 1990s the more business-friendly US boosted the service sector part of its economy, generating jobs and increasing productivity, but Europe stayed behind. You won't be welcome to talk about the service sector with former European Commission member Frits Bolkestein these days: in 2006 his proposed 'Bolkestein Directive', the objective of which was liberalization of the service sector throughout Europe, got very publicly downed by the French, whose commentators and politicians went on to revile him as 'Frankenstein'. Once more Old Europe could not stomach the idea of liberalizing and opening itself to competition, fearing it would somehow threaten social privileges. Once more, the lowest common denominator won and things stayed the way they were, with no chance for the service sector to take off in Europe. But the opportunity is not lost on everybody: if Europeans don't develop their own infrastructure to make their economies more efficient, China will help them do it – witness China's decision to invest 5 billion euros in the development of the Greek port of Piraeus in order to facilitate the entry of Chinese and Asian products in Europe.[3]

The People's Republic of Paradise

In the watershed year of 2005, Paul Krugman, the *New York Times* columnist who won the Nobel Prize for economics in 2008, wrote an article in which he reiterated the often heard argument that 'differences in the French and US economies are largely a matter of choice'.[4] The way he saw it (read Old Europe for France), the French are content with earning less money than the Americans because they chose instead to have a higher quality of life, better schools, longer holidays, workers spending more time with their families, better healthcare and so on. To cap it all, Krugman reported that 'working fewer hours makes Europeans happier, despite their loss of potential income'. In this he joined Mark Leonard who saw the value of Europe's model as coming from the quality of life Europeans enjoy.[5] That Old Europeans deliberately choose to work less hours, take longer holidays and retire earlier is undeniably true. In fact Europe holds the world record for longest vacations and shortest workweeks.[6]

But Krugman's people's paradise turns out to be an illusion. He may have glossed over OECD data showing Europeans generally 30 per cent poorer than Americans as the price to pay for this lifestyle.[7] He can be forgiven for not anticipating the 2010 survey by the French institute BVA that placed the French as the most unhappy people in the EU.[8] He omitted to mention the legions of unemployed, especially the young who cannot find a job and have little hope of ever finding one. He forgot to talk to the vast majority of Europeans who are seeing their quality of life eroded year by year, to the majority of young couples who cannot afford to buy a home and will probably never be able to. 'We can't make it': that's what he would have heard if he had talked to these people back in 2005, and in 2010 the situation is even worse. Things are getting tougher and tougher for everybody across Europe, particularly in its southern half, and people are terrified, especially the young. The double blow of the post-2008 recession and the debt/currency crisis hit the economies and everybody's pockets and prospects very hard and confronted people with the reality of their bleak future for the first time. These two crises cannot be blamed, however, for all the ills affecting the region. More sinister and structural forces have been at work for a long time in Europe. The European system suffers from an inability to create the wealth that would be necessary to sustain it. It generates more and more spending, less and less income, a real mismatch. The fabled quality of life of Europe may have been a reality for a while, but one that could not last because Europe was simply living beyond its means. Erosion of the quality of life is now palpable wherever you turn in Europe as people earn less and spend less. Their children will be even worse off. It will get worse before it gets even worse.

They used to say that the only two sure things in life are taxes and death. There are two more things you can count on this system to deliver without failure: unemployment and slow growth. Eurosclerosis leading to impoverishment. Several elements in this system are at work to ensure this outcome and reinforce each other. First, the high level of social benefits, especially pensions and welfare, gobbles more and more money, particularly as the population ages and life expectancy goes up. But at the same time the total population dwindles because couples are too busy trying to make ends meet instead of producing babies. So the number of people in the active workforce decreases, and you have less and less young people working to support more and more retiring old people for longer and longer, as we saw earlier. Unless you drastically cut down the level of support you give people (tantamount to political suicide), the only ways you can try to fill the gap (other than an increased birthrate or opening the doors to massive immigration) is with longer working hours, increasing retirement age so that people contribute longer into the pot, and increasing taxes.

Second, Old Europe in particular has been diabolically creative in finding every possible way to disincentivize business from flourishing, oblivious that the better business does, the more taxes the government can collect from it and the more people get jobs. Europe (as always, when we speak about the economy we are particularly singling out its southern half) killed the goose that laid the golden eggs through a combination of rigid and costly employment rules (which tell an employer he should think twice before hiring anyone), high and rigid corporate taxes and overregulation (which choke off business and act as a disincentive to investment). In Singapore and certain other places, if you are bringing good business to the country, tax authorities are ready to cut a deal with you to keep you there. This does not apply in Old Europe, where the authorities have little or no flexibility and don't care. The system stifles innovation and works against the creation of new wealth-generating enterprises by making life very hard for them. Ask any entrepreneur in Old Europe and they will shake their heads and tell you the system is unworkable: too many regulations, too many taxes from day one, too costly a labour force. Taxes, always more taxes to pay. There comes a point when people with drive and new ideas don't feel like creating the new companies that will spawn new jobs and growth. There comes a time when existing companies, tired of costs and complications at home, decide to delocalize or at the very least stop investing at home and thus stop creating jobs. So the equation does not compute, something has to give. In the absence of a growth engine the system needs to drastically cut social benefits and/or get more tax money from employees and companies. Whichever way you look at it the result is a decreasing quality of life, and this is happening in front of our eyes.

The French (again, read Old Europe) are scared of anything that may threaten their paradise, their *acquis-sociaux*, by which they mean the cradle to grave range of benefits the maintaining of which is more important to them than their children's future. Low self-confidence in the face of foreign competition from globalization and EU enlargement was already obvious in 2005. Remember the Polish plumber scare during the EU Constitution referendum campaign? French populist politicians at the time feared an invasion of Polish plumbers who would put their French counterparts out of work with their lower wage requirements and longer working hours (incidentally, none of these politicians said a word against the legions of jobs being exported to China at the time through delocalization, maybe because the Poles, next door, were easier to attack and less likely to react). Another convenient culprit was the European Central Bank, regularly accused of causing stagnation by keeping interest rates too high in the Eurozone. Every excuse has been good enough to avoid facing reality and enact badly needed structural reforms. Yet some elites have been aware of the writing on the wall and have been clamouring for reform for a long time. Former French high official Michel Camdessus wrote in his famous 2004 Rapport Camdessus that 'France is heading straight into a wall'. The model Krugman described turns out to be a utopian relic of the leftist political movements of the 1960s that simply became unsustainable in today's world.

In the 1970s, France's GDP was substantially larger than Britain's. But then something happened and recently British GDP has caught up with that of France. Not only did the British, whose system is more liberal and pro-business, catch up in terms of GDP, but they did it with unemployment at roughly half that of the French. Pre-crisis, quantitative yardsticks of growth and unemployment showed the British system was doing better. From a qualitative point of view, it was a matter of opinion: was the French system with its higher social protection and shorter working hours really more humane than the British system if people had less chances to make a living? In more general terms, per capita GDP is substantially lower in Europe than in the US, standards of living in Europe have been said to be about 30 per cent lower than in the US, and the gap is widening. In 2005 Bolkestein himself questioned a European model that produced unemployment in excess of 10 per cent. In the absence of high growth the model does not work, especially in the age of globalization when a country cannot hide its inefficiencies behind frontiers and is compelled to compete with every other country in the world.

The sustainability of this model is coming to an end. The tragedy is that Old Europe does not have a plan B. Compound this problem with that of the aging of the population and the result is gradual impoverishment; the only question is the degree of the declining slope. Yet Europeans don't want to let go of their ways and privileges, in the illusion they are part of the natural order of things and that the all-powerful government will somehow make things work at the end.

Welcome to the Roach Motel

Ten years after the event, many of the same countries that rushed in to join the Eurozone, the group of European countries sharing the common euro currency, wish they had never done so. Nostalgia for the old currencies set in but leaving the Eurozone was not an option because, like the fabled Roach Motel (a popular American trap for cockroaches), you can get in but you can't get out. The costs of leaving are just too high. What makes them want to leave today? Why is the cost of leaving so high? Has the euro effectively turned into an obstacle to growth?

Take the example of Spain. It seemed to be a miracle economy as a flood of cheap Eurozone loans and EU funds kept pouring in during the earlier part of the decade. But instead of investing these funds in value-added industries and increasing competitiveness to secure the future, Spaniards and their bankers took the easy road, fuelling a property construction bubble rather like Ireland (bankers notoriously lack imagination, except where stress tests are concerned). Spain built, built and built as if there was no end to it. Property prices went up fivefold in a decade. The basis of the economic growth model was a property bubble, with the construction sector amounting to 18 per cent of the country's GDP (double what it was in France or the UK) and employing 13 per cent of the workforce, and tourism and industry contributed little to growth.[9] The land of Cervantes and Real Madrid had turned into a big construction site. To compound this, as living standards were improving and money was coming in easily, Spanish industry, already burdened by a particularly rigid labour market, let its wages rise and increasingly priced itself out of the market. Compared with that of Germany, Spain's competitiveness is said to have dropped by 33 per cent during this period.[10] Credit must be given where it belongs: Spain's economy had its bright spots, with public debt as a share of GDP one of the lowest in Europe at 43.1 per cent, even lower than Germany's, although the deficit came to equal the UK's 11 per cent. The other side of the coin is that private debt (in particular, mortgages) rose to a startling 210 per cent of GDP, well above the 130 per cent of France, Italy or Germany. When the property bubble imploded in 2009, the growth engine stopped dead in its tracks. The collapse of the property market is said to have left over one million unoccupied homes and little else to show for all the money Spain had borrowed. The country was hit by a severe recession and very high unemployment. Once more, it was found that the emperor had no clothes. Spanish industry was flat on its back and hardly competitive. Spain could theoretically have tried to get out of the hole it had dug for itself by stimulating export-led growth, if it had still had its old currency, the peseta, and let it fall, undergoing a competitive devaluation. This would have made its products cheaper on international markets, reviving exports and industry. But Spain's new currency, the euro, was no longer in the control of Spain's central bank, but of a European Central Bundesbank intent on the primary aim of price stability. This remedy was also used in Italy, where the lira was frequently devalued to boost growth. Growth stimulation based on currency devaluation is no longer an option for a country in the Eurozone. The other option is pain. Spain had no choice but to take harsh medicine and dramatically cut its deficit in the short term. This measure was, however, not going to resolve the structural issues of growth and competitiveness. If you are a young Spaniard today, your chances of finding a job are rather poor. Your standard of living is likely to be lower than that of your parents. It is no surprise that many Spaniards are nostalgic for the peseta or are taking to the streets.

What about leaving the Eurozone? The consequences would be unfathomable not only for Spain but for the rest of Europe too. People would rush to take their euros out of Spanish banks and deposit them in non-Spanish banks. They would also rush to sell Spanish assets before they become depreciated into pesetas 2.0. Debt owed by Spaniards would still need to be repaid in high-value euros while their income would now be in low-value peseta 2.0 (according to some experts weak currencies leaving the euro could see their value slashed by half compared with the euro, so that would be like doubling your debt). A run on Spanish banks, leading to a collapse of the Spanish banking system, economic chaos and social instability would be the likely result. A run on Spanish banks could trigger a run on the banks of other peripheral countries. The impact would be felt far beyond the frontiers of Spain and even Europe. The country would see the doors of international capital markets shut for a long time. It would become a pariah in Europe because remaining Eurozone members would be left with a euro that may then, by default, become overvalued and hurt their exports.

But what if the one to leave the euro was Germany? What if the German economy slows down and Germans, fed up with having to pay for increasingly painful bailouts of weak Eurozone countries, decide to go back to their DM? The reverse of what we saw before would happen. Some experts predict that in such a far-fetched scenario the new-DM 2.0 would shoot up by 30 per cent against the euro. The euro may be undervalued by 30 per cent in relation to the German economy, which is why we said earlier that the weak euro has helped Germany's export-led growth: this would make German debt cheaper to service. Yet German exports, including the 40 per cent of its exports which ends up in the Eurozone, would take a very substantial hit as they would be priced in a higher-value currency. UBS was reported to have calculated that if Germany or Greece were to leave the Eurozone, the damage would be equivalent to respectively 20–25 per cent and 50 per cent of GDP just in the first year.[11] But the biggest issue by far, should Germany abandon the euro, would be the political fallout: Project Europe would come to a halt, and the core assumption behind it, that old rivalries between European nations would be buried forever, would be blown to pieces.

For countries with relatively weak economies such as Greece, Portugal, Ireland, Spain and even Italy, the euro has turned into a prison from which they can't escape, a Roach Motel, a Guantanamo that condemns them to perpetual pain and low growth. They can't devalue their currencies anymore, so they need to devalue their standards of living. They are stuck with a currency that is more a reflection of the economies of more successful and competitive Eurozone countries than their own weaker economies or perhaps represents a mean. To these weaklings the first decade of the new millennium was effectively a 'lost decade' as, in contrast to Germany, they failed to undertake the structural reforms that would have enabled them to streamline their economies, increase competitiveness and move up the value-added ladder when there was still time (and money) to do so. The opportunity has been lost, and unless they undertake at once a politically infeasible radical and extremely painful 180-degree structural turnaround, and reinvent themselves overnight, they don't stand a chance of recovery. For such countries, as far as sustained growth or stopping the slide towards lower and lower standards of living are concerned, it is the end of the road.

The euro has been hindering, not helping, the weaker countries of the Eurozone and lacked mechanisms to enhance competitiveness. One of the causes of last century's Great Depression was the trade wars unleashed by panicking nations. Fears of similar open trade wars during the recent crisis failed to materialize; yet country after country was taking measures to lower its currency to gain a trade advantage. America's 'quantitative easing' measures saw over

600 billion dollars injected into the US economy in 2010 to stimulate it but also ended up lowering the value of the dollar by about 10 per cent. China was forced to buy these dollars to avoid a further deterioration in the value of the American currency which would have put upward pressure on the renminbi and damaged Chinese exports. America was printing, China was buying. Emerging economies that could not follow China's example saw their currencies shoot up and too much money flow in, creating bubbles. Britain did the American thing and printed 200 billion sterling, and sterling expectedly lost 6.4 per cent against the euro at the time. This is a kind of zero-sum game, because when a currency goes down, another goes up and conventional wisdom says that the lower your currency goes, the easier it is for you to export and revive growth. What about the Eurozone in this particular currency war? The ECB's mandate is limited to fighting inflation; it had no power to intervene. So the euro was left to the vagaries of the markets. Its value remained relatively high just when a lower value could have helped exports.

While some were talking about leaving the Eurozone, someone was busy getting in. One country decided to enter the Roach Motel of its own free will, the 17th to do so, on 1 January 2011. This country's finances would put almost every other in the Eurozone to shame: a public deficit of only 1.7 per cent of GDP, a national debt of under 7 per cent of GDP and a growth rate of 8.5 per cent.[12] What a pity that Estonia represents only 2 per cent of Europe's GDP.

Forwards–backwards versus right–left

I met the gentleman in the vast and ornate lobby of a hotel, a short, stocky, jovial man in his fifties. A friend had arranged the introduction, saying this man's story was one I should hear. Over a cup of tea he proceeded to tell me how he had been dismissed from the army years ago, with a miserable severance pay, in line with a new drive to cut budgets. Not one to lose faith, he used this money and borrowed some more from the usual network of friends and family and, given that there was much construction going around and harsh winters, started a small business to make home-heaters. Now his company was grossing the equivalent of 100 million dollars in revenues. What gave this little man most pride is that his son had started a company to manufacture buses and was now going to list it on the stock exchange. This meeting didn't take place in Berlin, Bordeaux or Bilbao. It took place in Beijing in the mid-1990s. The man, a mid-ranking officer, had been dismissed years earlier by the PLA (the People's Liberation Army) with the equivalent in renminbi of less than 10,000 euros. In Asia, these days, the narrative is all about growth, about creating wealth. Whether you talk to young people, old people, men, women, government officials, company employees or students, rich or poor, that's what the talk is all about. In Europe, the narrative is all about fighting over whatever wealth there is still left. In Asia people talk about forwards or backwards: either you work hard and move forwards or you fall back. In Europe they talk about left or right, political discourse. It's all about directions – forwards–backwards in Asia, left–right in Europe. True, Asia is, to a degree, an enthusiastic newcomer of sorts in the game and the richer it gets the closer it may find itself moving to European ways. But it has a long way to go, and this convergence, if it ever comes true, should come as no consolation to Europeans.

Economic growth has, by and large, been absent from the European narrative, except after the crisis hit, when many governments suddenly 'discovered', too late, that without growth there was no way out. Growth, spectacular in the 1950s and 1960s, started to abate in the '70s and has since then mostly been eradicated from European culture and narrative. The instinctive reflex of European governments reacting from the crisis was to slash expenditures and raise taxes, not to stimulate growth. Former French Prime Minister Edouard Balladur recognized that the French first needed to 'get convinced that growth is the key issue, as it is basically absent from the public debate' and went on to state that 'the future is in opening ourselves to the world, not in closing and protectionism' and that 'increasing competitiveness is the only way to fight against unemployment, and this can be achieved by lighter social charges'.[13] The problem when growth disappears as a national priority is that you kill the goose that lays the golden eggs. Growth means the creation of new wealth and jobs, an increase in, or at least a chance of, maintaining standards of living and more taxes collected to fund government programmes and obligations. When growth slows down, less taxes are collected leading to a deterioration of the public goods and welfare delivered by the state and less money to repay national debt. It also impacts on budget deficits. If governments base their models on 3 per cent growth but the economy stagnates, their tax revenues take a hit and deficits shoot up, unless they increase taxes and/or cut down on public goods. Growth does not happen by itself; it needs to be promoted, nurtured, it needs smart choices, sacrifices, investments, hard work and dedication. Growth enlarges the pie shared by everybody. If you think growth is not really important and take your eye off that ball for as long as the Europeans have, you are in for a rough ride, because it is, after all, the most important factor.

Many European countries faced globalization mesmerized by anxiety and inaction. The French, for one, were conscious of not being able to adapt and be competitive in the new globalized world, and their biggest fear was to lose their privileges. Quintessentially Old European politician Dominique de Villepin's remark, when he became prime minister of France in 2005, speaks volumes: 'Globalization cannot be our destiny', the sort of philosophy espoused by Muslim civilizations when they decided to stay away from the modernization process Europe was going through a couple of centuries ago, only to find later on that they had totally missed out. The Italians just watched globalization pass them by, with less truculence, but numb and powerless. Countries like these became victims of globalization instead of taking advantage of it as an engine of growth, as Germany did, at least its *Mittelstand*. Not only did these countries export jobs, but they didn't hesitate to also export whole industries and the expertise with them. Countries such as China then used these not only to conquer their markets, but also sell back finished products to them. Europe took on the business of exporting industries, jobs and growth and became quite successful at it. Had they been able to insulate themselves from globalization, hide behind their frontiers, they might have had a chance of survival, but this was not an option; they were now suddenly competing with people in Eastern Europe and those on the other side of the world who had none of their burdens of social costs and high taxes, and were hungry. The European model is based on a social contract that is exactly the opposite of that in today's China. In Europe, a government's legitimacy rests on its ability to consistently deliver welfare, retirement and other benefits. In China, the Communist Party's legitimacy rests on its ability to consistently deliver growth. Italian Finance Minister Giulio Tremonti complained that Europe had been busying itself too much on regulating its internal market and competition and too little on competition from abroad, a sure way to keep agriculture and lose manufacturing.[14] He saw 1994 as a watershed year, the one when the World Trade Organization launched global free trade and globalization rushed from abroad into a Europe caught unprepared. Because of its reliance on labour-intensive, low value-added industries, Italy was the first to feel the impact of Chinese competition. It has not recovered since then.

Let my people go

Europe prides itself on being the world's most humane and generous society, the one that cares the most about the well-being of its people, especially its working classes. If this holds true, why is Europe's record in fighting unemployment so dismal? At the end of 2010, the unemployment rate in Spain topped 20 per cent in France it was almost 12 per cent. In Italy one in four young Italians was out of a job. There had just been a big crisis, but then why should the unemployment rate in Europe, historically hovering around 10 per cent, be double that of a US decried by many in Europe as a sort of purgatory for workers? Isn't putting as many people to work as possible and giving them the opportunity to earn a living one of the key goals of any government or system? Old Europe's employment regulations are widely known to be rigid and its unemployment chronically high. Evidence shows that more liberal employment regulations actually act as a catalyst to *increase* employment. Why does Old Europe cling to its sclerotic system? Albert Einstein famously defined madness as keeping doing the same thing while expecting different results.

Many knew that Old Europe needed a thorough and painful reform of its exceptionally rigid labour market, and needed it yesterday. Under Sarkozy, France's centre right government had been desperately trying to get rid of the 35-hour legal workweek, an aberration unique in the world. This regulation was finally watered down, but this was far from enough. The problem is not so much with those who don't have jobs. It is with those who actually *have* jobs. The jobless are held hostage by those who enjoy the privilege of a full benefits job, a situation that has been generally accepted. The problem starts with employment contracts that guarantee life-long tenure and make it extremely complicated, lengthy and costly for an employer to sack an employee unless he is caught dousing the factory with petrol, setting fire to it and dancing around. Every employee tries to lock into these full benefits contracts and the system helps them, as it limits the extent to which contracts of a more temporary nature can be renewed before they become full benefits ones. This is not very different from China's old 'iron rice bowl' policy, except that China wisely abolished it. When Sarkozy tried to introduce flexibility the entire leftist establishment took up arms, fearing a weakening of labour protection in general, and his proposals were watered down to the point of being meaningless. The left preferred to protect the existing privileges of those who already *have* jobs, rather than risk seeing some flexibility introduced in the system in order to give jobs to those who *do not have* them. As pointed out earlier, there thus exists a 'privileged working class', made up of people enjoying the advantages and armour-plated protection of full benefits contracts and not caring about others who can't find jobs. Any political leader attempting to tinker with the system and introduce some flexibility is pilloried because workers, employees, unions and the entire left (and some in the right) are ready to mobilize, take to the streets and fight to their last breath to protect these privileges.

In the People's Republic of Paradise, if you are an employer, and in particular if you have the misfortune to be an entrepreneur, the system is against you and your employees can turn into your worst nightmare. Whether they are good or bad performers, whether times are good or bad, whether you make a profit or a loss, you have to keep them. In some places you need to pay in excess of 40 per cent in social contributions on top of salaries; and if you are late with these payments you may be imprisoned. You need to contend with unions, strikes, holidays and sick pay, and more sick pay and more paid holidays and strikes. Above all, you have to contend with the employee's sacred right to do as little as possible. As an employer you have the duty of taking care of them, ensuring they get whatever they are entitled to, even if it means you need to run yourself and your enterprise into the ground. In times of crisis, when faced with a revenue drop, you can't readily reduce your payroll to cut costs. You are fighting an uphill battle against an entire system stacked against you, and spend your energies on issues related to personnel, bureaucracy, regulations and taxes. You are constantly paying taxes, more and more taxes, whether you make money or not. Business also has to contend with the notion, held by too many in the government and in the left, that business is a suspiciously fat chicken to be plucked, that it should be thankful for its being tolerated, that it grows at the expense of everybody else, and deserves little better than scorn. So what are you to do if you want your business to stay alive and compete in a market that is becoming more and more globalized and tougher and tougher? First, you reduce hiring to a minimum; you don't hire anyone unless you absolutely have to. Second, if you are an Italian employer you will probably employ people on the black market, undeclared. In general you are likely to outsource or move your production to China, Romania, Morocco or other places where labour is cheaper and regulations and taxes less burdensome. Old Europe has devised a system that is a perfect recipe to disincentivize the creation of new enterprises, employers, minimize employment, and export jobs and businesses. The bright and dynamic are today packing their bags and leaving Europe. The result is chronic anaemic growth.

The Nobel economics laureate Paul Samuelson warned that companies are not charitable enterprises and that they hire workers to make profits. That some European companies manage to thrive in the face of globalization challenges and despite such a system is remarkable in itself. There has nevertheless been a visible hollowing out of Europe's industrial base following the export of entire industries and jobs abroad. An obvious example is that of the British car industry. After the Rover deal fell through with China's Shanghai Automotive Industries Corp in 2005 Rover was heading for dire straits, and Britain no longer had much of a domestic car industry. It's mostly gone, along with the jobs. China has been exporting goods, we have been exporting jobs and industries. I've witnessed, firsthand, the fate of dozens of European SMEs that ended up being shut down or sold to (or joint ventured with) Asian or other interests, who often dismantled the enterprise, took it back home along with the expertise and established thriving businesses abroad with which they conquered some of the original company's markets. In all these cases the SME owners would say the same thing: they were fed up, their enterprises were not viable anymore in Europe because of the 'system', and their headaches and sacrifices were not worth anything.

The deindustrialization of Europe is a fact, especially in the south, but not only there. Textiles, shipbuilding, car production, chemicals, all have been hit. In *How the West was Lost* Dambisa Moyo reminds us that 'The West (Britain and America, in particular) has spent the better part of the last three decades dismantling its traditional industrial bases . . . and abandoning its once undisputed edge in training, science and technology, in favour of the more sanitized service industry. The net result, unsurprisingly, is the decline of the West's manufacturing capacity.'[15] More than a million manufacturing jobs were lost in Britain in the first years of Margaret Thatcher's rule; it is not only the left who are to blame. With the disappearance of so much productive capacity, will Europe ever come back to its former production levels? Has the recent crisis accelerated the deindustrialization and delocalization process that was already well under way? In France, for example, 2010 production levels dropped to those of 1997; 13 years of growth evaporated. The hollowing of its industrial base means Europe loses its manufacturing edge and R&D base. Compared with the US and Asia, Europe is investing less and less in R&D, which is not encouraging news for future growth. In 2008 Asian companies overtook the US for the first time in terms of R&D, with 387 billion dollars invested against 384 billion, leaving Europe far behind with only 280 billion dollars.[16] In global terms, Asia may soon eclipse the US as the world's innovation engine, at least in quantitative terms such as money invested and number of graduates. Europe, which invented the internet (but let the Americans commercialize it), will be left further and further behind. The students faring the best in international contests of reading, maths or science these days are those from Shanghai, Singapore or Korea. Europe's lack of enthusiasm for innovation can only mean that it will inevitably lose ground in future competitions and that the good jobs will be increasingly found outside Europe. And when it comes to R&D and the fate of researchers, the outlook is just as bleak: Europe's education system produces very good researchers (producing them comes at a substantial cost to their home societies). Yet many of the brightest, faced with the stifling system at home and poor incentives, emigrate to places such as America, where talent commands higher recognition and price. 'The acceleration of French scientific emigration to the US is recent and worrisome' warned France's Institut Montaigne in 2010.[17] The brain drain is real: the majority of those who go to the US to get a PhD stay there. The think-tank pointed out that France's best biologists and economists are found today in America, a more competitive and exciting environment with better facilities.

If you travel throughout the Far East today, you'll meet some of Europe's brightest, most promising and dynamic young men and women, working very hard and building themselves a future. In Italy, it used to be poor people who emigrated to find jobs. Now it is the well educated. The situation is radically different today: the proportion of highly educated Italians leaving the country has increased about four times in the last decade (they numbered 300,000 in total in 2005 according to OECD statistics) – not surprising since Italy has the lowest investment in R&D of the EU's original members. Italy probably has the worst of both worlds, with more and more educated people leaving the country and fewer and fewer educated people coming in: a net brain-drain not yet felt by Germany, France or the UK. These emigrants will tell you the same story: that they emigrated because there were no interesting opportunities back home, that the system is mired in the past and inefficient, and that they prefer to take their chances in Shanghai, Menlo Park or New York, where there are the opportunities. Europe is a net exporter of talent.

The factory of the factory of the world

Much has been said and written about the miraculous rise of China as the world's newest economic superpower, and how it is changing the world we live in. Less has been said about the no less miraculous recent success of Germany's 2.5 trillion euro economy. Having digested the huge cost of a reunification process with East Germany started two decades ago, by the end of 2010 Germany was a case apart, the one country in Old Europe to have embraced globalization and become the world's foremost export machine. Because Germany posted a spectacular 3.6 per cent growth rate in 2010, its highest since the 1990 reunification, well above its European peers and America's 2.9 per cent, it is, however, too often forgotten that the German economy *shrank* by a sizeable 4.7 per cent in 2009, its sharpest contraction since reunification and twice as bad as France's decline. Was this most spectacular *aufschwung* (upswing) as good as it seemed? Is Germany's success a reality with staying power or is it going to fade away soon? It is important to have an idea of where Germany is going because not only is it the continent's largest economy and the one whose growth helps pull the others, but it is also the one that foots most of the bill for the Eurozone's rescue packages. If Germany coughs, Europe catches pneumonia. Several factors have combined to bring this about for Germans and turn their economy into the only European one capable of competing with China or America, one that employs more than 40.5 million people (the highest level in 20 years) while maintaining its deficit at a reasonable 3.5 per cent of GDP and national debt at a manageable 83 per cent of GDP:

- During the decade that started in 2000, while many European countries were gorging themselves on cheap money brought about by the euro and creating property bubbles or piling up debt to finance their profligate lifestyles, Germany soberly undertook some structural reforms, fine-tuned its economy, keeping wages under control, deregulating labour markets, and reinvented itself as a manufacturing powerhouse.
- Reforms launched by the former chancellor Gerhard Schröder at the beginning of the decade resulted in labour costs in Germany staying flat for most of the decade.[18] If you adjust them for inflation, wages have actually *declined* by an estimated aggregate of 4.5 per cent in the past decade, according to the International Labour Organization, at a time when real wages were escalating beyond bounds in many European countries. At the same time, flexible arrangements were introduced to the effect that German workers could contribute additional hours when there was demand and take more time off when there was not, modulating

their contributions according to the actual needs of employers, with the government contributing when necessary to make the system work. In Germany, former co-leader of Old Europe with France, workers agreed to make sacrifices in order to keep their jobs and make companies competitive. Contrary to what was happening in many European countries, especially in the south, the German government made sure that working was made more attractive than living on government hand-outs. This new flexibility meant people held on to their jobs and companies held on to people, especially skilled ones, a gamble that paid off on the economic side with the spectacular results and on the social side with unemployment falling to an 18-year low of 7 per cent.

- While many European countries faced globalization as a bogey and became its victims, Germany fully embraced it. To take advantage of globalization, German companies didn't need to go very far: they could access plenty of low-cost skilled labour in former Eastern European countries a car drive away and used this opportunity to optimize their supply chain. The proportion of outsourced components going into the products Germany so successfully exported overseas went up. As a result of increasing the proportion of lower-cost components in their products, German companies, while maintaining strict control on end-product quality, managed to effect substantial cost-savings, thus remaining price-competitive and boosting profits.

- Germany's *Mittelstand*, its universe of countryside-based family-owned SMEs (one million more such enterprises than in France) has been the export engine driving the economic rebound. Michael Porter would find it a perfect case study for competitive analysis. The *Mittelstand* has been particularly good at reinventing itself, shedding its low value-added enterprises, focusing instead on niches of high-end durable goods with strong engineering content and requiring plenty of continuous innovation. German universities work hand in hand with researchers in these enterprises. These SMEs used their leadership in the domestic market to expand abroad and entrench themselves without fuss in leading positions in international B2B markets for items such as machine tools, printing presses, industrial cleaning systems, mechanical parts and the like. They focused on premium niches generally discarded by large multinationals, where reputation, reliability and servicing (bringing ongoing revenues) were key. About 80 per cent of the world's leading midsize enterprises are German.

- Germany's recent growth has been propelled by exports. Germany has been equipping China's factories. If China has become the factory of the world, Germany has become the factory of the factory of the world: it rode a wave of high demand for the capital goods and machines it was good at making, from developing economies, especially China. Worldwide exports from Germany shot up by more than 20 per cent in 2010. Germany's success shadowed China's as IMF data pointed to German exports to China having grown almost sixfold in the past decade. As Germany's and the Netherlands' shares of European exports went up, France's and Italy's went down: reform and embracing change pays. Germany exported higher-value-added goods, so it saw China as a market opportunity, whereas southern economies, with lower value-added content in the goods they produce, could only see China as a competitor.

- The misadventures of the euro may cost Germany's government dearly in the form of rescue packages to weaker countries, but had a beneficial effect on German export industries. Thanks to Greece and others, the euro is undervalued with respect to a performing German economy.

- Finally, Germans have been good at keeping their financial house in order, both in the public and the private sectors, with a not too unreasonable government debt at under 80 per cent of GDP and a small budget deficit in 2010, all the while having avoided an asset bubble. As a result Germany continues to borrow at reasonable rates and its levels of debt and deficit are sustainable.

At the end of 2010 polls indicated business confidence and general content among the German population at levels not seen for a very long time, as if the crisis hitting the rest of Europe had no impact in Germany. But every silver lining has a cloud. What could go wrong for Germany?

- First, a large part of Germany's recent success can be attributed to price competitiveness resulting from wages restraint on the part of a labour force scared that domestic companies would move production and jobs abroad. The remarkable discipline and sacrifice of German workers has a lot to do with keeping German companies competitive abroad, but, with discontent simmering among a working class that is now asking for its share of the spoils, this competitive advantage is bound to come to an end at some time soon. Labour costs are bound to go up in the short term.

- The growth of Germany's economy depends on sustained demand for exports, particularly from emerging economies. The miracle of Germany is the miracle of China and other developing markets such as Russia. The German car industry, for example, recovered because of demand from China. How long this export demand will persist depends on how long there will be strong demand in the developing world for German cars and machines. Moreover, 40 per cent of Germany's exports are to Eurozone countries, which happen to be in bad shape and subject to austerity measures that are likely to depress overall demand, including for German goods. At the same time domestic demand, which recently showed signs of picking up, has remained relatively low (56 per cent of GDP compared with 70 per cent in America), attesting to an unbalanced economy overreliant on exports. If growth slows in the developing world, as seems likely, Germany will be hit, all the harder because it won't have the possibility of relying on strong domestic demand or on the service sector to pick up the slack.

- Productivity, in the medium to long term is a challenge. As a result of relatively low investment at home, Germany's productivity growth has recently hovered around 0.4 per cent compared with 1.8 per cent in the US. Germany's productivity growth is the second lowest in Europe, just ahead of Italy.

- Germany's industrial sector has done well lately but its service sector remains inefficient and underdeveloped, saddled with low productivity. The *Mittelstand* may now be a good fighting machine but it is only one portion of the German economy. The rest is not as competitive, hindered by overregulation and a lack of innovation and investment, just like the rest of Old Europe. The government does not make things easier by clinging to a tax system that is one of the most arcane and complex in the world, to the extent that it damages competitiveness. You'll be surprised to learn that a World Bank survey placed Germany a disappointing 102nd out of 181 countries in which to start a new business.[19]

- Constant innovation has propelled the *Mittelstand* to where it is today, but when it comes to the industries of the future such as biotech, nanotechnologies or just software, Germany has been left way behind. What will the future source of growth be?

- The weakness of the euro has played in Germany's favour, assisting its export machine. Yet if the current crisis of the euro is over and markets calm down, or if weaker countries leave the euro, the currency could come back to levels that reflect more the German economy and less those of weaker countries in Europe, rendering the price of German products less competitive outside the Eurozone. And here is the most critical factor: many of Germany's banks are living on borrowed time. The money that fuelled asset bubbles or profligacy in countries such as Spain, Greece, Ireland or Portugal had to have a source, and German banks at the forefront. A default in any of these countries could mean gigantic write-offs in the German banking system that could provoke a very serious crisis in Germany and spread elsewhere.

Germany did far better than most of Europe in 2010, something that is not entirely new, since average growth rates in the couple of years leading to 2008 were 2.2 per cent against 1.6 in France, and the industrial sector, Germany's winning card, accounts for 26 per cent of GDP against 14 per cent in France, with exports representing 53 per cent of GDP against 27 per cent in France. Germany being an open, export-oriented economy, the collapse of global trade in 2009 hit it badly. But it had made the right choices and reinvented itself as a competitive industrial powerhouse: this paid off. The rebound was shared by Finland, Austria and the Netherlands but not by France or Italy, which, by virtue of being less open than Germany, were not hit as hard by the recession when global trade collapsed, but, having failed to readjust their competitiveness with structural changes, were not in a position to take advantage of export recovery abroad. Countries such as Germany, Austria and the Netherlands have been doing well despite the fact that they are *not* low-wage countries and have strong labour laws: these countries managed to benefit both ways because they invested in innovation and moved up the value-added ladder.

Yet the Germans themselves know that the current bonanza is unlikely to last forever. They remember that not so long ago, in 2005, Germany was considered Europe's sick man. Germany's economy was one of the weakest in Europe. Despite buoyant polls, when you talk to Germans and scratch the surface, they feel quite insecure about the future. Other European countries hoping to see Germany's success translate into a bout of domestic consumer spending that could drive their own exports have generally been left disappointed, although signs indicate that as unemployment is falling consumer demand and investments have been picking up. Yet, aside from considerations related to the future of demand for German goods in China and abroad, a continuation of Germany's success story in the medium to long term is by no means a given. The problems Germany's neighbours are going through could start affecting Germany not only because the government is forced to spend excessively to help some of them, but also because, as growth abates in these countries, they'll buy less goods made in Germany. The country's industry, aside from its *Mittelstand*, is in dire need of structural reforms like other European countries. Moreover, demographic pressures are going to start being felt soon. Should the German economy slow down, it will have a negative effect throughout Europe, and Germans will become increasingly reluctant to foot the bill for rescue packages of weak Eurozone economies. The words of Pier Carlo Padoan, Chief Economist of the OECD, are hardly reassuring: 'Germany should in principle grow less quickly in the long term than the United States . . . Europe has structural weaknesses that have to be corrected to increase the country's growth potential.'[20]

It is increasingly unlikely that Germany can be counted on to assume its traditional role as the locomotive of Europe. During the past decade German business has slowly but surely been shifting its sights away from Europe and towards developing economies. European markets may still represent a large 40 per cent share of Germany's exports, but they are becoming less and less important by the day in relative terms. German business and direct investments have been redirected to such countries as China, Russia, Eastern Europe and Brazil. This decoupling from Western Europe is likely to result in Germany feeling more and more independent and assertive, and less and less inclined to compromise with its Western European peers on any given subject, from strategic issues (Libya is a case in point) to Eurozone bailouts.

You can have it both ways

Here is the only good news in this book: the European model can work after all. 'The Nordic nations have shown how to successfully combine balanced budgets with economic fitness as well as smart, and fair, social policies.'[21] The fate of today's Germany, Austria and the Netherlands, and particularly of Nordic countries, shows that the delivery of high levels of public goods, relatively high wages and social protection is not inherently incompatible with a sound and sustainable economy. Having gone through hard times in the 1990s some of these countries managed to reinvent themselves, not unlike Germany, adopting austerity measures and fiscal discipline while keeping investments necessary for long-term global competitiveness and growth rolling. The exceptional sense of social responsibility and discipline of their populations made it possible to streamline their budgets and adopt intelligent social policies while maintaining growth as the driving factor. Their emphasis on free trade and open markets, investments in technology and competitiveness paid off. They reformed welfare so that people had more incentive to work than to stay home and live on unemployment benefits. They made day-care cheap so that more women could be free to join the workforce. In these countries the European dream is alive.

Consider Norway: its oil makes it rich. But Saudi Arabia has much much more oil and is far from successful. Norway's best guarded secret is that it put its female half of the population to work; 75 per cent of Norwegian women work compared with a 65 per cent EU average.[22] They pay taxes just as working men do; so the government collects more taxes and the country can more readily afford generous benefits. Scandinavian countries understood that equality between men and women can become a competitive advantage for a country. But who brings up the children? These countries have developed programmes that enable both parents to take long maternity leave, and children are also well taken care of by the system, which means that couples are encouraged to have children. Female participation in these economies has been increased, with the result that generous welfare programmes can be safely funded and with the added benefit of higher birthrates. The last ingredient in Nordic success is that, despite their high taxes, these are economies that focus on innovation and value-added industries. Entrepreneurship is very much alive in the north.

The good news is that the European model with a Nordic twist works. The bad news is that the rest of Europe has not cared to open its eyes to what has been going on in the north and to emulate the Nordic model. In general, countries which have adopted models based on high social costs and taxes and little discipline, while neglecting growth, find themselves in the position of companies with heavy overheads and dwindling markets and revenues. For systems such as these that operate on the razor edge of the cliff, sooner or later some event will trigger a catastrophe, with disastrous results for them. Most countries of Old Europe refused to face the music, failing to accept that in the absence of a growth engine social generosity would only be affordable for a short time, would doom future generations, and deliver stagnation and unemployment. Eastern Europeans generally fared better because they weren't yet fully Europeanized. Poland, helped by strong demand from Germany and having avoided Eurocurrency-induced hangovers (it has its own currency, the Zloty, which went down during the crisis, helping exports), sailed through the crisis like a breeze.

As pointed out earlier, one of the ingredients of the *Mittelstand's* recent success has been its ability to use low-cost skilled labour in neighbouring countries, especially in the East, as subcontractors for an increasing part of the components of its finished products. Once they had freed themselves from the USSR, these countries, having always looked up to the West, became even more free-enterprise oriented than the existing members of the EU they joined in 2004. They were hungry, aware that they had everything to gain by *not* adopting the system of the club they had just joined. So they went to work, kept labour costs low and regulations light, and focused on growth. The Lisbon Agenda, the competitive blueprint which Old Europe had first trumpeted then cast aside, was perfect medicine for the newcomers. Eastern Europeans were ideal subcontractors for a Germany that could focus its attention on higher value-added tasks, market expansion and innovation. Germany saw this opportunity and made the most of it. The question that arises is how long will these countries resist the temptations and pressures from their Western neighbours? How long will they resist the perverse pressure brought to bear by Old Europe towards fiscal and labour 'harmonization' – Old Europe, fearful of New Europe's higher competitiveness due to lower taxes and lower labour costs, wants to see these increased to 'even-up' the playing field, thus imposing on New Europe the same inefficiencies that plague its own economies? How long will the newcomers' societies resist the siren's song of the utopian European model with its high social benefits? How long will it be before Old Europe, intolerant of the dynamism of the newcomers, imposes its decaying system onto them? Whenever the word 'harmonization' is spoken by Old Europe politicians or regulators, it means they are trying to infect some country with the same virus that is bringing them down, that they are using the benchmark of the lowest common denominator to bring everybody to the same low level.

How not to do it

France could have been another Germany but missed the boat. Except for a few industries such as nuclear energy and aerospace, and despite its world class multinationals, goods made in France are not as competitive as Germany's, a reality reflected by French exports having fallen from being a little over half the size of Germany's at the beginning of the decade to 40 per cent in 2010.[23] In conquering foreign markets, France has been losing ground to its neighbour. The main reason is that the French could not let go of the Civilization of Entitlements. At the time German workers were tightening their belts and flexible labour systems were introduced, French workers increased their wages and cut down on working hours: the additional social costs a French company paid to its employees on top of salary increased to over 50 per cent of salary compared with 28 per cent in Germany. This was almost double Germany's costs, and almost four times those in the UK or Switzerland. The French priced themselves out of the market. In addition, Germany made over three times more use of subcontracting in Eastern Europe than France, which lost this opportunity too. French industry has been left behind and is unlikely to catch up soon. In 2009, 232,000 French people lost their jobs, about two-thirds of them in industry.[24] You would think French unions and other '*partenaires sociaux*' would read the writing on the wall. But, for example, French unions could not keep themselves from giving budget airline Ryanair such a hard time with their requests that it closed its base in Marseilles in 2010,[25] with another 200 jobs lost.

Take the case of Britain. Not only did Britain deindustrialize in the 1970s and 1980s, due in great part to an overly rigid labour market and powerful trade unions, but the government kept pouring money into industries that had no future instead of into new, high value-added ones. The problem of deindustrialization was in many areas of the country compounded by the barging in of the public sector.[26] Failing industries moved out, not necessarily a bad thing in itself, but were replaced not by new and promising industries and wealth generators, but by the government sector. And not only did the government sector move in, but it also moved in with wages and benefits substantially *above* what the private sector was offering. Why would anyone go to work for a private sector enterprise if they were going to make more money and get more retirement and other benefits holding a job in a government office? The end result of this madness is that any chance that business could flourish again in those areas (especially the north-west and north-east of the country) was reduced to nothing because private companies could not remain competitive if they paid the high wages the government was paying. The country not only lost industries, but remained saddled with a bloated and very costly public sector. Peripheral countries, instead of taking advantage of their entry into the Eurozone to become more competitive, took the exact opposite route, abusing easy cash to price themselves out of the market by pushing up the costs of manpower. Compared with the cost of labour in Germany as a benchmark, between 1999 and 2007 labour costs went up 31 per cent in Ireland, 27 per cent in Spain and Greece and 24 per cent in Portugal. These countries suddenly thought they were rich because they were using the same currency as the Germans. In terms of business and growth, many European countries first shot themselves in the foot then calmly reloaded and shot themselves in the other foot.

America also knows how to make mistakes over the economy, particularly in the outer galaxy of Wall Street. But it also knows how to get itself out of economic predicaments by focusing on what it is good at, growth. The initial response of the US government to the recent crisis was to provide massive stimulus to growth, such as the 858 billion dollar package of incentives and tax cuts passed by the US Congress in late December 2010, which led some economists to predict 4 per cent growth in 2011 (unrealistic in the light of subsequent events). Just as America's response to the crisis reflected its aggressive growth philosophy, Europe's response reflected its own philosophy, brutally slashing budgets and increasing taxes, with little talk of growth–two philosophies, two different responses, and it is difficult to get two economists to agree on which is better. But one thing seems sure: the harsh austerity measures introduced by most southern European countries may be necessary to put an end to the follies of the past, but they are likely to put a severe clamp on growth and it will take a very long time for these economies to recover, if ever. The IMF said that by 2015 the average growth rate in the Eurozone would hover around a meek 1.7 per cent, assuming the euro situation doesn't worsen. Recently about 40 per cent of Eurozone growth has come from export-oriented economies like Germany and Finland. Peripheral countries such as Italy, Spain, Greece, Portugal or Ireland, with their lack of international competitiveness, their low productivity and R&D investments, their large trade imbalances and weak finances, won't contribute to the region's growth soon, if at all. Due to its strong industrial base, France would, theoretically, be a candidate to contribute to European growth except that its large firms are dependent on government support. It has some of the weaknesses of peripheral countries and it innovates even less than Germany.

In terms of productivity, the value of goods and services a country generates per hour of work, Europe's per capita GDP is substantially lower than that of America, the current world leader in productivity. The productivity gap is said to be worth almost twice the size of the economy of Germany. Two-thirds of the productivity growth gap with America is said to come from the service sector. If the potential of the service sector was unleashed the European economy would look very different. Europeans, with their longer vacation time (30 days average vacation time in Germany, 25 in France, as against 12 in the US),[27] work fewer hours than Americans on average (in 1973 Europeans worked 2 per cent *more* hours than Americans, by 2004 they worked 18 per cent hours *less*[28]). What we forget is that during their working hours they work less productively than American workers. The McKinsey Global Institute calculated that Europe would need to accelerate productivity growth by well over 30 per cent per year to start to match America.[29] Some sources put the productivity gap at only 10 per cent, but there is still a gap, even if, 'Contrary to conventional wisdom, West European productivity growth outpaced that of the United States in the past 30 years'.[30] Europe is bound to fall behind as it will not bring itself to boost productivity, invest in R&D and innovation, and get rid of excessive labour market rigidity. Europe is definitely losing ground, and fast, relative to the economies of the US and of the emerging Asian giants. Of 139 countries surveyed by the World Economic Forum for competitiveness, America comes in 4th, ahead of Germany's 5th place and the Netherlands' 8th. France ranks 15th and Belgium 19th. The record for Europe's peripheral countries is dismal, as Ireland is 29th, Spain 42nd, Portugal 46th, Italy 48th and Greece 83rd. These statistics also attest to substantial divergences among European economies, a reality that contributed to the severity of the crisis addressed in the next chapter.

NINE

THE PERFECT STORM

*Europe hit by the subprime, sovereign debt and
currency crisis*

The stuff we are *not* made of

W here did it all go? Scientists have become better and better at exploring the far reaches of the universe, but remain puzzled by one question: according to theory, there should be an equal quantity of matter and antimatter in the universe, produced when the universe was born, some 13.6 billion years ago. But they can't find antimatter in space, they only find matter, the stuff we see and touch and feel, made of positively charged protons, negatively charged electrons and so forth. Antimatter, simplistically put, is the same but with the charges inverted, antiprotons, anti-electrons and so on. This is crucial not just because it keeps scientists awake at night but because when matter and antimatter meet the two instantly annihilate each other and 100 per cent of their mass becomes energy. There are only two things you need to remember from Albert Einstein's famous formula $E = mc^2$ – that, basically, mass and energy are the same thing and that 'c', the speed of light, is a very very large number, which means a tiny amount of matter is equivalent to a huge amount of energy. The hydrogen bomb, which uses the same fusion process as happens continuously in the sun, liberates only 1 per cent of the energy contained in matter when it detonates. One microgram of matter, much smaller than the smallest thing your eyes can perceive, contains enough energy to power an entire city for a day. The only process that converts the *entire* mass into energy, producing 100 times the bang of a hydrogen bomb, is the collision of matter and antimatter. If we could find a bit of antimatter, make it safely collide with matter and harness that immensely powerful process into producing energy for mankind, all our energy problems would be solved, forever. The problem is, where is the antimatter?

When they can't find something, scientists try to make it. In fact they have been creating antimatter for quite a while. To do so, they have to recreate conditions close to those that existed at the time of the Big Bang, when the universe was created. They do this by smashing components of matter into each other in huge, expensive and complex machines at speeds close to that of light and beyond our comprehension, and they study the products of collision – just like your child when he wants to see what his toy is made of, he smashes it on the floor and looks at the bits and pieces. But the bits of antimatter thus created are very few, just a few particles here and there, and they stay 'alive' for incredibly short amounts of time. Nine anti-atoms (anti-hydrogen, to be precise, as it's simpler, just one anti-electron swirling around an antiproton) were created this way in 1995 and lasted for only 40 billionths of a second. In 2010 Jeffrey Hangst and his Alpha team at Europe's CERN lab located in Geneva managed to produce and trap 38 anti-atoms for 0.2 thousandths of a second.[1] They used machinery that produces antiprotons by bombarding copper with protons and decelerating it, and they produced anti-electrons from a decaying radioactive source. They gently nudged the two streams of particles into each other, producing these few bits of antimatter that they kept 'alive' for a fleeting instant by using an electromagnetic trap. Similar advances are being made in other scientific fields from biotechnology to quantum computing and fusion. They could revolutionize the world we live in.

When the invisible hand became a raised middle finger

The point of this digression? You and I probably think that Hangst and other such scientists working at the edge of human knowledge are very clever people. But according to the average investment banker we are wrong: the banker will tell you that he and his colleagues are far cleverer than Hangst, so clever and precious to society that it is only fair that they should be paid colossal amounts of money. And society accepts it. An average investment banker probably earns, in an average year, ten or twenty times what Hangst makes.

And bankers even manage to hold on to profits when things go well and get the taxpayer to pay the bills when things go bad. Governments, elected to run the country for us, seem perfectly happy with this, especially in America since bankers hold the purse strings. Wall Streeters managed to convince gullible Americans that they are indispensable. In 2010, a couple of years after the biggest ever taxpayer-financed government bailouts of the financial industry, it was reported that these Wall Streeters collectively received 140 billion dollars in bonuses, a world record. The fact that they managed to throw most of the world into an abyss with their greed and recklessness is mere detail and please don't mention this in conversations with them, or the 20 million jobs lost across G20 countries in the last three years.[2] Sam Hayes, my investment banking professor at Harvard, should redefine a banker as someone who wears a pinstripe suit and is able to lose a billion dollars in one day. Banks should have been deemed to be too important to be left to bankers alone. Of course, these bankers look down on entrepreneurs and will not want to hear that *nearly all* new jobs created in America are created by companies that didn't even exist five years ago. But bankers apparently don't have to worry about creating jobs – far too mundane a subject for them.

The American-born subprime crisis was the product of a perversion of capitalism that is testimony to the cancer pervading the financial sector. The origins of this crisis are believed to lay in the deregulation binge launched by Reagan and pursued by Clinton. Remember Reagan's famous joke: 'The nine most terrifying words in the English language are: "I'm from the government and I'm here to help"'? The last of tight regulation disappeared when a pillar, the Glass-Stiegel Act, which separated commercial banking from investment banking and insurance, was repealed by the Gramm-Leach-Biley Act in 1999. The idea that markets worked for the benefit of society and were best left alone was back – the 'invisible hand' paradigm in its purest form. The old partnership structures, where investment bankers were liable for their firms' debts, became a thing of the past. That was just what the investment bankers had been waiting for. They began concocting all sorts of arcane financial products that escaped regulations, making the world of finance much riskier with products American business magnate Warren

Buffet called 'weapons of mass destruction'. The subprime scam itself was massive, clever and everybody was in on it. In retrospect, it was beautifully simple: using 'predatory lending' methods, mortgage lenders pushed people to buy up dream houses all over the US, taking up mortgages they couldn't afford to repay. These mortgage lenders passed the hot potato onto the next player in the chain, investment bankers who eagerly sliced and diced them, bundled them with other types of debts to produce the infamous CDOs (collateralized debt obligations) securities and other alphabet-soup products. Bankers could in turn count on rating agencies (that they were paying billions) to give the ultimate AAA gold-plated stamp of approval to their concoctions. Now magically labelled safe, these high yielding securities were irresistible, especially to institutions in the developed world. Insurers such as AIG even sold insurance against their default, so what was there to fear? This well-organized, vertically integrated production line ended up producing the biggest bubble the world had seen. Although some economists, such as Nouriel Roubini, had been crying wolf, they were few and preaching in the desert. The mother of all scams was making good money for everybody, so why worry about a few party poopers?

What goes up generally comes down, as economists showed long ago. The dot com bubble provoked the 2000 crash. Before that there was the savings and loans crisis, and before that other crises. In 2008 it was the turn of subprime mortgages. Every time the financial world rediscovers the perfect investment, a low-risk high-return panacea, it pours more and more money into it until the bubble explodes. *Homo Financialis* never learns. The volume of financial transactions in the world is estimated at about ten times the volume of trade transactions. The financial economy dwarfs the 'real' economy and its raw material, money, doesn't move in planes, containers or freight trains but at the speed of light. It has no master, no feeling, no consideration for social justice and follows no rule. In a new globalized world where financial markets rather than governments rule, damage can happen very fast and those with a hand in it can make large fortunes very fast.

A few people correctly predicted that the orgy of easy money and credit could not go on forever. A handful even bet against conventional wisdom and made lots of money, a famous case being that of my former Harvard classmate John Paulson, a nice guy with an easy smile and approachable demeanour who made a few billion dollars for himself. China, for one, sailed through this and other recent crises like a breeze, looking like an island of macroeconomic stability in sharp contrast with what can be taken as American recklessness. Where America piled up trillions of dollars of sovereign debt, China piled up trillions of dollars of foreign reserves. All is not rosy in the Middle Kingdom, but one would be at a loss to point to macroeconomic mistakes since Zhu Rongzhi became the economic czar in the 1980s and the country's political class shed its ideologues, filling its ranks with technocrats.

The subprime crisis was a crisis of the finance industry, an industry in which corruption and incompetence are pervasive and where money is a raw material too often used to make even more money mostly for itself, with manoeuvres that add little value to the real economy. Few still believe that modern finance made the world safer and more stable. In early 2011 Mervyn King, Governor of the Bank of England, warning that imbalances in the British banking system were growing again, accused banks of making money from gullible customers, being overly interested in short-term profits, of betting with other people's money on things they didn't fully understand, a culture that he blamed on the payment of bonuses. King pointed out that 'We allowed a (banking) system to build up which contained the seeds of its own destruction',[3] and that while hedge funds had been allowed to fail, banks hadn't and were at it again: 'The banks I should worry about are not only the ones that are losing money but the ones who are making a lot of money.' Dambisa Moyo added in *How the West Was Lost*: 'the propensity for high salaries in ostensibly non-productive areas is another example of the misallocation of labour, further contributing to the economic demise of the West'.[4]

By the end of 2009 the American banking system had lost 4 trillion dollars and the government was forced to issue massive amounts of debt to finance most of these losses. The result was the worst recession since the Second World War and a doubling of America's national debt. Yet, adding insult to injury, many of the top executives of financial institutions that went down or were rescued by taxpayers went home with tens of millions of dollars in their pockets. And why should they worry when billions are spent every year by the financial industry on lobbying and contributions to politicians to ensure the continued support of the American government for this state of affairs? The average American is the one getting trampled on in the process but accepts it, having been fed the illusion that these are necessary bumps on the road to free enterprise prosperity, oblivious that America is the developed country with the most unequal distribution of wealth.

Published in January 2011, the American Financial Crisis Inquiry Commission's Report concluded that the 2008 crisis was avoidable. It laid the blame squarely on Wall Street's greed,[5] recklessness and mismanagement, as well as on the banks, the Fed, the SEC and regulators, decrying overall ineptitude and lack of accountability. Nothing less than the entire American financial system and government were to blame. Icons of American finance such as Alan Greenspan, Larry Summers, Hank Paulson, Ben Bernanke and others were said by some to have been involved in institutionalized highway robbery or at the very least to have condoned this madness, having refused to heed warning calls. Perhaps they were just incompetent. In 2007, Ben Bernanke, Chairman of the Federal Reserve, went out of his way to convince the markets that things were under control and the problem of subprime mortgage loans would be contained. His ECB counterpart, Jean-Claude Trichet, later went out of his way to convince markets that Europe's sovereign debt crisis was going to be contained and wouldn't threaten the overall economy. So are we to trust what a central banker tells us or what we see?

A mighty one-two

In Europe the aftershocks of the subprime crisis brutally hit weak economies at the wrong time. More importantly, it provoked a sovereign debt crisis which evolved into a full-blown crisis of the euro that, in turn, threatened the Eurozone and with it Project Europe. A perfect storm had gathered over the continent.

The Great Recession that followed the subprime meltdown brought entire European economies to a halt and provoked the rapid destruction of wealth on a massive scale. Money stopped flowing, banks ceased lending, financial markets collapsed and the crisis hit every sector, driving unemployment up to unprecedented levels. Because of their interdependency and sophistication advanced economies were paradoxically hit the hardest. The American government had intervened and became the owner of some of America's largest companies, giving America's economy a socialist bias just when China was becoming more capitalist. Similarly, in Europe scores of governments were forced to assume colossal debt and pump in huge amounts of money to save the system. The resulting brutal economic contraction had the worst possible effect at the worst possible time on the structurally weak economies. Their weaknesses, which had not so far attracted much attention, were now suddenly in the spotlight. All sorts of risks, including sovereign risks – that is, a country's ability to repay its debts – started attracting scrutiny from the markets in a world where money was suddenly hard to come by and the virtues of sound finances rediscovered. Nervous markets had suddenly discovered that many European countries had been living way beyond their means for years, accumulating mountains of debt and suffering from chronic budget deficits, that Eurozone economies diverged in a substantial way and that growth was missing. The spotlight was now on these issues, and it brought about a crisis of the *entire* Eurozone. And so it was that on the heels of the Great Recession came Europe's home-made sovereign debt crisis, which had its roots in a culture of profligacy related in no small way to the Civilization of Entitlements and to the perverse effects of the euro on some economies.

With markets now upset, the sovereign bond yields of weaker countries started taking off, making it increasingly difficult for them to borrow the money they needed to survive. In the best case the structural reforms they had refused to go through in the past would now be forced down their throats; in the worst case they would crash. To compound difficulties, the European banking system started looking unsafe, its banks not only infected by loads of toxic American subprime paper but now also by their exposure to crisis countries. The year 2010 was a watershed as people everywhere started waking up to the shortcomings of the European model, as if hit in the face by a freight train carrying a big billboard spelling 'unsustainable'. Things started rapidly unravelling at the periphery.

The chicken finally came home to roost

Once the bubble burst the world suddenly 'discovered' that Greece headed the list of risky countries with a gargantuan 400 billion euro national debt (140 per cent of GDP) and that it had cooked the books to become a Eurozone member in 2001, having failed entrance criteria two years earlier. The Greek bond market collapsed and the economy stopped dead. Greeks took to the streets as they realized the extent of the catastrophe that had fallen upon them and got a taste of the brutal belt-tightening awaiting them. Prime Minister George Papandreou was forced to go to the EU and the IMF to obtain a 110 billion euro credit line to save his country from immediate bankruptcy. The money came with strings attached, requiring overnight a surgical restructuring of the economy. Greece reinvented itself overnight (or so it seemed on paper), introducing regulations to make government spending transparent, abolishing the tight controls that had been choking its economy, opening the economy to competition and foreign investment, reforming the pension system and abolishing collective bargaining. But in the unlikely event that these reforms were not just ink on paper and would work, with GDP having contracted 4 per cent in 2010, government spending being cut to the bone and an economy that had little to offer to the rest of the world (this is a country that imports even most of its food), where would the growth necessary to repay Greek debts come from?

The Greeks brought the disaster on themselves. In Greece, profligacy and social benefits taken to absurd levels had combined with pervasive financial mismanagement, institutionalized waste, corruption and tax avoidance (only one Greek in seven pays taxes), a pervasive lack of social discipline or sense of responsibility and an anaemic economy to ensure that disaster would hit sooner rather than later. About 20 per cent of Greece's workforce was employed on a lifelong basis by the government in a wasteful system related to political patronage. During the decade preceding the crisis Athens' structural deficit shot up almost ninefold to reach an unprecedented 18 per cent of GDP, and its national debt doubled. With hindsight, the Greek crisis of 2010 was inevitable and Greece was saved from bankruptcy *in extremis* by the combined financial backing of the

EU (i.e. an unwilling Germany) and the IMF. But a leopard does not change its spots, and Greece was Greece again as bureaucratic inefficiencies ensured that cost-cutting and revenue-raising measures missed deadlines and the drive for reforms slackened off as rapidly as it had started. To protest against the necessary liberalization of their sector, Greek taxi drivers (like their French colleagues previously) undertook a strike right in the middle of the 2011 summer holidays, damaging the country's reputation with the tourists it dearly needed. Measures to reform the labour market and put its fiscal house in order would certainly help, but in the absence of a credible engine for growth, and given the shackles the euro imposes on competitive devaluations, it was difficult to see how Greeks could regain their previous standards of living in real terms in the foreseeable future, let alone repay their debt. How credible were government declarations that Greece would develop 'green industries' that would create 200,000 new jobs by 2015? Moreover, the specificity of the Greek economy had to be taken into account: 96 per cent of all enterprises are not even SMEs but in fact microbusinesses employing just a few people.[6] For good or for worse they have been the backbone of the country's economy, employing almost 40 per cent of the country's workforce. They survived somehow over the years and make, by and large, low-end goods that can no longer compete with cheaper imports. These businesses have been severely hit by the recession and the difficulty in obtaining credit. It was estimated that 65,000 enterprises went under in Greece in 2010 and that another 220,000 were threatened. Jacques Attali pointed out that for a country with a national debt of 100 per cent of GDP and public spending of 40 per cent of GDP, 1 per cent additional growth per year translates into slashing debt to 86 per cent in ten years.[7] Growth is very important, in theory the one factor that has the best chance to help an economy come out of its debt predicament. But in reality how can Greece repay its gargantuan debt given its barren economic landscape? When a government is faced with having to cut its deficit the easy way out is to focus on the top line and increase taxes rather than slash expenses. The problem is that high taxes choke the economy, so you need to do a bit of both. But in the absence of growth, how far can a government tax people and business and slash spending before the entire edifice falls apart? What if Greece cannot survive?

Ireland had, in recent years, turned a past history of poverty into an economic miracle to the extent of being dubbed the 'Celtic tiger'. Its high productivity, innovation and low tax structure (12.5 per cent corporate tax, or about a third of that of countries such as France or Germany) lured foreign companies, more and more women entered the workforce and yearly GDP growth at one point came close to an astonishing 10 per cent. Ireland, which had suffered from famine in the past, briefly became the second richest country in the EU. Exports doubled between 1995 and 2000.[8] Apart from a budget deficit that exploded to 32 per cent of GDP (over ten times the magic Eurozone number) attesting to profligacy recently gone out of control, things were going reasonably well until the bankers became excited. At the beginning of 2008 Ireland's debt was a mere 25 per cent of GDP. But since Ireland was in the Eurozone, it was easy for an Irish banker to borrow cheaply abroad and funnel the money back home. For simple-minded people such as bankers, the easiest thing to do with money (other than losing it) is to lend it to the property sector: it gives them the reassuring feeling that they can kick the bricks, there is a real asset there.

Undeniably, the euro indirectly helped to bring about the crisis in countries such as Ireland and Spain. Interest rate differentials among countries in the Eurozone had been shrinking over the years, as if financial markets, having swallowed euro rhetoric, naively considered these widely disparate economies to be one and the same and their debt virtually risk-free, just because they shared a single currency and Germany was the Eurozone bulwark. Weaker countries got a free ride on the back of stronger countries as they saw their cost of raising debt shrink. They couldn't resist the temptation and borrowed more and more of this easy money, fuelling a property and construction bubble that saw politicians, developers and bankers living in dangerous promiscuity. Previously poor countries felt rich, wages went up and up, and they too bought into the Civilization of Entitlements. Initially markets failed to understand the difference between these economies and that of, say, Germany, which was tightening its belt and reforming while others were partying. But Irish property prices finally started falling in 2006 and an overexposed and bloated banking sector imploded. Ireland itself was not saddled with particularly high levels of national debt, but its banks were. Some governments seem to love bankers more than their electors, and in September 2008 Brian Cowen's Fianna Fáil government made the fateful and hasty decision to bail out the country's shaky banks by guaranteeing all their debts. In other words, what was a problem for private Irish banks and the foreign lenders who gave them the cash suddenly became a national debt problem for every Irish citizen. The invisible hand gave way to the raised middle finger once more; thanks to the bankers, and the banking crisis became a sovereign debt crisis. About 30 per cent of Irish GDP was used to bail out the Irish banks, that is, to save the French and German banks and investors who had recklessly lent to reckless Irish banks.

Doubts about the soundness of the European banking system prompted banking authorities to launch a series of so-called 'stress tests' to great fanfare, the objective of which was to check the health of European banks and give a thumbs up sign to reassure the financial community. Tests undertaken in the summer of 2010 seemed to indicate that the European banking system was generally healthy, but nobody looked close enough to see what was in the tests – and the tests didn't include a scenario in which a sovereign default occurred. This was simply another masquerade which indicated in the summer that Irish banks were generally sound, when, just a few months later, they were shown to be so fragile that they brought the entire country down with them. Not only Greeks like to play games, or perhaps the regulators were sleeping. As a result of the nationalization of bank debt there are today 4.6 million Irish citizens sharing a 100 billion euro debt, that's about 20,000 euros for every man, woman and child in the country. The situation was exacerbated by the alleged flight of 100 to 150 billion euros in capital during the crisis and the downgrading of Irish debt to junk status by Moody's during the summer of 2011. Guinness beer consumption went down 10 per cent, and that, in Ireland, is a sign things are really bad. The stoic children and grandchildren of Ireland will be toiling for a long time to pay for this folly. But the bankers, especially the foreign lenders who gave money to Irish banks, were saved.

Across the North Atlantic, Iceland had been in a similar predicament with a bloated banking sector that underwent a meltdown in 2008. Deregulation, started in 2000, resulted in local banks going into a frenzy of international borrowing to fuel a domestic property bubble (rating agencies gave these banks AAA ratings) – a classic case. Bank losses came to total more than seven times the country's GDP of about 10 billion euros. Yet, contrary to the situation in Ireland, Iceland's government refused to bail out the banks and foreign creditors. Some banks were annihilated, the country saw the doors of international capital markets close for a long time and GDP took a 15 per cent drop. Not being in the Eurozone, Iceland let its currency, the krona, fall, fuelling export growth. Iceland persisted in this direction as its president vetoed the repayment to the Netherlands and Britain of over 3 billion euros lost by depositors in the Icesave bank failure, a move that may come to haunt Iceland as it needs these countries' support to join the EU.[9] Nevertheless, Iceland seems to be recovering well today: the OECD reported that its economy is projected to grow faster than the Eurozone's in 2012, and with a lower budget deficit to boot. Did the Irish miss something?

Not only did Ireland not have the luxury of letting its currency fall, but it faced growing pressure from France and Germany to increase its relatively low corporate taxes to nearer their own levels (the process of tax 'normalization' derided earlier), a move that could have disastrous consequences for an economy that started showing some signs of an export-led recovery following the brutal internal devaluation it went through in 2009. France and Germany didn't seem to worry over the fact that, if Ireland were forced to raise taxes, it would lose its growth engine, however artificial an engine that was. This is another case of the more powerful European countries imposing the lowest common denominator onto everybody else, making sure Europe will stay uncompetitive.

From PIGS to bacon

Portugal, Ireland, Greece and Spain (the so-called PIGS) grew when money was cheap and the markets were little concerned with sovereign credit risk or fiscal orthodoxy. Being in the Eurozone they took advantage of low interest rates practised by the ECB to gorge themselves on easy cash, pushing up domestic demand, prices and wages. But this internal inflation was not being balanced by increases in productivity, and their industries inevitably lost competitiveness.

Moreover, the financial systems of these countries didn't do their jobs properly: instead of channelling money into productive investments they misallocated it and also enabled people to live well beyond their means. Greece and Ireland had actually to run to the EFSF and the IMF to save themselves from immediate collapse. The markets then wondered who would be next.

The most obvious candidate was Portugal. Its predicament was different from that of Greece or Ireland in that it hadn't fallen prey to a property bubble or severe banking crisis, nor had it fiddled the numbers to get in the Eurozone. Portugal's problem was its lack of growth. This made its high level of debt (especially private sector debt, which foreign banks funnelled through local banks) unsustainable. In the 1990s, Portugal was looking good, with high growth, low unemployment hovering at 4.5 per cent, European companies and capital flowing in to take advantage of cheap labour. When the country entered the Eurozone it was underdeveloped and suddenly thought itself rich. Here too, easy money from the EU and from membership in the Eurozone resulted in large government borrowings and inflated wages that, combined with labour market rigidity, resulted in low value-added industries and textiles from the north pricing themselves out of the market and being wiped out by Asian imports.[10] In a sense Portugal's industry, which rested on low value-added SMEs and agriculture, was killed by its integration into Europe, the Eurozone and globalization. In fact, since Portugal adopted the euro, its growth has hovered around a minimal 0.8 per cent or half of the Eurozone's average. Here too the medicine was now brutal, with drastic welfare cuts, tax increases and reductions in wages hitting the economy in order to bring a deficit which stood at 7.3 per cent of GDP in 2010 down to 4.6 per cent by the end of 2011. When Portuguese debt, amounting to 80 per cent of GDP, was downgraded in the spring of 2010, Portugal was effectively shut out of bond markets and had to turn to the ECB as lender of last resort, which is how the country managed to hold on for a while before it had to run to the EFSF. Hit by the crisis and by brutal austerity measures, the Portuguese economy went into a coma and was estimated to have shrunk by 2 per cent in 2011. Assuming Portugal would hold its own, the question was, once more, where growth would come from.

The cost of bailing out Greece and Ireland was tremendous but sustainable, as the eventual cost of a Portuguese rescue would be. These were relatively small economies. But since the world of finance is characterized by a herd mentality, the markets were now doubting everything and everyone, going through the medical file of each country with a magnifying glass, looking for signs of weakness in much larger economies such as Spain, and even Italy and Belgium. Moreover, contagion from one country to another was a distinct possibility because banks from healthier countries had been lending to weaker countries, exposing themselves to debt repayment problems. The implication was that no country, weak or strong, small or large, was really safe anymore, and everybody realized that the system could not absorb the gargantuan rescue packages any of the larger countries would require. However unlikely it was that any of these larger economies would actually need a bailout, they didn't project very encouraging pictures.

The fundamental problem with Spain, the last of the PIGS, was not so much one of profligacy run amok as one of misallocation of funds. What the markets were now worried about in the case of Spain was not so much the level of sovereign debt or the fiscal deficit but the health of a banking system overexposed to a collapsed property sector, as had happened in Ireland. Spanish banks, especially the tiny *cajas* that financed the property bubble, collectively held over 300 billion euros in lending exposure to property developers alone. If we include construction also, their aggregate exposure to the property sector amounted to over 40 per cent of GDP. Bailing out Spain was estimated to be a 420 billion euro operation, a totally different scale from Greece or Ireland. Madrid was trying to consolidate and reform the *cajas*, saying that it would need about 15 billion to do so, while the market thought it would need in excess of 40 billion euros if not more. Inevitably, Moody's downgraded Spanish sovereign debt in March 2011. Spanish banks were still on their feet; the largest ones remained relatively strong and public finances were not as bad as those of other peripheral countries. But one question remained unanswered: with the property sector, which represented a large portion of Spain's economy, now defunct, where would Spanish growth really come from? From where would Spain generate the cash to repay its debts? Even when hit by this unprecedented crisis and the resulting high overall unemployment (60 per cent in the construction sector), the socialist Zapatero government didn't at first seem to fully grasp the need for serious structural reforms. No serious moves were made to tackle an overly rigid labour market characterized by mandatory yearly increases in wages and centralized wage bargaining that had made its industry uncompetitive during the boom years. How difficult it is to let go of the comfortable Civilization of Entitlements! Even at the end of 2010 Madrid was refusing to face the facts as the cost of Spanish labour remained higher than the European average. The retirement age was raised from 65 to 67, but even this modest reform would kick in only in 2027. Similarly, no serious moves were made to rein in the profligate and inefficient health care sector. With credit dried up, where would enterprises get the fuel for growth at a time of drastic austerity measures?

The Andromeda strain

The sovereign debt of Italy and Belgium may be relatively high, but these were countries with finances in far better shape than the PIGS. They relied less heavily on foreign borrowings and their primary budgets (before interest payments) were nearly balanced. Yet by the end of 2010 markets were doubting everything and everybody's capacity to survive. Contagion was the word of the day. By forcing governments to commit large amounts of financial resources to prop up their banks, the banking crisis had generated a fiscal crisis and this crisis of government money in turn added oil to the fire of the banking crisis, resulting in an additional credit crunch in the system – a vicious spiral. The markets knew that should contagion spread to larger economies such as Spain or Italy, it would be game over for the Eurozone. Italy, the 7th largest economy in the world and third largest in the Eurozone, now found itself in the market's sights.

Italy's social model is like the French one with added twists *al dente*. The backbone of Italy's postwar economy has traditionally been its nimble, family-owned SMEs exporting garments, shoes, furniture, light specialized machinery and similar items. A lot of these businesses thrived in Italy's '*economia sommersa*', the shadow economy said to amount to about 20 per cent of total real GDP and based on undeclared labour and tax avoidance.[11] Competitive devaluations of the lira meant Italy could periodically boost these export industries when things slowed down, before the age of the euro. Change came with the advent of globalization and the ascent of countries such as China and Eastern Europe which, thanks to low labour costs, could outcompete Italy in these low-tech low-investment industries. Contrary to Germany's *Mittelstand* SMEs, most of Italy's SMEs were, for all their success, not competing in specialized B2B niches requiring innovation and high premium services, but in branded consumer goods or in industries with low know-how, low investment and low barriers to entry. Moreover, globalization meant Italy's SMEs were now also competing with foreign producers enjoying larger economies of scale and lower labour costs, taxes and regulations. To compound the problem, most Italian entrepreneurs, having had enough of the absurd complexities of doing business at home, soon started moving their own production abroad, exporting jobs and know-how at the same time. Like Greece, the Italian economy counts a huge number of microenterprises (defined as businesses employing fewer than ten people), said to be more than 5 million and counting for 47 per cent of Italy's employment. Very small enterprises are particularly fragile and often have difficulty in keeping their heads above water in normal times, let alone when confronted with a crisis of this magnitude and the subsequent credit crunch. No help is likely from your banker when you need it: these enterprises were devastated by an Italian banking system that felt no pity towards these weaklings, overcharging them, drowning them in bureaucracy and drying up credit. Italian banks are responsible for a great part of the 45 billion euro loss these microenterprises are collectively said to have suffered and a great many of them will fail.[12]

Italy suffers from the southern European chronic disease of high wages, low productivity (no increase over the last ten years) and little to show in terms of growth. Added to this is a stifling and inefficient bureaucracy, corruption, clientelism, a third-rate geriatric political class and punitively high taxes. Growth, competitiveness and economic strategy don't appear in the national narrative of Italy these days. Italy has taken a leave of absence from the serious world. The country's deindustrialization has been severe, having applied almost entirely to sectors offering growth and value-added and requiring substantial R&D expenses, such as pharmaceuticals and electronics. The final nail in the coffin was the advent of the euro (how many economies has this new currency killed?), which made Italian products overvalued, took away the country's ability to resort to competitive devaluations and cost its SMEs dearly. As in France, Italy's system caused economic stagnation and high unemployment. Italy, however, is worse off, lacking multinationals with their economies of scale and market strengths.

Finally, Italy is faced with the ticking bomb of rapidly declining demography. It is now paying the price of its refusal to face reality in the past and its having systematically hidden behind its weak currency instead of enacting structural reforms when time and money were available. It can expect no leadership from an incompetent, lethargic and overpaid political class mired for years in ridiculous political infighting. As a Japanese businessman once told me, 'Italy is not a serious country', and he could have added that it was becoming irrelevant too. The Italian left cannot get rid of its outdated class struggle paradigm and has turned into the most conservative force in society, as is witnessed by Susanna Camusso, head of the largest trade union, CGIL, being unable to propose anything better than a general strike to protest against austerity and labour reform measures.[13] From 2009 Italy enacted severe budget cuts, a step on the road to financial rectitude imposed by the markets. Under Giulio Tremonti's stewardship it reduced its deficit to 4.6 per cent and reached a reassuring 2 per cent primary budget surplus (before interest payments) and its debt has not increased. Moreover, it has not been hit by a property bubble and its banking system remains relatively solid. Yet, as in the case of Greece and Spain, fiscal rectitude is a condition necessary but not sufficient. There needs to be an engine of growth somewhere to enable a country to repay its debt. The fact that Italy doesn't have growth prospects scared the markets and caused the country to come under attack in July 2011. Additionally, most new planned deficit reductions were to come from tax increases, which would impede growth. The bright spot that is northern Italy, a highly productive region said to be growing at a remarkable 3–4 per cent per year (while the inefficient *mezzogiorno* south shrinks by 2 per cent) won't change the fact that the future of the land of Dante and AC Milan is bleak indeed; one of rapid decline, impoverishment and growing irrelevance in the twenty-first century.

One cannot fail to be surprised by the fact that Belgium too, the quintessential European country, came under fire from the markets. The case of Belgium was unusual as markets were not punishing the country for financial but for political reasons. Here was a country with good economic fundamentals, growing 2 per cent in 2010 (thanks to its German neighbour), high private savings, a relatively low budget deficit and a current account surplus. Its banking sector was not very healthy and, at 100 per cent of GDP, its national debt was the third largest in Europe behind Greece and Italy.[14] But Belgium was generally sound. In fact it has a dynamic economy and its exports per capita beat Germany, China and the US. But a very European thing happened: language and ethnicity got in the way. The political crisis between Belgium's French-speaking Walloons and Dutch-speaking Flemish that threatened to physically split the country apart resulted in a drawn-out political paralysis that unnerved the financial markets. Belgium had agreed to cut its deficit from 4.8 per cent of GDP to 4.1 per cent, almost 2 billion euros in savings. Yet, in the absence of a strong government, who was going to make the tough decisions?

France initially narrowly escaped the fate of the so-called peripheral countries because of what seemed to be a solid banking system and the absence of an asset bubble. Nor did French industry, despite its woes, have the acute competitiveness problems of the peripheral countries. Yet its national debt doubled in the last decade to reach 1.5 trillion euros in 2010, at 85 per cent of GDP one of the highest among AAA rated nations. Its deficit was an unhealthy 7 per cent of GDP and the country has had a hard time enacting any effective structural reforms. The problem for France is that it fully espoused the siren song of the Civilization of Entitlements and its welfare state has turned into a burden which its economy cannot sustain. The 50,000 bankruptcies per year before the crisis increased by 20 per cent; and it was difficult to see where help would come from for SMEs in the face of government budget cuts, and where growth would come from in an economy saddled by very high labour costs. Nothing was sacred anymore after America's sovereign debt was downgraded in the summer of 2011. France's sovereign debt, under threat from a market worried about the burden the country would have to carry to bail out its weak neighbours, managed to retain its gold medal AAA status only after Sarkozy agreed to enact austerity measures, only to lose it in early 2012 and economic growth, having ground to a halt in the second quarter of 2011 (mainly due to slower consumer spending), was sure to take a further drop, prompting the government to revise 2011 GDP growth forecasts down from 2 per cent to 1.5 per cent, killing its plans to bring down the deficit. French banks, among those most exposed to Greek and Italian debt, inevitably came under attack in the summer of 2011, with shares of some top institutions losing more than half their value.

Germany seemed to come through the crisis unscathed, except that it is the one that has to pick up most of the bills for the laggards. The markets know that, and it's not over yet. Germany remains the pillar, but, as pointed out earlier, its economy, overdependent on exports to the developing world, is not entirely sound and its banks are overexposed to the weaker Eurozone countries. As with France, the markets, looking for any potential causes of trouble, would now worry about the cost of Germany's participation in rescue packages. If you see German bond yields start to climb up, it means the markets are getting nervous about Germany too and will raise its cost of borrowing. In this case, only a miracle could save the Eurozone.

TEN

THE DAY AFTER

Dealing with the Eurozone crisis

The good Samaritan

In every group of rowdy friends there is one who does not drink or drew the shortest straw and has to stay sober to drive the car after the party in order to take his friends safely home. In Europe this role belongs to Germany. Most of Europe, especially in the south, parties: Germany drives the car. This way every country does what it is best at doing. As the Eurozone's leading economy and the euro currency's anchor, Germany was naturally expected to be the main contributor to Greek and other rescue packages. Understandably, the disciplined and hardworking Germans were not happy about this, to the extent of German tabloid *Bild* yelling 'Sell your islands, you bankrupt Greeks!'.[1] Not only has Germany recently become an example of fiscal rectitude in the Eurozone (memories of Germany and France being the first to flout Eurozone rules in 2003 seem to have conveniently faded) but it has even passed a *Schulden-bremse* law which forces its government to balance budgets: after 2016 budget deficits will be illegal.

But what could Germans do now? Having given up the DM for the euro on the assumption that it would be as stable and strong they were now in a quandary. To say *nein* to rescue packages meant the fall of the euro and the catastrophic demise of Project Europe. Saying *ja* meant paying large sums to save Greece and a possible unknown number of others, over an unknown period. Going back to the DM would be impossible. In any case, the country would see its export competitiveness vanish in smoke as the DM, free from the burden of the weaker countries, would soar like an eagle, not a good prospect for German industries and jobs. They had no choice but to bite the bullet and Merkel was compelled to say 'We will stand by the euro'. Germans, after having made sacrifices to pay for their country's reunification, having worked hard to make ends meet, having kept their salaries down while everybody else in Europe was increasing theirs, were now asked to pay for the folly of PIGS and maybe others too. At the very least Germans would lose interest in Project Europe, the Franco-German axis, and all those concepts. They would become more self-centred and independent. It is thus not entirely surprising that, since the 1992 Maastricht Treaty defining the euro had no bailout provisions (anathema to German constitutional courts), Merkel demanded the reopening of the Lisbon Treaty, the watered-down successor to the European Constitution finally ratified in 2009, to insert German discipline into the Eurozone.

It is with extreme reluctance that Germany agreed to setting up a bailout facility in the spring of 2010 after failing to convince other European countries to reopen Lisbon. The European Financial Stabilization Facility (EFSF), a rescue fund for Eurozone countries, was put together following much delay with a German at its head, Klaus Regling. The EFSF was but a 440 billion euro facility, itself part of a larger 750 billion euro rescue package that included funds from the IMF and the EU. Unlike the ECB, an independent institution, the EFSF was an intergovernmental agency that borrowed with the backing of 440 billion euros' worth of credit guarantees from Eurozone governments. Unlike Germany and France, some 11 Eurozone governments were not AAA rated; so in order to obtain AAA rating the EFSF had to retain additional collateral, reducing its firepower to 250 billion euros. The rescue package for Greece was thus cobbled together late and hesitantly, further unnerving the markets. To its credit, after Greece, Europe moved relatively fast to rescue Ireland, which was at first refusing help for fear of having to abandon its low corporate taxes.

Treading water

The EFSF packed enough of a punch to bail out Greece with 110 billion euros in the spring of 2010, followed by Ireland with

85 billion euros in December. Nevertheless, the EFSF was charging a hefty 3 per cent more than market rates, adding to the debtors' burden, but at least the debtors avoided immediate default. It was estimated that a bailout of the next potential victim, Portugal, would require an additional 70 billion euros. This was practicable, except that, with markets becoming hostile to the EFSF and much larger economies such as those of Spain and Italy now getting in the sights of such markets, the EFSF would need a far bigger punch. Estimates for a fully fledged facility providing *total* Eurozone protection reached 2 trillion euros.

This time the Germans baulked. Merkel pressed again for changes to the Lisbon Treaty that would impose *real* penalties on profligate countries. Again the rest of Europe resisted the idea: the memories of years of endless negotiations to put Lisbon together in the first place were too fresh, and they didn't want to go through it again. When a country is bailed out, it is essentially given money to repay its debts to bondholders; so it is really bailing out the bondholders. Berlin had also insisted that these private bondholders should become part of the solution, that they should take a 'haircut' after 2013, that is accept some losses on their holdings (in effect triggering a partial default), instead of the taxpayers having to shoulder everything. This position was rejected outright by the ECB's Trichet, fearful that the markets would panic and spread contagion to sounder countries in an uncontrollable domino effect. As French and German leaders met in the French seaside resort of Deauville, Merkel, who needed to show her electorate something, demanded automatic sanctions against those who flouted currency rules, such as loss of voting rights, a proposal France watered down by requiring the European Council to approve such sanctions. Germany decided to collaborate when France finally agreed to reopen the Lisbon Treaty, but without the approval of other member countries the idea didn't go very far.

Another idea posited by the Italian Finance Minister Giulio Tremonti and the head of the Euro group of finance ministers, Jean-Claude Juncker, at the end of 2010 was that of Eurobonds, bonds issued with the joint backing of *all* Eurozone members. This went much further than the EFSF, mutualizing debt, turning the debt of individual nations into the debt of *all* Eurozone nations – a big step towards fiscal union that many in Europe were not ready to contemplate. German Finance Minister Wolfgang Schäuble feared undisciplined countries would hide behind this collective borrowing scheme backed by richer countries to avoid putting their own houses in order. Eurobonds implied weak countries raising money on the back of stronger economies, that is, paying cheaper interest rates than they normally would on their own, the other side of the coin being that the debt of strong borrowers such as Germany, the Netherlands, Finland and Austria would see its quality tainted by the weak members, sparking higher costs. Creditor countries, abhorring the idea of a transfer union in which they subsidized the profligacy of their undisciplined neighbours and institutionalized profligacy and inefficiencies, could be expected to resist the idea. Yet the rationale was compelling. Based on a credible unified Eurozone with its 10 trillion euro economy and reasonable aggregate deficit (4.4 per cent of GDP) and debt (87 per cent of GDP),[2] Eurobonds would make it possible to raise a considerable amount of money, underpinning the euro as a reserve currency and creating a market estimated at 8 trillion euros, rivalling that of US treasuries (a development China would doubtless welcome), for which there could be substantial demand (thus resulting in low rates).

There were more talks, more meetings, but little action. And all the while, the time bomb was ticking...

In February 2011 a revived Franco-German axis laid down what appeared to be a far-reaching plan to bring about finally some measure of economic integration within the Eurozone. Labelled the 'Pact for Competitiveness' by a Merkel intent on pushing weaker Eurozone economies to emulate the German economy, or at least its discipline, it was proposed in exchange for Germany backing the development of the EFSF into a larger and more permanent rescue mechanism. This amounted to a volte-face for Germany, which had so far been preaching *less* Eurozone economic coordination and political oversight, and a vindication for a *dirigiste* France, pushing for more. Measures proposed included convergence of economic, fiscal and labour policies, areas where countries so far had been jealously guarding their sovereignty, constitutional limits on debt, and changes destined to enhance competitiveness. The plan immediately ran into hostility from countries such as Belgium and Luxembourg, which refused to abandon wage indexation and saw no reason to submit to such punishment since they had not themselves been victims of the crisis.[3] Others, such as Ireland, Estonia, Slovakia and Luxembourg, viewed with suspicion any attempt at 'tax harmonization' that threatened to wipe out their competitive fiscal advantage. Some objected to the increase in retirement age. Convergence imposed from above wouldn't be easily accepted because each country, as usual, was vying for its own interests. Once more the plan was negated.

Some important issues were missing in all these discussions, including the problem of an undercapitalized European banking system. Yet the mere fact that a serious debate about the pooling of economic sovereignty was finally taking place was remarkable.

Disparate and desperate

It was difficult to imagine the Eurozone's 17 disparate countries agreeing to a permanent bailout mechanism, let alone to structural changes. Yet the more they delayed producing a common and convincing solution, the worse the crisis would get. The only realistic thing to do, a restructuring of the debt of the troubled countries, was not even on the agenda. Everybody knew the EFSF was a temporary scheme to provide emergency support to countries shut out of markets by sky-high borrowing costs, in order to prevent immediate defaults and to calm the financial markets. But what then? The March 2011 Pact for the euro was basically calling for an enhanced version of the EFSF, an EFSF Mark 2.0 in which actual firepower was to increase from 250 to 440 billion euros. This would, however, only buy time, and wouldn't be enough for Italy or Spain. Was it realistic to expect that troubled countries would use the extra time to reinvent themselves, become competitive and grow out of their debt problems? Would they achieve, in a year or two, what they had not been able to achieve in a decade? This was highly unlikely. The one thing they did, though, was to accept bitter austerity medicine and drastically slash budgets. Unable to devalue their currencies, they had to undergo painful 'internal devaluations', significantly lowering their living standards.

The markets were increasingly fearful that these countries would soon opt out from the challenge and choose the only alternative that made sense, debt rescheduling, anathema to the markets. By now these countries' paper was radioactive. In mid-March 2011 the ten-year Greek bond was trading at around 12.4 (it went to 16.8 per cent two months later, with two-year bonds hitting a 27 per cent yield), more than 9 per cent over the benchmark German bund. At 9.65 per cent, Irish debt was not much better and Portugal's 7.5 per cent yield remained unsustainable (6 per cent is widely considered as the upper limit of sustainability). The rating agency Moody's had downgraded Greece's debt to the level of Egypt's and Spain's, Aa2, to the great outcry of EU finance ministers hard at work to stabilize the situation. Rating agencies were not in the mood to spare anyone, and Portugal's sovereign rating was lowered too as was that of many Spanish banks.

Finally, in April 2011 the next domino fell. With borrowing costs having reached an unsustainable 9 per cent, Portugal had no choice but to apply to the EFSF, the third Eurozone country to enter intensive care. Eyes now inevitably turned to Spain, the fourth and last of the PIGS. If Spain didn't hold, Europe would confront a problem of a much larger scale. And what of the banking system? It was estimated that another 20 billion euro would be needed to shore up Irish banks, bringing the total to over 70 billion euros. Spanish estimates of 15 billion euros for its own banks were dwarfed by the 40–50 billion estimate from Moody's (who said in the worse case it could even go to 120 billion). No wonder the markets remained fearful about Spain's prospects, effectively shutting its overexposed banks out of the debt markets. By the end of the first quarter of 2011 the market believed that the last of the PIGS was by no means out of the woods.

Enter the dragon

Just as Germany had pumped some of its hard-earned cash into the EFSF, China started injecting some of its own into European sovereign bonds and other items. Like the Germans, they had no choice. The Chinese were not bullish on Europe but Europe has overtaken the US in becoming China's largest trading partner (363 billion euros against 292 billion in trade volume) and export market, buying one-quarter of all goods made in China. Moreover, for geopolitical reasons Beijing prefers Europe to be strong, believing that Europe can have a moderating influence on American actions. China had been diversifying some 25 per cent of its gargantuan foreign reserves away from overdependence on the dollar and into the euro. Beijing thus took steps to support the euro, buying large sums of Portuguese and other troubled Eurozone government bonds. In Africa and Brazil, China has been buying into resources and emerging economies; in Europe, China was now buying into submerging economies. Once China had entered the fray, Japan was not far behind and declared that it would buy Eurozone debt to help Ireland just a few days after China reiterated that it would buy Spanish debt.[4] A weak euro would hurt Japanese exports to Europe just as it would hurt Chinese exports. Moreover, since the Japanese yen is a freely convertible currency, should investors flee the euro they would buy yen, pushing up its value and hurting Japanese exports even more. The euro had lost 20 per cent against the Chinese yuan and 23 per cent against the Japanese yen in less than two years; so there was little surprise that these two countries, enjoying the world's largest foreign reserve troves, would take steps to prop up the euro. It is very rarely that one sees the interests of China and Japan thus aligned.

Yet these moves were made more out of necessity than conviction. China's involvement in Europe remains quite selective. When it comes to spending its money, China is mainly after US securities and worldwide natural resources. In Europe, China looks mainly for brands and technology: Europe represents only 3 per cent or so of China's overseas investments. France, for one, invested ten times more in China than the 200 million euros China invested in France.[5] The Chinese know when to press for an advantage, and the crisis provided opportunities for Beijing to shop for bargains while making new friends. China has been resisting efforts by the US and Europe to push up the value of its undervalued currency in order to level out the playing field. It is thus not surprising that, just as China was helping Europe, China's Prime Minister Wen Jiabao reminded Europeans 'not to pressure China on the yuan's appreciation'.[6] The Chinese shipping giant Cosco was already involved in expanding the capacity of the southern Italian port of Naples and at the height of the crisis secured management of a gateway to Europe, the Greek port of Piraeus, with plans to turn it into a major container-receiving hub and boost traffic to 3.7 million containers within five years. China also won a bid to build a highway in Poland. What does all this tell you? That China, a country with an average income per capita of about half that of Turkey or Mexico, is working to improve European logistics and infrastructure the better to move Chinese goods into the European market. We'll see later that at the end of October 2011 Europe didn't shy away from going to China hat in hand to ask for more.

Crucially, the ECB too turned into a good Samaritan, the only European institution standing between the euro and catastrophe. Virtually shut-out of debt markets, many weaker banks came to rely on the ECB for their liquidity. When Portugal issued new bonds in 2010, the ECB bought, for the first time, contributing to their demand and lowering borrowing costs. The ECB's capital reserves stood at just under 5.8 billion euros, and it was reported that ECB purchases of Greek, Irish and Portuguese bonds came to a total of almost 72 billion euros. A 10–15 per cent decrease in their value (quite possible) would wipe its capital out, and if it didn't turn out to be that bad, the ECB would in any case find itself awash with junk bonds – not exactly what the European Central Bundesbank had been created for. Moreover, the ECB had indirectly helped affected countries by keeping untouched its historically low 1 per cent benchmark interest rate. This was not going to last forever. With inflation increasing, the ECB finally raised its rate to 1.25 per cent in April 2011, the first increase since 2008; not good news for the troubled countries of the Eurozone. A frustrated ECB had become Europe's crisis manager. But how long could it go on doing this sort of patch-up, a very long way from its original mandate, and involving risky endeavours to the great displeasure of many parties, especially in conservative Germany. Otmar Issing, the former chief economist of the ECB, gloomily spoke of the central bank having 'crossed the Rubicon'.[7]

Dracula and the taxman

When Harry Potter, Peter Pan or Dracula are required to pay taxes, you know governments have become serious about balancing budgets. Romania is a land where superstition has been embedded in the national culture for a very long time. Even politicians take it seriously, paying witches to cast spells on their enemies (it beats having to go through an election!). So it took great courage for the Romanian government to declare in 2010 that witches and astrologers were, after all, entrepreneurs that needed to pay income tax on their meagre earnings.[8] Governments throughout Europe had finally become serious about putting their financial houses in order.

The world's 6th manufacturing power, Britain is ranked 12th in global competitiveness by the World Economic Forum, and the country still keeps its AAA rating from Moody's.[9] The recent deindustrialization of Britain meant, however, that the country became over-reliant on London as a financial and service centre. When the financial sector was hit by the crisis, the shrinkage of tax income contributed to the budget deficit leaping from 3 per cent to 11 per cent of GDP in 2010 – with more than a little help from Britain's profligate Labour government. Although Eurosceptic Britain never adopted the euro, the country had caught the European-model disease and its national debt ballooned to 82 per cent of GDP and its fiscal deficit had risen sharply. Britain's bloated state had grown to represent over 40 per cent of GDP, 5 million people were living on government handouts, National Health Service budgets had exploded and in a fit of universal generosity children of well-to-do families had become entitled to the same government benefits as those of poor families. George Osborne, Chancellor of the Exchequer in David Cameron's Tory government, started cutting and slashing government department budgets with a vengeance, resulting in average cuts of 19 per cent across the board for the five years ending in 2015.[10] The welfare state was thrown into a washing machine for a heavy dose of shrinkage. Half a million government employees would be laid off. With Price Waterhouse's forecast of over 450,000 jobs lost in the private sector the result approached 1 million jobs lost in the UK. And millions of people would receive reduced welfare payments. From 11 per cent of GDP, the deficit is expected to be cut to 1.1 per cent by 2016, possibly the most brutal austerity package in the OECD. Yet 46 per cent of Britons seemed to understand the need for such measures, according to a *Times* survey. Money would be saved, and that was necessary. But this money was badly needed in an economy just coming out of deep recession.

By the summer of 2011 it became obvious that austerity measures had resulted in an economy more sluggish than expected and tax revenues had fallen even faster than expenses; this gave rise to a wider than expected budget deficit. The IMF warned that British families would on average be £1500 worse off for the next five years, aggregating to 35 billion pounds in loss of disposable income.[11] The surgery had been working too well. How long would Britain's economy and citizens withstand this brutal treatment?

Most of the decade had been an easy time. By the end of 2010, however, all over Europe problem countries had enacted overnight austerity measures the like of which had not been seen since the Second World War. Fiscal rectitude suddenly became the flavour of the day. Lowering pensions, minimum salaries, social benefits, slashing the number of public servants, increasing taxes and cutting spending in every way possible to reduce debts swollen up by the cost of rescuing banks during the financial crisis: everything went. Putting the financial house in order is all very well. But doing overnight what should have been done over a decade comes with risks. The question was what would this sudden bout of slashing do to economies that were already moribund? Would shock therapy revive them or finish them?

The hare and the turtle

The British economist John Maynard Keynes was a fervent proponent of the need for governments to spend *more* money, not less, in times of economic downturn, to replace the demand from the private sector that evaporates. Europeans set exactly the opposite course for themselves. America's initial response to its crisis was to stimulate, reflecting its different, pro-growth mentality: it decided to pump large quantities of money into the economy to revive it, with the added benefit of decreasing the value of the dollar to facilitate exports. Yet America made a spectacular turnaround. At the time of the well-publicized downgrade of American sovereign debt in the summer of 2011, the House of Representatives' Republican majority went European, replacing stimulus measures with spending cuts. Then in late September 2011 the Bank of England and the Fed, recognizing that their economies were going into a coma, started again taking modest steps to stimulate them. Both sides of the Atlantic were by now afflicted by slow growth and austerity and risked falling back into recession. Keynesians have been declaring loudly that overly severe austerity measures are what turned a great depression into *the* Great Depression in the thirties and that it is only after an economy recovers that tax increases and budget reductions should be contemplated. In fact there is no proven recipe.

Brutal austerity measures being deeply deflationary, economic growth in the Eurozone was bound to suffer a big hit. That zombie economies could grow fast enough in order to raise enough taxes to repay their huge debts was in the realm of the fantastic. Spain, Ireland and Greece tried nevertheless to introduce measures designed to boost growth. Ireland had been doing well in the recent past and its exports had been an important component of its success: could Irish exports now help fuel a recovery? Maybe, but it would need to be a stupendous recovery to compensate for the brutal cuts in government spending, and the data were not encouraging, showing economic contraction at the end of 2010. Self-inflicted 'internal deflation' risked seeing them all falling into a classic debt trap by which the value of the debt to be repaid, in real terms, would be going up, making its repayment increasingly painful; if the interest rate on their debt turned out to be higher than their growth rates, debt would just keep accumulating. There is, moreover, a minimum amount of public goods governments need to deliver beyond which people take to the streets and torch cars. In order to recover these countries needed growth, fast growth. But for most of them, growth was no longer in their DNA, and it was denied by a currency they were not free to devalue. What chance did these countries stand? At what point are people unwilling to continue suffering to repay their country's sovereign debt held by foreign lenders? An early 2010 Barclays Capital survey of money managers, investors and others showed 70 per cent of them believing there would be defaults or restructurings in the coming few years (only 2 per cent foresaw a break-up of the Eurozone) for Portugal, Greece and Ireland. During the past half-century Greece has frequently been in debt default mode. Spain is the historical champion of defaults, with 13 during the past two centuries. France itself defaulted 8 times several centuries ago.[12] Default is a definite possibility when citizens can't take any more pain, but the threshold is unclear: Mexico defaulted in 1982 with debt of under 50 per cent of GDP, while there is not even talk of Japan defaulting despite its debt standing at over 200 per cent of GDP. Other factors are obviously at play. One thing is certain: if a country goes into default, it better be at 'primary balance' (the expenses in its budget are matched by its home tax and other revenues, before interest payments), because the moment it defaults it will be shut out from the markets and won't be able to borrow to fill the deficit gap. For its basic expenses it will have to rely only on itself. Greece, for example, did not have a primary budget surplus and a default would thus be likely to result in very serious social upheaval.

It takes two to tango

If some countries have been borrowing easy money as if they could go on doing so indefinitely, the money must have come from somewhere. There must have been someone willing to lend it, and lenders must have expected to make a nice profit. They were mainly German, French and British banks, as well as others. It is easy for stronger countries to lay blame on weaker ones, but the stronger countries' banks launched an orgy of reckless lending (not unlike America's predatory mortgage lenders) to countries that couldn't afford to borrow so much yet started their own orgy of borrowing. Reckless lenders were just as much to blame as reckless borrowers for the situation. European banks and their governments did their best to avoid the topic of their exposure to the sovereign debt of weak countries.

George Soros pointed out that Germany's view that the countries in trouble became uncompetitive and overburdened with debt by their own choosing and thus should bear the entire burden of adjustment was biased, and in fact Germany had a big share of responsibility for this crisis. The banking crisis was affecting German banks more than others, and sovereign bailouts were tantamount to barely disguised bailouts of German banks. For Soros,

> The European Union will suffer something worse than a lost decade;
> it will endure a chronic divergence in which the surplus countries

forge ahead and the deficit countries are dragged down by the burden of accumulated debt. The competitiveness requirements will be imposed on an uneven playing field, putting deficit countries into an untenable position.[13]

The banking crisis was just starting. It could suddenly explode and spread across the continent and beyond like wildfire with catastrophic consequences, because of the interconnection of the international banking system. The aggregate sovereign debt of Europe's peripheral nations amounts to more than 2 trillion euros; most of it is in the hands of European banks, particularly those of so-called 'stronger' European countries. How solid could these banks be, given the levels of risky debt they carried in their books? The IMF estimated the overall bank risk due to the crisis at roughly 300 billion euros.[14] French and German banks were said by some sources to hold nearly 600 billion euros of debt from the PIGS, of which less than 20 per cent was sovereign debt and the rest private (individuals and companies). Goldman Sachs calculated the exposure of European banks to Irish, Portuguese and Greek bonds alone to be 192 billion euros, with German banks leading with 44 billion euros. The Bank for International Settlements (BIS) estimated that French banks, holding the largest aggregate exposure to Greece's public and private sectors, held Greek debt for over 57 billion euros, followed by Germany with 34 billion euros. More frightening, the total exposure of European banks to Spanish debt was said to be over 700 billion euros, with French and German banks again in the lead. Whichever way you looked at it, these were very big numbers. One needs to keep in mind that when a bank buys a sovereign bond, it carries it in its books permanently at the price it originally bought it, even if the bond subsequently falls in value in the market. If banks' books were to suddenly reflect reality and carry these bonds at their 'real' current market price (a practice known as 'mark to market'), it would punch a gaping hole in their balance sheets because some of these bonds are now trading at half their original value or less. In other words, the real health of many banks was far worse than it appeared. But how did it come to that? Once more, you don't need to look much further than to the bankers to find the causes.

Eurozone bankers have, in the past, been more European than Monnet. In the years before the crisis, they dramatically increased cross-border lending within Europe, treating disparate countries as if they were one and the same, as if country risk had been eliminated. European economies were not converging but bond yields were. Just before the sovereign debt crisis hit, over three-quarters of aggregate banking exposure to *peripheral* countries came from banks in core Eurozone countries and the UK. The PIGS' problem thus becomes the problem of Europe as a whole. A substantial default in Europe could suddenly turn many big European banks into insolvent institutions (this is also why Ireland was 'forced' to bail out its banks so that continental banks be saved, with the technical detail of the Irish taxpayer ending up paying the cost – collateral damage). Germany would be in big trouble should this happen. Large amounts of money were needed to recapitalize this house of cards lest it fell apart. In September 2011 Goldman Sachs estimated that somewhere between 32 and 92 billion euros would be needed to recapitalize the 38 largest European banks to protect them against potential losses from peripheral countries' bond write-downs,[15] but a month later it said as much as 298 million euros would be needed to recapitalize 50 of the 91 European banks if banking authorities raised capital requirements from 6 to 9 per cent as was contemplated.[16] Europe was in effect bankrupt, its governments and its banking system. The crisis was three crises in one – a currency crisis, a sovereign debt crisis and also a banking crisis, all interrelated and feeding on each other. It was also a political crisis.

Still treading water . . .

Greece's first bailout had done little but postpone the inevitable and caused its deficit to grow due to tax income having shrunk faster than expenses had been cut, a result of austerity measures, as in the UK. Its debt was expected to rise to 172 per cent of GDP in 2012. By the summer of 2011 Greece needed a second bailout. Worried about the consequences to the banking system, about reactions from their constituencies and about other countries demanding the same relief treatment, Eurozone leaders could still not bring themselves to the idea of restructuring Greece's debt, the only measure that could give it a chance. So they continued playing for time with half-measures. More cash was thrown in to buy a little more time, in exchange for additional austerity. The cash would end up increasing the pile of debt already owned by debtor countries which were unable to repay, a Ponzi scheme concocted in the vain hope of a miracle. In the eyes of the Greek Prime Minister Andreas Papandreou it was 'too little, too late to convince markets'.[17] The world's biggest garage sale got under way as Greece was pushed to launch ambitious privatization programmes to raise extra cash.

Creativity reached new heights with the notion that banks should undertake 'voluntary reschedulings' in the useless hope that rating agencies would close an eye and not consider them as de facto defaults. The economist Jeffrey Sachs joined the chorus with his own solution: since defaulting could not be managed in today's global financial system and may lead to the unravelling of the euro, he advocated stretching Greece's repayments over two decades and lowering the interest rate burden through Europe-wide guarantees to ease the strain.[18] But this solution partly rested on the dubious assumption that Greece could grow at 3 per cent by reinventing itself as an exporter of wind and solar power to the rest of Europe. Certainly, in 2009 Greece produced 50MW of solar energy and, with project Helios, intended to turn this into 10,000MW by 2025,[19] but it was unrealistic to expect it to provide relief to the crisis. The ECB's Trichet proposed the establishment of a pan-European finance ministry to control how Eurozone countries were spending their money, effectively proposing that countries give away some of their fiscal sovereignty. But given the 'success and credibility' of the European Foreign Ministry experiment, would an unelected European finance minister really have an impact? Real monetary union remained a pipe dream and the markets knew it. Some observers, including the Harvard economist Kenneth S. Rogoff,[20] pointed out that a bout of artificially induced inflation would help alleviate part of the burden of debt: a 5 per cent yearly inflation rate translates into debt depreciated by 22 per cent within five years and by 40 per cent within ten. But to do this a country would need its own currency and central bank. The reality was that in the absence of debt reduction, insolvent countries would remain insolvent. In the absence of a substantially increased EFSF (or of Eurobonds), the resources to fight the conflagration would not be there. In the absence of serious recapitalization, the European banking system would be close to collapse. In the absence of a credible firewall protecting Spain and Italy, contagion would spread from the periphery to the core.

By the summer of 2011 there were ominous signs that rating agencies were now threatening Italy, prompting an angry head of the European Commission José Manuel Barroso to accuse them of Anglo-Saxon bias against Europe. In July Italy saw its ten-year bond yields reach unprecedented levels, over the 6 per cent limit of sustainability. Jittery markets worried about the country's solvency due to chronic lack of growth given that Italian debt had piled up to 1.9 trillion euros, far more than any European rescue mechanism could deal with. It was now clear that it was not just the PIGS that could fail: contagion was turning into a reality. Italian Finance Minister Giulio Tremonti quipped that this was increasingly looking like the *Titanic* where not even first-class passengers (Germany and core Eurozone countries) would come out unscathed. An Italian default would probably destroy the entire European banking system. For one, the French banks held over 100 billion euros of Italian debt. The crisis had entered a new and frightening phase, jolting Eurozone leaders into action.

News that a compromise had been reached at the 59th minute of the 11th hour on 21 July 2011 to produce a second rescue package for Greece was greeted by European leaders and markets alike with the same relief they would have received the news that a large meteorite about to hit planet Earth had narrowly missed its target. The Eurozone suddenly seemed to have resolved its problems. Leaders congratulated themselves for having saved the currency, the continent and the Earth. Some talked of a new Marshall Plan and of remaking Europe in Germany's more disciplined image. In Gallic fashion the French press praised Sarkozy–Merkel as the saviours of Europe, spoke of a revival of the Franco-German axis and of Sarkozy having convinced Merkel to embrace his federalist views. In typical European fashion the new 109 billion euro rescue plan was, however, a compromise intended to make everybody happy. The Greeks got their money, with interest rates slashed from 5.5 to 3.5 per cent and bailout loan maturities extended. Germany got its prescription for across-the-board austerity packages confirmed and for banks to indirectly 'participate' in the rescue package by taking a 21 per cent haircut, a loss estimated at 37 billion euros on the Greek bonds they owned, a condition sine qua non for German voters to provide an estimated 45 billion euros. While this measure precipitated the partial Greek default that the ECB had fought so hard against, the ECB handed the responsibility to an enlarged and more permanent EFSF (to be renamed ESM, for European Stability Mechanism), and to European governments that promised to work together to shore up Greece's economy, to somehow guarantee Greek bonds and strengthen Eurozone discipline by increasing central control over tax policies and national budgets. The ECB could now go back to its original central banking job. France was happy because its banks, overexposed to peripheral countries, were temporarily out of the woods and because the plan brought about the sort of increased European integration, governance and centralization dear to Paris. The EFSF saw its mandate enlarged with authority to buy government bonds on the secondary market to shore up their prices, and to intervene pre-emptively by lending to countries about to get attacked (Spain, Italy), and to finance the recapitalization of banks. The EFSF was going to be a sort of European IMF, effectively 'Europeanizing' the debts of individual nations.

Was this the final solution everybody had been hoping for? Few concrete details had been worked out and, as the saying goes, the devil is in the details. In late September Wolfgang Schäuble, German finance minister, expressed his own serious doubts: 'One has to see whether what has been envisaged in June, July is still sustainable in the light of more recent developments.'[21] What would happen when the excitement subsided, pressure decreased and these measures needed to go through parliaments and be turned into laws and regulations? It would take months for the beefed up EFSF to secure the approval of various governments, assuming everything went to plan; so would the ECB continue playing firefighter in the meantime? What value could be given to promises of more central control of individual countries' fiscal discipline? In addition, the plan changed nothing in respect of Greece being unable to repay its debt and didn't address the need to recapitalize European banks. Germany and the Netherlands didn't want to have to continually subsidise others for ever. Greeks didn't want to suffer the pains of austerity for ever and their *anakistimenoi* (the outraged) were taking to the streets to make their point.

And just when you think it can't get worse . . .

The former UK Prime Minister Gordon Brown recognized that 'Europe has a deeply flawed banking system, a widening competitiveness gap, and a debt crisis that cannot get much better if the economy gets worse . . . I reached the conclusion that there was no solution possible within the existing Euro structure . . . Either the Euro has to be fundamentally reformed by Europe's political leaders and the European Central Bank or it will collapse . . . there is not even a chance of a middle way.'[22] The Bank of England Governor Sir Mervyn King added 'the world is facing nothing less than the worst financial crisis since at least the 1930s if not ever'.[23] The unthinkable had entered the realm of the possible, on the way to reaching the probable. The worsening debt crisis brought about a worsening banking and liquidity crisis causing a severe contraction of overall business activity. In the summer of 2011, a bad situation became worse:

- America's sovereign debt downgrade rattled markets and raised the spectre of downgrades in France (and even Germany), prompting Sarkozy to enact austerity measures that were bound to dent France's low growth prospects further. France's loss of its AAA status would raise its borrowing costs but also adversely affect the firepower of the EFSF.
- Eurozone industrial production went down 0.7 per cent in June compared with the previous month and GDP growth slowed from 0.8 per cent in the first quarter to 0.3 per cent. Greece, having seen its economy contract 2.2 per cent in 2009, then to 4.4 per cent in 2010, was projected to shrink by another 3.9 per cent in 2011, its third consecutive year of recession. Portugal was also in the midst of its worse recession in 30 years, with a 5 per cent shrinkage, and Italy and the UK were barely growing.
- Europe's best hope in the short term had been for the German economy to keep forging ahead and German domestic demand to pick up, helping inject some life into the other economies. This

was not to be. In the second quarter of 2011 Germany's economy was growing at a paltry 0.1 per cent, and the OECD forecast
negative growth for the fourth quarter (and the same for France
and Italy). Was Germany's boom cycle over? Could its economy,
over-dependent on exports, risk being hit as severely as in 2008/9
by a fall in export demand? With America now embracing fiscal austerity too, the entire West could fall back into recession.
Moreover, global manufacturing data attested to a broad and deep
slowdown of world economies, including that of China. Since
China exports 40 per cent of its output to developed nations, the
European and US slowdown affected it and in turn it was buying
less, which affected Germany. The problems of an undercapitalized and overexposed European banking system started to make
themselves felt, with major bank stocks taking a brutal beating,
especially in France and Italy. Banks were finding it increasingly
difficult to access money for day-to-day operations. That some big
banks could soon fail and be nationalized was increasingly possible. The IMF estimated that about 200 billion euros were needed
to recapitalize Europe's banks.[24] Trust among banks was down to
such low levels that those with excess cash preferred to put their
money safely with the ECB, even if they were earning less than
they would by lending to other banks.[25] At the same time, peripheral banks in need of cash had nowhere to go but to the ECB for
liquidity. American money-market funds were moving away from
Europe. The financial system was effectively drying out. To check
how healthy financial markets think banks are, one need look no
further than the spread of their credit default swaps, the cost of
insuring against their default. From an average of around 150
basis points in 2010 it had more than doubled by autumn 2011.[26]

Facing the music

By the autumn of 2011 the slippery slope had become a downward
spiral. Germany seemed still unable to figure out what it wanted
and how far it was ready to go to achieve it. Additional austerity
measures passed in Italy didn't calm markets, to the dismay of Prime
Minister Silvio Berlusconi who lamented 'Our heart bleeds to have
to do this' and feared he may need to raise taxes and slash pensions,

thus possibly leading to social disorder. Contagion had now become a reality as the sovereign ratings of Italy and Spain were degraded and France's AAA rating was threatened. Moody's had further downgraded Greek debt and considered the probability of a Greek default (an orderly one, it was hoped) to have become a certainty,[27] something taken for granted except by delusional European politicians. To the question 'can a recession be avoided', economist Nouriel Roubini answered 'It may simply be mission impossible'.[28] Talk of Greece leaving the euro (implying Portugal and Italy might also leave) increased and a *Bild am Sonntag* poll showed that 31 per cent of Germans were convinced that the euro would disappear within a decade.[29] A few German officials resigned from the ECB, highlighting its internal divisions. The Franco-Belgian bank Dexia collapsed. The 21 July plan was by now obsolete and the usual last minute half-hearted deals were clearly not going to work anymore. In the absence of a coherent and comprehensive strategy Europe now faced no less than 'the collapse of the most successful project of economic integration in the history of mankind' according to the former ECB Chief Economist Otmar Issing.[30] As David Cameron warned fellow leaders that they would now only have 'weeks to avoid an economic disaster' there came a general feeling that the crisis had reached its peak.[31]

Any solution would still need to take into account the following:

- The most urgent task was to confine the conflagration once and for all. The Eurozone needed to show the markets that it held the bigger stick and that the arsenal so far deployed was inadequate. Only bold, decisive and coordinated action involving the ECB, the EFSF, the EU, national governments and other actors such as the IMF and possibly cash-rich BRICs (Brazil, Russia, India, China) would put an end to market nervousness, contagion and the immediate crisis. If what was needed to kill the fire once and for all was a 2 trillion euro commitment, then that is what must happen. Only then could structural issues be tackled and, if the euro was to survive, it needed a comprehensive plan backed by the commitment of all parties acting in concert.
- Europeans needed to make a political choice with profound implications. How much did they really want to stay together? Since creditor countries wouldn't accept a true transfer union in which

they would keep on subsidising weaker ones, a sort of fiscal union would be one solution, at least for the 17 Eurozone countries; this would be the true monetary integration they eschewed when the euro was launched. This would entail substantial losses of sovereignty in areas such as taxes and budgets, which would need to be overseen by a central authority, and elements of a transfer union, with collective borrowing schemes such as Eurobonds, a strengthened EFSF and the like. Germany would want to be in the driving seat of such a union, leading to the question of how committed Germany was to Europe, and whether it could make the right decisions. The other solution for Europeans was the break-up of the Eurozone, with its catastrophic economic and political consequences. The sovereign debt of Greece (and of other economies) needed to be very substantially restructured, essentially creating an orderly default, to give it breathing space to recover. A bout of controlled inflation, anathema to Germany, may be necessary for a few years in order to alleviate the burden of debt.

- The good news was that given the current wave of austerity, profligacy and oversized deficits would probably be things of the past. Yet, led by a Germany convinced that the problem of the Eurozone was only profligacy and indiscipline and that the solution was simply fiscal – that austerity was the universal cure – Eurozone leaders were oblivious to the fact that too much austerity too fast everywhere was becoming the problem, killing growth. They forgot that Ireland and Spain didn't actually have budget deficits before the crisis: they had budget *surpluses* and relatively low sovereign debt. There is a difference between cutting into fat and cutting into muscle, and this oversimplification risked plunging Europe into a deep recession. Everything should have be done instead to stimulate economies in general and demand in the stronger economies in particular. Only after recovery should real austerity packages be implemented, and then gradually. A surprising August 2011 1.2 per cent jump in Eurozone industrial production from Italy, Ireland and Portugal, showed there was still vitality there.[32]

- The European banking system, dangerously exposed and more leveraged than the American one, needed hefty recapitalization.

There was no point in hiding behind sham stress tests or pretending the problem would go away. Banks were, however, being banks again: fearful of having to sell shares to increase their capital at a time when share prices were extremely low, they were taking the easy route and shrinking their balance sheets by reducing lending, damaging business and growth in general, a practice that needed to be curtailed.

- There was no escaping the fact that mutualizing debt, one way or another, would be the only realistic solution to avoid a Eurozone break-up. If Eurobonds were not an immediate solution because they would require an integrated budgetary policy and the time to amend treaties, an increase in the EFSF and/or use of the ECB's power to print euros or to lend massive amounts of money to banks would suffice, provided it was big and fast enough.

- *Dulcis in fundo*, no solution would work without a comprehensive growth agenda. This was the most worrying point because many European nations have done such a thorough job of eradicating growth from their DNA. A rethinking of the European model would be necessary, a nearly impossible task.

Addressing the Bundestag at the end of October 2011 Angela Merkel said 'The world is looking at Germany, whether we are strong enough to accept responsibility for the biggest crisis since the Second World War . . . it would be irresponsible not to assume the risk'.[33] It seemed Eurozone leaders, confronting an imminent meltdown, were finally ready to face the challenge at the well-publicized Wednesday, 26 October 2011 summit in Brussels. To its credit, the all-night summit achieved a few milestones. Apart from Greece getting its second bailout money and thus averting default, the main concrete result was to wipe out half of Greece's debt held by private creditors, that is, banks. Banks exposed to Greek debt had a 50 per cent haircut forced on them under the guise of a 'voluntary' settlement in order to try to avoid a 'credit event' (euphemism for default) that would have plunged markets into further turmoil by triggering credit default-swaps insurance repayments. As a result, Greece's 350 billion euro debt was reduced to 260 billion euros and the country was temporarily saved; but it would remain subject to 'intrusive surveillance'. An agreement was also reached to recapitalize European banks to the tune of more than 100 billion euros, have them mark their government bond holdings to market and boost their reserves to 9 per cent of money at risk by June 2012. It was also decided that the EFSF would be expanded to a trillion euros as a firewall to protect Spain and Italy. A separate IMF-managed fund would be set up to attract money from the BRICs.

News that a 'grand bargain' agreement had been reached sent euphoric markets up, just as it had after the 21 July summit. Germany had set the agenda, but would the plan work? As usual, the devil is in the details and most details were left, to be worked out in the coming months. Nevertheless, Greece's debt, set to peak at 186 per cent of GDP in 2013, would decrease thereafter but still amount to 120 per cent of GDP by 2020, a similar percentage to Italy's today and twice the limit imposed by Maastricht. Could Greece grow to repay its debt? Hardly, and in all likelihood the country would soon be back drowning in debt. The forced recapitalization of European banks was a step in the right direction, but the sum contemplated was probably not enough to restore full confidence in the banking system. And what to make of the decision to increase the EFSF's firepower to 1 trillion euros? Germany had rejected France's 'big bazooka' proposal to have the EFSF access the unlimited financial resources of the ECB; so the hands remained tied of the only institution with enough resources to put an end to the conflagration with quantitative-easing-type measures. Since the size of the EFSF remained insufficient to tackle Italy's 1.9 trillion euro debt problem, the whole plan hinged on the ability of the embattled Berlusconi government to pass draconian austerity measures and at the same time reform and revive Italy's economy so as to show markets that the country could indeed repay its debt and stop contagion. If this didn't succeed, Italy would be the next Greece, only bigger, and the recapitalization of European banks would not help much. The unsustainably high 6.06 per cent rate that Italy had to pay on a new ten-year bond issue held right after the Brussels summit and the fact that the ECB remained the key player in Italy's bond market showed how little markets were convinced about Italy's good health. In addition, Germany's central bank itself immediately decried the plan to boost the EFSF as risky, since it was not based on injecting additional money but on leveraging the 250 or so billion euros left in the existing fund after this second Greek bailout about four or five times, with financial derivative instruments such as the infamous credit default swaps. The mandatory increase of bank reserves to 9 per cent may be a good idea, except that, as pointed out earlier, in a time when low share prices make it unpalatable to raise capital in the markets, banks take the easy route, that is, shrink their balance sheets and curtail credit, with dire consequences for businesses and growth in general. And China's involvement in the rescue would surely carry an economic and political price, as the last thing Beijing's leaders would want to elicit from their people was accusations of helping rich countries with hard-won money. In the words of Germany's BDI industry association president Hans-Peter Keitel, 'Asking a non-eurozone nation to help the euro would give the other nation the power to decide the fate of the single currency'.[34] The Brussels summit was a step in the right direction but, as usual, not enough. It focused on the symptoms rather than the causes of the disease. Whatever the result of all this might be, in the short to medium term the deadly cocktail of brutal austerity measures, higher borrowing costs and economies in recession would remain in place, and in the long term the euro's fundamental flaws would still be there. Only economic growth could help Europe recover, but, as usual, a Eurozone growth strategy was not even part of the discussion.

The blind leading the blind

The Eurozone crisis may have been a sovereign debt, currency and banking crisis rolled into one, but it was also a political and leadership crisis. The flaws inherent in the Eurozone construct originated when the euro was created, with Europe running ahead of itself without a well-thought-out plan and politicians unable to accept real monetary union. Used to compromise among self-interested actors and to step-by-step action, Europe is simply unable, in its essence, to tackle crises and important issues in an effective and decisive manner. The former British Prime Minister Gordon Brown didn't mince his words 'Europe has flinched at every turn',[35] and neither did UK Chancellor of the Exchequer George Osborne when he reflected the despair of the rest of the world with Eurozone leadership: 'Patience is running out in the international community'.[36] The IMF was a little more diplomatic when it said that 'political differences within economies undergoing adjustment and among economies providing support have impeded achievement of a lasting solution'.[37] Only when standing on the edge of the abyss did Europeans take action, mostly half-measures, only postponing the inevitable and making things worse. According to Gordon Brown: 'When the history of the twenty-first century is written people will ask why it was that Europe was found wanting during its most intractable economic crisis. They will ask why Europe slept as an undercapitalized banking system floundered, unemployment remained unacceptably high, and the Continent's growth and competitiveness plummeted... Europe's leaders will be charged with the "decline of the West" .....'.[38]

Appointed leader by default, a delusional Germany dragged its feet at every occasion, making things worse. Merkel had to contend with Germany's fragmented federal system and an electorate not inclined to pay for the mistakes of others. She knew the stakes, having said 'If the euro fails, then Europe fails', adding that the euro was 'the glue that holds Europe together'.[39] Yet Germany had a hard time recognizing that it has been the biggest beneficiary of the euro. Germany initially refused to bailout affected countries despite the risks of a meltdown, vetoed an increase in EFSF firepower, and fought the notion of Eurobonds and ECB bond purchases. It only agreed to a minimalist approach, obsessed by its belief that the crisis was due to profligacy and that the culprits should pay the price. True, when the ECB buys a country's sovereign bonds, it is tantamount to the entire Eurozone lending to it and the action dangerously intervenes in budgets and politics. But did Germany not realize that had the ECB *not* purchased Italian or Spanish bonds, a financial meltdown would have resulted? That without Eurobonds, a beefed up EFSF or ECB intervention, nothing would protect Italy or Spain and prevent catastrophe? Berlin failed also to recognize that no matter the amount of austerity forced on countries like Greece, they wouldn't be able to repay their debts and that Germany and other creditor countries were going to have to plug the hole one way or another. Germany is likely to set Europe's agenda for a while, but, given its recent performance, how good a leader will it be? Will German austerity and discipline make

Eurozone economies less divergent? Some would say this is hardly likely.

The bumpy road ahead

Who would have commented a few years ago that Europe was going to be shaken to the core by a sovereign debt crisis? In 2005 Mark Leonard wrote in *Why Europe Will Run the 21ˢᵗ Century* that the euro was one of three reasons why he was optimistic about Europe's economy.[40] Yet a mere decade after the currency was created its survival was at stake and with it that of the entire edifice of Project Europe. In a sense, the fault does not lie with the euro itself. Members of the Eurozone were supposed to adhere to the Maastricht Treaty's magic numbers, but political leaders made a mockery of the rules they had themselves devised. As the former ECB board member Otmar Issing put it bluntly: 'Almost all treaties promising European fiscal discipline have been broken time and again. The worse example was delivered by France and Germany in 2002–03 when they violated the Stability and Growth Pact, and even organized a political majority against the application of its rules.'[41]

Can the euro problems be fixed? Not if the euro remains in its present form. In what form can it survive? Will Greece be able to repay its debts? Will Italy reform? Will the Eurozone inevitably lose some members as Nouriel Roubini predicted? Will there be a new version of the euro? Will the euro actually disappear and every country go back to its own currency? Is it realistic to expect that the south will accept the severe pain of austerity forever, just to maintain membership in the Eurozone? Looking at the other side of the coin, is it realistic to expect that the taxpayers of the north will accept continuing to pick up the bills to save the south? How realistic is it to expect that Germany will always have the necessary *means* to pay the bills for others? What if Germany slows down? Nobody knows.

Europe never expected the successive shocks of the Great Recession followed by the sovereign debt and currency crisis and then by the hardships of forced brutal austerity; nor was it ready to have to shoulder so much to bail out countries and banks. Will European economies ever recover? An end of 2010 OECD report on growth in the Eurozone left little room for hope: the shocks may have crippled European economies to a point where growth may *never* catch up with projections made before the crisis and GDP growth may need to be reviewed by 3 per cent downwards *overall*. It is difficult, in the medium term at least, to envision for Europe as a whole a scenario other than low growth across the Continent, with economic stagnation and deflation in the periphery, leading to impoverishment. Germany sailed through the crisis, posting a 6 per cent annualized growth rate in early 2011 (while Greece was *minus* 6 per cent). Sweden followed a similar path with its export-dependent economy first hit by the global recession in 2009 but then saw its GDP shoot up by 6.9 per cent. Countries such as the Czech Republic have latched on to Germany as suppliers and benefited from the German rebound. Poland's economy held its own, thanks to fiscal stimulus and domestic spending from its 40 million-strong population. So in the centre, north and east of the continent things are not going too badly for now. The southern belt, with the UK and Ireland, is another matter, another Europe. When it comes to divergence the understatement of 2010 may turn out to be the European Commissioner for Economic and Monetary Affairs Olli Rehn's 'There is a certain dualism in Europe'.[42] The European model, at least in its southern sybaritic version, came to a premature end due to its unsustainability and, with it, the social contract that had underpinned social stability for the past half-century, leading millions to take to the streets across Europe, especially in France and Greece (joint champions of street demonstrations and strikes). Unions and other forces are likely to fight austerity, labor market and other reforms to their last breath.

Will Project Europe survive if the euro doesn't? Van Rompuy warned 'If the Eurozone had fallen apart it would have been the end of the European Union.'[43] One thing Europeans do agree on: if the euro fails, Project Europe is finished. And the euro has shown that it can fail. But here is a question just as important: will Project Europe survive if the euro survives? George Soros feared 'a real danger that the euro may destroy the political and social cohesion of the EU'.[44] In 1997 Harvard's Martin Feldstein had warned that the currency's flaws would not only result in its demise but also revive nationalism.[45] The euro indeed seems like the curse of Europe. No matter what the end result of the crisis will be, it will have dented the cohesion among European nations in no small way. Instead of the euro promoting economic convergence as had originally been hoped, it turns out to have cemented and even exacerbated differences.

One immediate consequence of the crisis is that further European integration will probably happen among the 17 Eurozone countries, the 'ins'. But what about the relationship between these 'ins' and the 'outs', the other ten members of the EU who are *not* in the Eurozone? Closer integration of the ins profoundly alters the EU's political landscape and will inevitably come at the expense of the power of the outs, eliciting a hostile response from the outs led by a London more Eurosceptic than ever. It comes as no surprise that after the Brussels summit the former UK Foreign Secretary Lord Owen advocated the creation of a 'Non-Euro Group', a NEG made of the outs in contrast to French proposals for a core European group made up of the ins,[46] and David Cameron's rhetoric against Europe stiffened noticeably, echoing growing calls within his own Tory party to 'repatriate' some powers from the EU. Europe is likely to see a widening and destabilizing split between its 17 Eurozone nations and the other 10. At the very least, post-2010 Europe risks being deeply divided between creditor/core and debtor/peripheral Eurozone countries and also between Eurozone ins and outs.

In general terms one can see a Europe centred on Germany and characterized by discipline, a push for innovation and productivity gains, more flexible labour markets, and openness to the world. And then there is this other Europe, mainly a Europe of the south, clinging to its utopian model that doesn't work and its undisciplined habits. Some observers foresee a European landscape evolving into three tiers, with top performers Germany and a few similar countries such as the Netherlands in one corner, intermediates France and Italy in another, and a poorer southern belt. Others see a two-tier Eurozone with Germany, the Netherlands, France and Italy in the top tier and the PIGS in the second. A split also exists between the ins and outs. Countries will have to choose where they want to belong and adjust their habits accordingly: France, for example, cannot have a 35-hour week philosophy and belong to the top tier at the same time for much longer. As a result, one can't talk about a single Europe anymore. Nobody actually knows what will happen except that a multi-lane, politically unstable Europe is likely to be a reality in the years ahead.

The crisis has profoundly altered the European landscape in other ways as well. In the past, Germany was very European, the Franco-German pair dominated European politics, with France in the political driving seat. Germany obtained political legitimacy from its alliance with France. Today's shift of the economic tectonic plates has resulted in a France so far behind Germany that Germany has little need of France and is more than ever dominant, even if it may still pretend to need the French from time to time. The vast differences in the two countries' economic and political structures have been laid bare despite Sarkozy's calls, after the Brussels summit, for France to be more like Germany. The New Germany that emerged from reunification and years of reform has finally come of age: it is much stronger in relative and in absolute terms than before: it is once more Europe's colossus. But it is profoundly disillusioned with Project Europe and looks East and abroad. Its economy has grown at more than double France's rate and its 2011 estimated budget deficit is half that of France's. The relative power of France and Germany in Europe will never be the same again after the crisis. The centre of gravity of power on the continent has decisively shifted towards Germany, a trend that had already started before the crisis with Europe's enlargement towards the east. Monnet cleverly invented Project Europe to keep Germany in check. It worked for over half a century, but would you bet that it will work for another half-century?

CONCLUSION: THE END OF THE GOLDEN AGE

The inevitable decline and impoverishment of Europe

'May you live in interesting times'
An old Chinese curse

Europe has lost its mojo

After swarms of British students had taken to the streets to vent their anger at cuts in education and increases in tuition fees, it was the turn of tens of thousands of public-sector workers who, in July 2011, protested against the brutal austerity measures imposed by David Cameron's government. They were followed by rampaging youths a month later who turned some British cities into war zones. In Greece street protests, sometimes violent, have become a daily occurrence. Young Spanish *indignados*, facing a bleak future, took over the famous Puerta del Sol in Madrid's centre, camping day and night for months to vent their frustrations. The list continues, and social strife is likely to worsen and become part of the European landscape. Though Europe has seen protests before, some larger and more intense, the difference this time is the general feeling of helplessness, a sense that there is little hope in terms of solutions or of a future, that there is no light at the end of this tunnel. For young people, there is also a feeling that their future has been stolen from them. It is not just a question of tightening belts for a while to get over a slump: this is how people's lives are going to be from now on. Governments are at a loss to offer any remedy except for more taxes and austerity measures. Across most of Europe is settling the feeling of a hangover after a party.

Europe is seriously sick. This much is obvious from the journey we have just taken through its landscape. For Europeans, there is good and bad news. The good news is that decline takes time, it is not an overnight affair. We can, however, safely and sadly infer that, due to the forces of history and a series of socio-politico-economic choices made by the nations of Europe and their leaders in the past half-century, many countries in Europe have entered an era of irreversible decline, impoverishment and social instability. Europe as a whole may slowly lose its cohesion and geopolitical relevance. The Golden Age of Europe is over. With a trajectory of decline inevitable, the natural question is what will be the speed and gradient of this decline, in individual countries and in aggregate. One may also speculate whether it will be a soft or a hard landing, how to best manage it, and one may ponder issues of absolute and relative decline.

Regarding national wealth and the economy, some countries, particularly in the south, are likely to undergo a swift decline and may become, by mid-century, mere shadows of what we know them to be today. Others may hold on for longer. A few, particularly in the north, may even know prosperous times. Yet, by and large, Europe will inevitably decline, like a greying rich old lady. But this will be not only in the economic dimension but also in terms of relevance, population trends, innovation and social cohesion, among others. In an enlarged yet increasingly divergent and divided Europe, as the EU continues to lose traction, politics on the continent are likely to become more and more national in character and less and less European. European ideals will probably end up taking a back seat as countries increasingly look after their own interests.

There is little comfort in knowing that this was the good news. The bad news is that, given what has been happening in the Eurozone, the likelihood of a catastrophic event cannot be dismissed, an event that could suddenly devastate Europe with the potential to hasten its demise. The disintegration of the Eurozone would be such an event. Were it to happen, Project Europe would be finished and no one would be able to see where the continent's future lay. In such an unlikely, but not impossible, doomsday scenario, a slow demise would be replaced by massive and sudden uncertainty and fragmentation. A return to old rivalries, nationalism and balance-of-power politics and their devastating effects could not be entirely ruled out.

The colour of fear

Europeans, particularly in the south, fell prey to the belief that governments have an obligation to look after their constituencies like benevolent parents looking after children, that they have infinite resources to do so and can solve every problem. They also convinced themselves that they were entitled by birthright to a certain quality of life and, to maintain it, they had to break the bank, borrow to the hilt and make future generations pay. They also bought into the illusion that the natural course of things is that their lives will always get better. In this post-Second World War European philosophical construct, pragmatism had no place. Unfortunately for Europeans, life is what happens when you make other plans. The only plausible solution to the complex equation relating the unsustainable costs of the Civilization of Entitlements to chronic low growth, unfavourable demographics and other socio-economic factors examined in this book is gradual and irreversible impoverishment, in particular in relation to southern Europe. Compelled to choose between structural reforms and decline, many European countries chose decline by default, because the only reforms they can implement are marginal. The decade and a half that ended in 2008 represented a golden age for the EU not unlike that of the 1950s and 1960s. With the advent of the 2008 crisis every problem lurking below the surface came out with a vengeance. Germany alone (with its satellites) was reprieved because it reinvented itself as the factory of the factory of the world, but for how long?

In *The Geopolitics of Emotion*, the French geopolitical expert Dominique Moisi speaks of a 'culture of hope' mostly found in Asia (and also in northern Europe) as against a 'culture of fear' now pervading most of the rest of Europe.[1] Fear of the future, fear of where the European construct is heading, fear of globalization, fear of enlargement, fear of Turkey in and of Turkey out, fear of a reunited Germany, fear that Europe has 'lost it' and fear that there is no coming back to the decades of hope and prosperity. To Moisi,

Asia exemplifies the future while 'Europe stands for a glorious but fading past', and 'fear today is Europe's dominant color'.[2]

We are the champions, my friend

Propelled by the Industrial Revolution and the ideals of free markets, imperialist Europe became the world's centre of gravity. Despite constant infighting, for centuries it came to control most of the world. About a hundred years ago it was replaced in this role by a young and dynamic America. Writing about Western civilization in general Sam Huntington said:

> All civilizations go through similar processes of emergence, rise, and decline... The West differs from other civilizations not in the way it has developed but in the distinctive character of its values and institutions. These include most notably its Christianity, pluralism, individualism, and rule of law, which made it possible for the West to invent modernity, expand throughout the world, and become the envy of other societies... the West won the world not by the superiority of its ideas or values or religion (to which few members of other civilizations were converted) but rather by its superiority in applying organized violence.[3]

We are currently witnessing another shift of the tectonic plates as China overtook Japan in 2010 to become the world's second largest economy and, according to some estimates, is bound to overtake that of the US to become number one within a couple of decades. The fall of the Soviet Union removed the clear and present danger that kept the West cohesive and unleashed the forces of globalization that allowed China to triple its share of world GDP and bring about a immense shift of economic power in a very short time. It is easy to forget that a long time ago China was for centuries the world's foremost economic power, with a share of world GDP close to a third until as recently as 1820. Its recent return to the scene has had an impact on every sector of economy and industry the world over. Having caused Europe to lose many of its low value-added industries, China has been moving with just as much determination into higher value-added industries. In a not too distant future Europeans may see Chinese cars on their streets and Chinese aeroplanes in their skies.

Divergence is not limited only to Europe. Public finances in America too have been wrecked by the recent crisis: its outlook for growth is questionable. Contrast this with a developing world where many countries retained healthier finances and growth outlooks. The 'rise of the Rest' is not a notion, it is a fact. The 'West' and the 'Rest' diverge. In most of the 'Rest's' economies it is not stimulation that leaders worry about, but overheating. Goldman Sachs expects the four BRICs to be among the top five economies by mid-century.[4] The relative fact of the decline of Europe (and the West) compared with these countries is not even being questioned.

Predicting the future is impossible and it isn't certain that China and India, which face daunting challenges of their own, will continue their successful trajectories in the coming decades. A lot can happen to derail the BRIC's rise. Yet one thing is certain: how Europe responds to the new challenges posed by these new giants will greatly impact its own future and well-being. In the short to medium term a hard landing of these developing economies would undoubtedly wreak havoc on Germany's export industries, with consequences across Europe. In the medium to long term, China is likely to displace many European value-added industries on the world stage and its currency is bound to become as important as the dollar and (if it survives) the euro. The question of whether America or China will be number one in 2050 is open, but one thing is sure: Europe will be lucky if it makes it to third place.

It's not just Europe

Who can laugh today at Fidel Castro for saying 'My idea, as the whole world knows, is that the capitalist system now doesn't work either for the United Sates or the world, driving it from crisis to crisis, which are each time more serious'? The Great Recession of 2008 resulted in a worldwide loss of trust in America and its financial system that compounded Europe's own problems. The unexpected downgrade of America's sovereign debt was a watershed event as the markets had 'discovered' that America, like most of Europe, had been living way beyond its means and that its own third-rate and polarized political class was unable to offer solutions. Europe overindulged in butter, America indulged in guns *and* butter. The post-war financial order we used to know has little left of an order. Similarities in the crises in the US and Europe induced many to speak of a more generalized 'decline of the West'. Given the disastrous state of public finances, recklessness, profligacy, slow growth, high youth unemployment, mediocre and paralysed leadership on both sides of the Atlantic, who would disagree? One wonders whether we are seeing today the limits of modern democratic systems. In Europe the social democratic model has failed in its quest to sustainably deliver high levels of welfare, and in the US there is a feeling that 'insider capitalism', a free market model rigged to enrich a small elite, has failed in its quest to sustainably deliver growing prosperity to all. What next? Protests may be becoming the norm in Europe, but America is not immune to them as the spread of the Occupy Wall Street protests across the US in the autumn of 2011 indicated. Fear of the future, discontent about rising inequalities and a sense of disengagement have settled across the West.

In *How the West was Lost*, Dambisa Moyo predicts that

The US and much of Western Europe are running out of capital, their labour dynamics are damaged...and their grip is loosening more and more on the monopoly they once held in technology. The rising Rest, led by China...have money in the bank, a superior labour outlook and a drive to take the technological lead.[5]

To Moyo the fate of the West is sealed: it is losing the world leadership position held for close to five centuries in economic, military and political terms, due to a 'sustained catalogue of fundamentally flawed economic policies'; 'the behaviour of the West in the last fifty years has been like that of a profligate son, squandering the family wealth garnered over the centuries'. One culprit is the systematic misallocation of resources, capital, labour and technology. The West now finds itself out of cash because it misallocated money when it had it and 'people grew comfortable with the idea of living beyond one's means'. The strategy of home-ownership for all promoted a culture of debt and resulted in asset bubbles and capital being allocated to unproductive assets instead of cashflow generating investments (in that sense the housing bubbles in Spain and the US are not very different).

'Europe's crisis will lap on US shores and America's economic woes will lap on Europe's – a two way tsunami.'[6] Yet there are fundamental differences between America and Europe. Growth is part of America's DNA and America knows how to periodically reinvent itself, although it may have more difficulty this time, having squandered its treasure in useless wars and let its insatiable appetite for oil and consumer goods get the better of itself. The case of Europe is different because its Civilization of Entitlements is as unsustainable as it is ingrained: Europe cannot bring itself to let it go. In most of Europe growth is no longer part of the culture and young people have become a conservative force against change. Europeans have become used to contenting themselves with mediocrity. Social cohesion and stability cannot be taken for granted.

So what?

If you are European, the simple answer to this question is that your own standards of living will drop and your children's standards of living won't even come close to yours. Overall youth unemployment across the EU is over 20 per cent, and young Europeans in the continent's southern belt looking for a job, may never be able to find a *real* one: their well-being may forever remain subordinate to that of the older generation and of the privileged class holding permanent jobs. For those approaching retirement, retirement benefits are under very serious threat, and they should ponder how to make ends meet in a few years, as their governments won't be able to keep the pension promises they have made to them. And pensioners over 65 in need of health care may soon have to sell their home to pay for support because government help will decline sharply. For Greeks or Portuguese the question is whether savings in the local bank are safe. Germans must pray for the good of key export markets such as China and Russia.

But the economy is not the only aspect. What sort of Europe will future generations inherit? Will the relative political stability, peace and unity Europeans have got used to in the past half-century be still there in ten or twenty years' time? Will it still be possible to move freely across the Continent a few years from now or will the freedom of Schengen be remembered as a short-term aberration?

Will businesses still be able to take advantage of Europe as a single market in a few years? Those who have felt the brunt of recent severe austerity measures must know that they are only the beginning.

If you are an immigrant from the Maghreb, Turkey or Africa, or a European of such origin, you know that, as the economy of the country you live in deteriorates, not only will your prospects for finding a job grow increasingly dimmer but you will increasingly be treated as an unwanted alien because, in times of crisis, immigrants are always perceived as competing with locals for jobs and benefits. If you are an American, you may worry whether your government may be taking steps to make America more European, with all the inherent implications. If you are sitting in a political office in Washington, you are probably already convinced that this declining Europe is not going to be a useful strategic partner anyway; yet you try to make the best of it, hoping it won't completely fall apart. If you are part of the elite in Beijing, you wonder how much of a counterweight a weaker and fragmented Europe is going to be to American ambitions, whether the euro is going to be stable enough to allow you to diversify away from US dollars, what will happen to the billions you invested in Greek and other bonds, and what will happen to your number one export market. In a globalized world decoupling is an illusion, and everything and everybody inside and outside Europe will be, one way or another, sooner rather than later, affected by its decline.

As the general situation worsens, European politics are likely to become increasingly nationalist, populist, xenophobic. Populist platforms are likely to be increasingly anti-EU and anti-globalization. A corresponding change has already been taking place in Europe's political landscape, possibly the most defining one since the fall of communism. The suggestion of Poland's finance minister that a break-up of the euro could mean a *real war* breaking out in Europe within a decade reflects the darkest fear of some.[7]

The poor and the less rich

According to the OECD definition of relative poverty, you are considered 'relatively poor' if you earn less than your country's average. It is said that there are over 50 million people qualifying in the EU today as relatively poor, with 25 million additionally at risk, close to the *Science Daily* estimate of 75 million people at risk of poverty across the EU. The Caritas organization places the total number at 85 million, not far from Eurostat's 81 million. The rate of poverty varies considerably within the EU, attesting to the divergence of its economies, oscillating between 10 per cent and 23 per cent. The most affected countries in terms of poor population absolute numbers are France, Germany, Italy (13 per cent), Poland, Spain and the UK (11 per cent).[8] In France, statistics showed that poverty, which declined for decades after the Second World War, started rearing its ugly head again and increased after 2001, and that 52 per cent of French people feel that their purchasing power has been declining.[9] Across the Alps, Italy's statistics bureau ISTAT reported that a quarter of all Italians (15 million people) risk falling into poverty, that one in three Italian families could not sustain unexpected expenses (i.e. have been truly living on the edge), and that one in four Italian youths was unemployed (half a million jobs lost in the past two years). Further, 3 million Italians (5.2 per cent of the total population) are said to live in absolute poverty. Some 20 per cent of *all* Spaniards can't find a job. In the hardest hit countries young people drop out of school prematurely at an alarming rate, approaching 19 per cent in Italy and over 30 per cent in Spain and Portugal.

The impoverishment of Western Europe, mostly now its southern belt, Ireland and Britain, is not the hypothetical outcome of some hypothetical scenario. It's something real that has already started. Europe may be the world's largest trading bloc, it may be relatively rich today, but it is quickly becoming a lot poorer. The trend is unlikely to be reversed.

Less than the sum of its parts

Europe remains, as we have seen, a union of convenience. That it would constantly be torn by conflicting forces was known since Project Europe was launched in the 1950s. Europe is a process, not the end result of a journey. As long as there is life in the process, there is Europe, independently of how far Europe is from being Europe. Mark Leonard aptly compared it to a bicycle that will fall down if you stop pedalling.[10]

Below the surface the most powerful countries still try to balance each other. Each of the 27 countries that constitute the EU today still puts its own narrow national interest first, justifiably given the profound distrust they have for each other, the EU government and bureaucracy. No country is ready to let its sovereignty go entirely, especially when it comes to budgets, foreign policy and, to some extent, defence. As a consequence Europe will keep punching below its weight on the international arena. It will never turn into the power it could have been. Europe turns out to be less than the sum of its parts. Perhaps Europe never really had particular geopolitical ambitions and is perfectly content with sinking into irrelevance, unconcerned with any existential threat from outside because there is none. Frustrated by Europe's shortcomings on the occasion of the Gulf War of 1991, a high government official from Belgium was reported to have portrayed Europe as 'an economic giant, a political dwarf and a military worm'. *Washington Post* journalist Robert Samuelson called Europe 'history's has been'.[11] Others call it now a 'sideshow'.

Soviet occupation resulted in Eastern Europe and part of the Balkans removing themselves from European history during the Cold War. When these countries re-emerged after the fall of the Berlin Wall in 1989, TV pictures showed surrealist scenes, a forgotten world next door, of old ladies wearing black shawls and old men looking lost among decrepit buildings. If someone took leave from the EU today and came back in 50 years' time, what would this someone find? 'Did France walk out of history without realizing it?' asked French politician Jean Pierre Chevènement in his book *La France est elle finie?*,[12] adding that his own country was heading for the precipice. Polls taken in early 2011 show almost 60 per cent of the French population saying that the situation will worsen in the next decades. They are right.

A busy radar screen

The title I have chosen for this book, *The Decline and Fall of Europe*, implies two different notions, one of 'decline', a slow and inexorable process of decay, and one of 'fall', something more sudden, brutal and final from which there is no return. I trust few people will argue today that Europe is not declining: the question is how steep is this decline. But will it also 'fall'? The Eurozone crisis shows that the possibility of a brutal fall is not mere fantasy. The absence of *external* existential threats to Europe does not mean there aren't any existential threats. But they are more likely to come from within. Chief among them is the question of demographics which, as we have seen, represents a ticking bomb, one that will explode in slow motion with diabolical inevitability, with disastrous continent-wide consequences. Longer life expectancies, low fertility rates and an aging population combined with the high cost of elderly care and pensions and early retirement age resulting from the Civilization of Entitlements, make this a slow-motion explosion. Massive immigration is not going to take place and would tear the continent apart. The unsustainability of the whole construct will eventually catch up and overwhelm the entire system if current trends are maintained.

And what of the old German question? The post-2010 reality is that Europe is facing a Germany that, having finally been reunited, having left France and most European economies in the dust, having realized that it has much to gain by looking outside Western Europe, is feeling increasingly self-assured, independent and assertive. Germany is not 'merely' European anymore and won't be kept bottled up. Germany motivated the creation of Europe: its resurgence and decoupling from Europe, left unchecked, could lead to Project Europe's demise. The euro that was supposed to cement the unity of Europe and contain a reunited Germany could achieve the exact opposite. As a result of the recent sovereign debt and currency crisis, this construct threatens to come apart. Jean Monnet, the 'inventor' of Europe and a realist who shunned grand narratives, famously predicted that Europe would be 'forged in crisis'. In fact, it is more like two or more Europes, separate continents drifting apart from the force of tectonic plates. It is today widely recognized that the Eurozone cannot exist in its current state, with such diverging economies, and since convergence is a utopia (unless Germany converges *down* to the level of the weaker), either the weak or the strong will leave it altogether or at the very least somehow restructure it as a two-speed zone. The political result would be nearly the same. A split in the overall European construct seems inevitable, with political implications bringing about the start of either the de-Europeanization of

Germany or the de-Germanization of Europe. The worst scenario is if France cannot stay in the same speed lane as Germany. The Franco-German axis has worried many, but it had the benefit of keeping Germany in check and Europe whole. An unravelling of this axis would be far more worrying than its resurgence.

Europe was not designed to handle that much stress and the Europe that will emerge a decade or two from now is likely to be very different from the Europe of the past decades. Already the two pillars of European integration, the euro and the Schengen treaty on the free flow of people, have come under serious attack. In the political sphere, the return of nationalism, populism and xenophobic politics is a distinct possibility, as beleaguered countries will realize that jobs are not coming back. As populist politicians may see the closing of frontiers as the only way to save jobs and industries at home and reverse the consequences of globalization may come protectionism. It could happen again despite the much heralded intertwining of European economies. After all, Germany used to be France's largest trading partner until they went to war in 1914 and a very globalized world shut down. With a resurgence of protectionism, the question is how long before some countries, suffering the pain of brutal austerity with no real remedy in sight, fall prey to the idea that the open, globalized system has only resulted in the export of jobs and industries, and that the one way to get them back is to close frontiers and force a rebirth of these industries and jobs at home. Talk of such 'deglobalization', however unlikely it may seem today, has already been heard from some European politicians. French presidential candidate Arnaud Montebourg won almost 20 per cent of the votes in October 2011's socialist primaries on a platform of deglobalization and hostility to free trade, an indication of what may come.

A world without a strong, cohesive and stable Europe would undoubtedly be worse off. Despite its many shortcomings the EU has, in general, been a force for good and moderation in world affairs, and not only for peace and human rights. The 'transformative' power of Project Europe and EU enlargement have influenced its neighbourhood for the better. The EU remains the planet's largest market. To America Europe is, despite its shortcomings, an ally. To China it is a moderator of America's actions and the euro is an alternative to dollar dependency. Everybody stands to gain if this unassertive giant does well. Everybody stands to lose if it does badly. Europe is, it would seem, too important to be left to Europeans to run alone.

It's up to you after all

The French eighteenth-century playwright Jean de Molière wisely said 'La critique est aisée mais l'art est difficile'. Proposing specific remedies to Europe's woes is no easy chore and is the work of experts and politicians. But if you are European, after all you live in a democracy and your vote counts. Change starts with you. You actually don't need to be a genius to understand the problems and figure out broad responses. In fact you have probably, by now, worked out most of it, and I hope this book has helped a little.

If you felt a sense of inevitability of Europe's decline when reading this book it is because my own analysis led me to the unpleasant conclusion that the various forces at play and the many self-generated constraints and limitations on Europe's ability to act combine to bring about such an outcome. Being content with mediocrity, clinging to an outdated and unsustainable model, systematically applying the law of the lowest common denominator to joint endeavours, failing to confront reality, lacking leadership, a common vision and solidarity, are features that have become ingrained in today's European psyche. I simply don't see Europeans rising to the challenge, having the stomach, creativity, pragmatism and courage to effect the extraordinarily broad and deep changes that would be needed to reverse the current decline of Europe. Moreover, to have the slightest chance, any radical reform movement would, in any case, need to originate from and be promoted by the Franco-German couple, something which is unlikely given the extent of Germany's drift and disenchantment with Europe, the absence of a shared vision and the fact that these countries don't have equal influence. Any reforms will either be imposed by events or be marginal.

It would, however, be callous and cowardly to say why bother. I may well be wrong (and I certainly hope so) in my assessments. Inevitability may not be inevitable after all. Every solution that makes sense should be tried to attempt to extricate Europe from its predicament or at least let it down gently. Apart from pointing out that it may be advisable to hurry because we are running out of time,

the only thing I can say when it comes to finding concrete remedies is that Europeans need to come back to Earth first. They need
to regain the pragmatism and survival instinct they have so utterly
lost to ensure that political ideals, taboos, political correctness and
wishful thinking don't stand in the way of realistic assessments and
pragmatic solutions. Europeans need to take a good look at themselves in the mirror. Only when everything is laid bare in cold light –
when they look at reality face to face and talk about things the way
they really are – can a meaningful search for practical solutions really
start.

May I venture a last piece of advice for my fellow Europeans?
Despite everything that is written in this book, despite all the feelings
of misgiving you may have about Europe, the EU, Brussels, Europeans and their shortcomings, we cannot afford to let go of Project
Europe. Nowhere is the threat of pulling away from Project Europe
as worrying as in Germany, the linchpin of European unity. Poland,
which joined Europe in 2004, assumed the rotating EU presidency
in the summer of 2011 and the first thing Prime Minister Donald Tusk did was to wisely remind his fellow Europeans that 'The
most important task is to rebuild trust and faith in the idea that
Europe makes sense, that the EU is truly a worthwhile invention.'[13]
Former French Foreign Minister Michel Barnier asked, 'Who can
believe and seriously say, today, that each of us (European countries)
would carry more weight in world affairs if we were not united?'[14]
They are right. Project Europe itself, as an ideology promoting unity
and integration across the continent, has little to do with most of
our predicaments. Most of what is good about Europe today *comes*
from Project Europe. Most of what is bad comes from choices we,
as Europeans, have been making over half a century of democratic
politics and which have little to do with the Project Europe ideology.
If we let go of Project Europe, Europe will be left with the worse and
the continent risks turning back to its former nasty habits. We cannot afford to forget or let our children forget why a few wise men
decided to launch Project Europe in the first place.

We started with China, so let's end with China. The French
statesman Charles de Gaulle said that 'It will not be any European statesman who will unite Europe: Europe will be united by
the Chinese.'[15] Whether one agrees or not with this strange forecast,

this country matters tremendously to Europe and the trek Eurozone leaders recently undertook to Beijing hat in hand asking for rescue funds shows how much world economic power has already shifted there. China used to be the planet's most advanced civilization and ruled a good portion of it a long time ago. It then went through a long period of decline lasting centuries, only to rise again today, like the phoenix. So even if Europe's destiny is one of decline, there may be a prospect for a turnaround at some point. Let's just hope it won't take that long.

EPILOGUE

In the autumn of 2011 I made an experiment. Having just put the final touches to *The Decline and Fall of Europe* and been told by my publisher that it would take a few months before the book was actually launched, I decided to take a short leave of absence from things European. During this time I forced myself to look the other way when confronted with this topic in the media or conversations. Surely, one wouldn't realistically expect to witness any significant change after such a short period? To the contrary, what I found when I reopened my eyes was enough to prompt me to add this short epilogue.

By early 2012, there were an estimated 23 million Europeans unemployed.[1] German Chancellor Angela Merkel predicted the year would be tougher than 2011 and French President Nicolas Sarkozy called it 'the year of all risks'.[2] Labelling Europe a 'global has-been', the *Wall Street Journal* observed that a 'historic change' had taken place in the first two weeks of 2012 with global investors now favouring emerging market bonds over those of European countries.[3] *The Economist* spoke of Standard and Poor's having changed the balance in Europe, restoring the dividing line down the Rhine with its degrading of the sovereign ratings of nine European countries, most notably France, in January.[4] French Finance Minister François Baroin had warned that France had to keep its AAA status to preserve its social model.[5] The unsustainability of this model, with an economy dominated by the government sector and people working even fewer hours than the Greeks,[6] had finally caught up with France. It was likely that this loss of status would bring higher borrowing costs for France, worsening prospects for its banks. Germany could find itself compelled to inject more of its own cash into the EFSF, which had now lost its own AAA status. One can imagine the Germans being not particularly thrilled by this development, to say the least. The difference in power between Germany and France was now such that the fabled partnership would probably become a purely cosmetic affair. To some observers the European stage now seemed to be dominated by an assertive and inflexible Germany dictating conditions, policies and treaties to the rest of Europe.

The one thing that had not changed in these few months was the sense of surrealism surrounding the crisis. Europeans 'discovered' in early 2012 that Greece had never stopped being Greece and had, by and large, failed to make good on its promises to restructure itself. Germany now insisted that Greece cede sovereignty on spending and taxes to Eurozone authorities in order to get additional bailout money, something the Greeks furiously resisted as an offence to 'national dignity'. How long before debtor countries begin to revolt against creditor countries? Clearly, austerity wasn't working. The likelihood of a Greek default had not decreased, it had increased, despite the efforts of Greece's new Prime Minister, Lucas Papademos, and his technocratic government. Greece remained insolvent, unable to repay its debts and would need help for a long time. If, after more than a year of trying, Europeans remained unable to come up with a solution to restructure the debts of Greece, a country representing just a few per cent of Eurozone GDP, could they realistically be expected to find solutions to the larger problems posed by Spain or Italy?

The other constant remained Berlin's obsession with fiscal discipline and punishment, which ensured that the only cure available to Eurozone debtors continued to be brutal austerity measures applied everywhere at the same time. This simplistic approach from the country that had most benefited from the euro misdiagnosed the crisis as being only about profligacy; but two of the most embattled countries, Ireland and Spain, had budget surpluses before the crisis and Italy had been running a primary surplus. The result could well be a downward spiral, which economist and Nobel laureate Joseph Stiglitz described as a 'suicide pact': austerity measures deepening the recession, making debt harder to service and risking widening budget deficits. As a result, by early 2012 most European economies were heading for shrinkage, with the risk of Germany joining them soon. It was not just in the Eurozone that the austerity doctrine seemed to be damaging economies: Paul Krugman pointed out that British GDP had recovered four years into the Great Depression whereas it was nowhere near recovering four years into this crisis.[7] Despite the radical austerity imposed, many economies were seeing their budget deficits *widening* instead of shrinking because falls in tax receipts – caused by lower than expected growth – were larger than the cuts imposed on budgets. The illegality of budget deficits was nevertheless to be enshrined in a new European treaty, a 'fiscal compact' promoted by Germany, that would in effect eliminate Keynesian-style stimulus from the shrinking number of options available to governments. The doctor persisted in prescribing more of the same medicine despite the fact that it was not working and that at some point austerity might plunge the entire continent into a protracted recession and even greater unemployment, which could become too much for ordinary people to bear, raising the spectre of social instability and unrest in debtor countries.

At the World Economic Forum meeting in Davos at the end of January 2012, economist Nouriel Roubini, one of the few who had predicted the crisis, warned 'What Europe needs is less austerity and more growth', and George Soros lamented that 'Europe did too little too late and the crisis snowballed'.[8] Throughout the crisis measures to stimulate growth were not even discussed seriously in European media or political narrative. Other than the pursuit of austerity, governments were at a loss what to do. As it became increasingly obvious in early 2012 that most European economies would shrink and that unemployment would continue to rise (almost 300,000 additional jobs were expected to be lost in France in 2012), the most astonishing development was that governments were wondering why it was so. They had taken a patient in coma, shut off the oxygen, cut off his leg, and were now wondering why he wasn't recovering and walking. It is not entirely surprising that the political left doesn't concern itself with the creation of new wealth – given its roots in an ideology of wealth redistribution – and offers little these days apart from its outdated mantra and conservatism in the face of reform. What is more surprising is that the centre right has generally abdicated its promotion of free enterprise, growth and the creation of wealth. As a result of this sterile ideological backdrop, growth is to remain an orphan in most of Europe.

In early 2012, the ECB, now headed by a more flexible Mario Draghi, was still trying everything except for measures that would put a stop to the crisis such as acting as lender of last resort. A late December decision by 'Super Mario' to lend half a trillion euros to banks for an unusually long three years at low interest rates eliminated the immediate prospect of a credit crunch-induced 'Lehman moment' in Europe. Banks figured that the best use they could make of this bonanza was to buy short-term sovereign securities which were yielding substantially more – pocketing a nice profit in the process. This measure was also an indirect way to inject money into sovereign bonds without overly ruffling German feathers. Hooked on such easy money, by the end of January banks let it be known that they would tap the ECB's three-year facility for *double* the December amount: 1 trillion euros.[9] These ECB funds wouldn't find their way into a real economy that desperately needed them. Moreover, how easy would it be to wean the banking sector from this panacea in the future? Interbank lending rates remained at high levels, and banks rushed to deposit excess liquidity with the ECB in record amounts instead of lending it to other banks, thus attesting to continued mistrust. In the first days of 2012, Italy's UniCredit bank saw the price of its shares plummet after it announced its decision to issue shares to raise funds in order to meet the new capital adequacy requirements imposed by the EBA (European Banking Authorities). Its shares later recovered but the episode was a signal to the banking sector that raising capital in the market was not an option. The other option, reducing assets in order to indirectly increase capital ratios, required a substantial reduction in lending, almost ten to one, as a result of which banks now had even less incentive to lend to real businesses and people. A brutal credit crunch in the real economy was looming in early 2012, one which could make the downturn deeper and longer.

In weaker countries, which Soros now likened to 'third world countries highly indebted in a foreign currency',[10] people continued to be subjected to heavy doses of harsh medicine combining tax hikes, budget cuts and more. Italy, now rated BBB+, like Lithuania and Peru, remained the crucial country in the crisis, yet there was still no credible European firewall to protect it despite appeals by the IMF's Christine Lagarde and others. Under the new technocratic leadership of Mario Monti, Italy – whose social contract had been based for a half century on the government stealing from the people and the people stealing from the government – was, by early 2012, turning into a sort of fiscal police state with, among others, new regulations that required its citizens having to justify taking out sums over 1000 euros from their bank accounts. Big Brother wanted to know where every penny was every minute of the day so that it could tax it. Yet, at the same time, it was reported that Italian members of parliament, already the highest paid in Europe, had voted to increase their own benefits. As it was raising taxes and slashing expenses, Monti's unelected and apolitical government launched an ambitious programme of measures aimed at liberalizing Italy's notoriously inefficient and opaque economy to revive growth, which met stiff resistance from entrenched interest groups. How could such countries reconcile the clashing imperatives of austerity and growth? The net result, in Italy, was an economy expected to shrink by 1 per cent in 2012.[11] Spain's was expected to shrink by 1.5 per cent and under its new Prime Minister Mariano Rajoy was now turning into one of the EU's highest taxed countries,[12] one where unemployment reached 22.8 per cent and more than 1.6 million households had no single member holding a job.[13] A vicious spiral of austerity, growing budget deficits and negative growth with rising unemployment was being set in affected countries. How long would it be before people took to the streets in droves? By early 2012, Europe had become the 'weak link' in a global economy in which even emerging markets were starting to slow down. The only good news was that the American economy – which, contrary to that of the EU, had subjected itself to stimulus – seemed to show signs of waking up from its torpor and was expected by some to post a 2 per cent growth rate.

On a cold January afternoon I found myself with a business associate looking for a place to get a hot drink. We entered a pastry/coffee shop and asked for two cappuccinos. The lady behind the counter replied that she couldn't serve us hot drinks. To our astonishment her excuse was that there were not enough clients that day for her to go through the chore of preparing hot beverages. This may be an extreme, colourful and rare case even in France, but it is a true story. Despite the economic crisis hitting everyone savagely, certain attitudes will not change. In the firm grip of the Civilization of Entitlements, too many Europeans continue clinging to their sacred right to do as little as possible, oblivious that the price they may soon have to pay could be all the steeper.

On 22 January 2012 Croatia voted by popular referendum to become the 28th member of the EU, to come into effect in 2013. Gone, however, were the days when newcomers were conspicuous by their enthusiasm to join the Union. With the backdrop of the current EU crisis, Croatia's population was deeply divided between those who wished the country to join and those who wanted it to stay out. Only 44 per cent of eligible voters bothered to vote, with less than 70 per cent of them saying 'yes', a net result of just about 30 per cent in favour. The outcome in Croatia was nevertheless a victory for the 'yes', and polls showing pro-EU candidates ahead in Finland's presidential elections being held at about the same time proved there was still life in Project Europe after all. Yet moves within the EU to work out ways to get around countries' vetoes by devising plans that could be approved by a few key members rather than by all 27 of them (such as plans for new taxes which were opposed by the UK), represented a significant departure from the usual ways of Project Europe. Had Europeans given up the idea of consensus-based decision-making in the Union? Within the 27-member EU, the Eurozone was also likely to become an inner club of 17 in which France and Germany would have an easier time calling the shots.

These developments were among signs of a rapid change in the relationship between members of the Union. Europe's fragmentation can be visualized with the image of plate tectonics: if at the time of the Cold War the continent was divided in a western plate and an eastern plate, by early 2012 the reality is vastly different. The first plate detaching itself from the continent is the Britannic plate, to the west. Coined for the British, the word 'Eurosceptic' seems by now *passé*, as it is difficult today to find a EU country that is *not* Eurosceptic. A large part of the British political class now sees Britain's future away from Europe and its mission that of turning London into *the* financial centre of a globalized world. Sarkozy's insistence on a financial transactions tax that would dent London's competitiveness may have been the last straw for the British. So is it goodbye euro, hello renminbi? How realistic, durable and welcome this vision is remains to be seen, given that Britain, whether it wants it or not, is just a few kilometres from a continent that matters tremendously to its economy and that a single EU market without Britain may well become more protectionist. To the east, the disillusioned Germanic plate is accelerating its drift away and up, towering over the continent and taking with it satellites and some of central and north-eastern Europe. To the north the Scandinavian plate is taking with it the 'smart Europe' that has (so far) managed to have its cake and eat it, lessons which 'dumb Europe' chose to not learn. A southern plate encompassing the continental arch bordering the Mediterranean running from Portugal to the southern Balkans is not so much drifting as sinking. There remains the question of France, a geological oddity with a foot firmly planted on the southern plate and the other desperately clinging to the Germanic plate but losing its grip.

Scenarios leading to a collapse of the euro or a political breakdown of the Union remain extreme. Muddling through for a long time appears more likely. Yet, according to some, like Soros, 'Europe is confronting a descent into chaos and conflict'.[14] At the very least, the answer to the question 'will the euro still be there in the coming few years' is not obvious, and the fault lines between plates seem to be widening by the day.

Ask yourself: if, by magic, some hypothetical outside power paid off half of Europe's debts in a fit of generosity, would Europe suddenly find itself out of its predicament? Hardly. Since fear is a motivator of European actions, what may save the euro at the end of the day may be the fear of the disastrous and unfathomable consequences of its breakdown. Nevertheless, curing the euro, if it can be done, would only cure the symptoms and not the illness of Europe. The currency and debt crisis may be the headline-grabbing topic, but it is only the tip of an 'iceberg of challenges' that Europe faces today. The word 'crisis' is, in truth, a misnomer in that it incorporates the notion of something adverse yet temporary, a brief and painful dip expected to be followed sooner or later by a return to the *status quo ante*. What Europe is starting to go through, and at an accelerating pace, is not temporary. It should be clear to Europeans by now that this is not just about the euro, it is a crisis of the entire European model, construct and philosophy of life, and so far there is no plan B. We are witnessing the dawn of a new era, one that could see standards of living drastically readjusted downwards throughout most of the region and the glue that has held together the European political construct melt like snow in the sun. By early 2012 it seems that the real danger in the coming few years is not so much that Europe's economic crisis becomes more severe, although this is already quite distressing in itself. The danger is that it moves from an economic crisis to a serious political crisis within nations and between the nations of Europe, with dire consequences.

Europe faces an existential crisis, but is not going to disappear into a hole tomorrow. Yet where it will be ten years from now depends on whether Europeans open their eyes and face reality today. If the severity of the current crisis doesn't break Europe, will it become its much needed wake-up call?

SOURCES AND ACKNOWLEDGEMENTS

Allow me to let you in on a little secret: the best source of information in any given country is the taxi driver. Taxi drivers are always plugged into local news, willing to talk, and they can rapidly give their charge the temperature of their country. This book is the result of personal reflexions but also of conversations with government officials, experts and scholars, businessmen, ordinary people and, yes, taxi drivers. It is also the result of going through many books as well as countless articles from newspapers and magazines from various countries in various languages for news, opinions, information, data, ideas and inspiration. I have been jolting down reams of notes, learning and borrowing from these works with the objective of trying to connect the dots they represented to see patterns emerge in order to form my own ideas.

As a consequence this book will inevitably contain material from these works and I humbly acknowledge my debt to their authors and rights holders, including to those not explicitly credited herein, if they have been overlooked or where I have lost trace of the source. Every effort has been made to trace rights holders, but if any have been inadvertently overlooked the publishers and I would be pleased to make the necessary arrangements at the first opportunity.

The Decline and Fall of Europe was written during my free personal time. I gathered and checked facts and figures as best as I could without the benefit of any staff or resources. I am not a writer, economist, politician or historian, nor am I an expert in any of the topics touched upon in this book. In a sense, mine has been a journey of personal discovery.

Except where specifically indicated, opinions expressed here are my own. I was reckless enough to choose to write the original version of this book in English, which is not my mother tongue. All this points to the fact that there are inevitably shortcomings in this book. Any mistakes I make are entirely mine and I hope that the reader will be forgiving.

I am grateful to Palgrave Macmillan for having taken the plunge with this novice author and to Taiba Batool, Ellie Shillito, Claire Morrison and the editorial, marketing and production teams for their patience and invaluable help. I would like to also thank all the people who knowingly or unknowingly contributed to my journey and to this book.

NOTES

Introduction

1. Samuel P. Huntington, 'The U.S.-Decline or renewal?', *Foreign Affairs*, Winter 1988/89.
2. Gordon Brown, 'Europe's real problems', *International Herald Tribune*, 12 July 2011, p. 8.
3. Paul Krugman, 'Euro zone death trip', *International Herald Tribune*, 27 September 2011, p. 7.
4. Bret Stephens, 'What Comes after "Europe"?', *Wall Street Journal*, 19 September 2011.
5. 'Monti: Italia verso la decadenza', *Corriere della Sera*, 27 September 2011, p. 15.
6. Bernard Lewis, *What Went Wrong?* (London: Phoenix, 2004).
7. Elaine Sciolino, 'Visions of a union: Europe gropes for an identity', *New York Times*, 15 December 2002.

Chapter 1

1. Philippe Mesmer and Brice Pedroletti, 'La montée en puissance de la Chine menace l'équilibre des forces en Asie', *Le Monde*, 14 September 2010, p. 6.
2. As reported by Ravi Velloor, 'India to deploy strike force at Tibet border', *Straits Times*, 1 September 2011, p. 22, and 'China warns off Indian ship in South China Sea', 2 September 2011, p. 26.
3. Edward Wong, 'Beijing lets a delicate issue lie', *International Herald Tribune*, 31 March 2011, p. 2.
4. R. M. Schneiderman, 'Temple of doom', *Newsweek*, 21 February 2011, p. 7.
5. 'China's military gets a rise', *Time*, 21 March 2011, p. 9.
6. Andrew Marshall, 'Military maneuvers', *Time*, 27 September 2010, p. 12.
7. *The Clash of Civilizations and the Remaking of World Order* (New York: The Free Press, 2002), p. 219.
8. Yoon Young-Kwan, 'Can East Asians cooperate?', *Straits Times*, 30 April 2011, p. 36.

9. Dominique Moisi, *The Geopolitics of Emotion* (New York: Anchor Books, 2010), p. 39.

10. Mark Mazower, *Dark Continent* (Harmondsworth: Penguin, 1998), Preface, p. xii.

11. Daniel Vernet, 'La guerre froide, une analogie trompeuse', *Le Monde*, 14 August 2008, p. 2.

12. Olli Rehn, Speech at the Plenary Session of the European Parliament in Strasbourg, 15 November 2005.

13. Roger Cohen, 'Europe! Europe! Europe!', *International Herald Tribune*, 7 October 2010.

14. Winston Churchill quotes are taken from Mark Grant, *Out of the Box and Onto Wall Street: Unorthodox Insights on Investments and the Economy* (New York: John Wiley & Sons, 2011) .

15. Mark Leonard, *Why Europe Will Run the 21st Century* (London and New York: Fourth Estate, 2005).

16. Jeremy Rifkin *The European Dream* (New York: Tarcher/Penguin, 2005), p. 385.

17. Ibid., p. 183.

18. Ibid., p. 3.

19. Ibid., p. 303.

20. T. R. Reid, *The United States of Europe* (Harmondsworth: Penguin, 2005), p. 1.

21. Ibid., p. 64.

22. Ibid., p. 232.

23. Paul Krugman, 'The great illusion', *International Herald Tribune*, 16–17 August 2008, p. 5.

24. Helmut Schmidt, 'Europe, slow and steady', *New York Times*, 13 June 2005.

Chapter 2

1. Alan Cowell, 'Britain suspends referendum on European constitution', *New York Times*, 7 June 2005.

2. John Vinocur, 'Hum of activity at EU, or is that a ho-hom?', *International Herald Tribune*, 18 May 2004, p. 2 .

3. Thomas Fuller and Katrin Bennhold, 'EU leaders face task of selling new charter', *International Herald Tribune*, 21 June 2004, p. 4.

4. *International Herald Tribune*, 13 June 2005.

5. Charles Kupchan, 'L'érosion de l'idéal Européen est préoccupante, même pour les Etats-Unis!', *Le Monde*, 14 October 2010, p. 22.

6. 'Chirac jokes about British food', BBC News, 4 July 2005.

7. George Soros, 'Germany must defend the EUro', available at GeorgeSoros.com (accessed 12 August 2011).

8. 'The divisiveness pact', *The Economist*, 12 March 2011, p. 34.

9. Joel Havemann, 'Market newsletter: Europe wonders: Buddy, can you spare an ECU? That stands for European Currency Unit, which is what the 12-nation European Community will be using if plans go forward for a unified currency', *Los Angeles Times*, 13 November 1990.

10. John Vinocur, 'Jospin envisions an alternative EU', *International Herald Tribune*, 29 May 2001.

11. 'The Italian's job', *The Economist*, 19 February 2011, p. 12.

Chapter 3

1. *Le Monde*, 6 August 2005.

2. Paul Kennedy, *Preparing for the Twenty-first Century* (London: Fontana, 1993), p. 259.

3. 'After D-Day', *The Economist*, 12 June 2004, p. 30.

4. Frédéric Lemaitre, 'Le refus de Berlin de soutnir l'intervention est critique en Allemagne', *Le Monde*, 23 March 2011, p. 10.

5. 'The unadventurous eagle', *The Economist*, 14 May 2011, p. 35.

6. *Il Sole 24 Ore*, 8 August 2011.

7. Bruno Waterfield, 'Cameron: Ashton is too soft on Egypt', *Daily Telegraph*, 5 February 2011, p. 13.

8. Robert Cooper, *The Breaking of Nations* (London: Atlantic Books, 2004), p. 155.

9. Robert Kagan, *Paradise and Power* (London: Atlantic Books, 2003), pp. 1 and 11.

10. Pascal Bruckner, *La tyrannie de la pénitence* (Paris: Bernard Grasset, 2006).

11. Kagan, *Paradise and Power*, pp. 1 and 25.

12. Joschka Fischer, Speech at Humboldt University, Germany, 12 May 2000.

13. Judy Dempsey, 'EU moves to block a Polish deal with Russia', *International Herald Tribune*, 11 October 2010, p. 1.

14. Niall Ferguson, *The War of the World* (London: Penguin Books, 2007), p. 610.

15. Dominique Moisi, *The Geopolitics of Emotion* (New York: Anchor Books, 2010), p. 119.

16. Thomas Friedman, 'Nato's new front', *International Herald Tribune*, 30 March 2003.

17. Zurab Tchiaberashvili, 'Une decision prise de longue date', *Le Figaro*, 27 August 2008, p. 12, translated by the author.

18. Doreen Carvajal, 'Sale of warships raises alarm', *International Herald Tribune*, 29 December 2010, p. 3.

19. Michael Richardson, 'US to match China's arms build-up:Gates', *Straits Times*, 10 January 2011, p. 1, and. 'Sino-US arms race: is the gap closing?', p. A23.

20. Judy Dempsey, 'The peril that NATO can't ignore', *International Herald Tribune*, 11 November 2010.

21. Ivo H. Daalder, 'Breaking a Brussels logjam', *International Herald Tribune*, 19 October 2010, p. 8.

22. James Blitz, 'Nato chief warns Europe over cutting defence budgets', *Financial Times*, 8 February 2011, p. 3.

23. Tom Shanker, Stephen Castle and Romain Parlier, 'Gates accuses allies of sidestepping military commitments', *International Herald Tribune*, 12 June 2011, p. 3.

24. *The Clash of Civilizations and the Remaking of World Order* (New York; The Free Press, 2002).

25. Ibid., p. 101.

26. Ibid., p. 31.

27. Ibid., p. 158.

Chapter 4

1. Roger Cohen, 'Erdogan may know best on Turkey's path to EU', *International Herald Tribune*, 19 May 2004, p. 2.

2. Huntingdon, *The Clash of Civilizations*.

3. Roger Cohen, 'Is EU ready for Turkey? Muslim world is waiting', *International Herald Tribune*, 12 May 2004, p. 2.

4. Roger Cohen, 'Erdogan may know best on Turkey's path to EU', *International Herald Tribune*, 19 May 2004, p. 2.

5. Laurent Arthur du Plessus, *Islam-Occident la guerre totale* (Paris: Jean-Cyrille Godefroy, 2004) , title translated by the author.

6. Elisabeth Bumiller and Christine Hauser, 'Bush courts Turks and presses NATO', *International Herald Tribune*, 28 June 2004, p. 1.

7. Joanna Kakissis, 'Postcard: Orestiada', *Time*, 31 January 2011, p. 3.

8. Recept Tayyip Erdogan, 'The Robust Man of Europe', *Newsweek*, 24 January 2011, p. 14.

9. Ibid., p. 14.

10. Daniel Dombey, 'Issues of trust add to Turkey's apathy over EU membership', *Financial Times*, 11 October 2011, p. 3.

11. 'An uncertain path', *The Economist*,15 October 2011, p. 30.

12. Kemal Koprulu, 'On Turkish political developments', email dated 17 April 2011 (sent to selected recipients, of which the author was one).
13. Guillaume Perrier, 'La Turquie veut accroître le commerce avec l'Iran, malgré les pressions internationales', *Le Monde*, 18 October 2010, p. 14.
14. Mensur Akgun, Sabica Senyucel Gundogar, Jonathan Levack and Gockce Percinoglu, *The Perception of Turkey in the Middle East 2010*, Turkish Economic and Social Studies Foundation, TESEV Publications.

Chapter 5

1. Suzanne Daley and Stephen Castle, 'A "traveling circus" for Europe', *International Herald Tribune*, 29 June 2011, p. 3.
2. Doreen Carvajal, 'EU deputies vowing to give up their perks', *International Herald Tribune*, 8 June 2004, p. 1.
3. Giulio Tremonti, *Rischi Fatali* (Milan: Mondadori, 2005).
4. Jeremy Rifkin, *The European Dream* (New York: Tarcher/Penguin, 2005), p. 227.
5. Margaret Thatcher, Speech at the College of Europe in Bruges, Belgium, 20 September 1988.
6. 'Charlemagne-Europe's need for e-freedom', *The Economist*, 28 October 2010.
7. Stephen Castle, 'Report faults EU regional aid spending', *International Herald Tribune*, 11 November 2010, p. 3.
8. Agence France-Presse, 'EU to cut costs amid fury over "fund misuse"', *Straits Times*, 14 February 2011, p. A16.
9. Stephen Castle, 'Cost of EU rises even as countries impose cuts', *International Herald Tribune*, 8 October 2010, p. 4.
10. Jean-Pierre Stroobants, 'Un ex-fonctionnaire Européen dénonce la "corruption" à bruxelles', *Le Monde*, 13 January 2011, p. 8.
11. Maia de la Baume and Scott Sayare, 'Weaker Euro nations test strength of union', *International Herald Tribune*, 4–5 December 2010, p. 13.
12. *Financial Times*, 17 June 2005.
13. 'Blair admits EU rebate difficulty', BBC News, 14 June 2005.

Chapter 6

1. 'Labour pains', *The Economist*, 4 November 2010.
2. Yves de Kerdrel, 'Comment la France perd le nord en étant gangrene par le sud!', *Le Figaro*, 20 October 2010, p. 17.

3. 'Getting it right', *The Economist*, 13 November 2010, p. 18.
4. Floyd Norris, 'France has no equal in retirement', *International Herald Tribune*, 30–31 October 2010, p. 9.
5. Jenny Barchfield, 'New strikes in France over retirement age', Yahoo! News, 23 September 2010, p. 1.
6. 'Struck off', *The Economist*, 16 October 2010, p. 30.
7. Katrin Bennhold, 'In student protests, fears of bleak future', *International herald Tribune*, 22 October 2010, p. 3.
8. Karl Marx and Friedrich Engels, *The Communist Manifesto* (London: Arcturus, 2010).
9. Ibid.
10. 'Marx, Mervyn or Mario?', *The Economist*, 26 March 2011, p. 75.
11. John Vinocur, 'Europe's left adrift in its inconsistency', *International Herald Tribune*, 2 November 2010, p. 2.
12. Olivier Truc, 'La notation précoce des élèves sème la zizanie en Suéde', *Le Monde*, 8 November 2010, p. 8.
13. See www.BrainyQuote.com.
14. Standard & Poor's Rating Services, 'Global aging 2010: the irreversible truth', 7 October 2010.
15. Fareed Zakaria, 'The hard truth about going "soft"', *Time*, 17 October 2011.p. 20.
16. James Hall, 'Time bomb as pension savings fall', *Daily Telegraph*, 28 October 2011, p. 2.
17. Mark Landler, 'Western Europe slowly comes to grips with working', *International Herald Tribune*.
18. Jacques Attali, *Tous ruinés dans dix ans?* (Paris : Fayard, 2010), p.137.

Chapter 7

1. 'Multikulturell? Wir?', *The Economist*, 13 November 2010, p. 36.
2. See www.BrainyQuote.com.
3. 'The old world shrinking with age', *Financial Times*, 1–2 March 2003.
4. Giulio Meotti, 'Italia, R.I.P.', *Wall Street Journal*, 7 September 2010, p. 13.
5. 'Replacement migration: Is it a solution to declining and ageing populations?', The United Nations, Population Division, 2001.
6. Massimo Introvigne, 'Mohammed supera Giuseppe Cosi spariscono I nomi cristiani', *Il Giornale*, 17 January 2011, p. 15.
7. Bruni and Frank, 'Persistent drop in fertility reshapes Europe's future', *New York Times*, 26 December 2002.

8. Quentin Peel, 'Merkel needs to reconcile the economic and political realities', *Financial Times*, 19 October 2010, p. 2.

9. Judy Dempsey, 'In Germany, a quandary of labour and timing', *International Herald Tribune*, 5–6 February 2011, p. 9.

10. Tracy McNicoll, 'France: le baby boom', *Newsweek*, 7 February 2011, p. 6.

11. Special report: Pensions, *The Economist*, 9 April 2011, p. 6.

12. '70 or bust!', *The Economist*, 9 April 2011, p. 13.

13. Samuel P. Huntington, *The Clash of Civilizations and the Remaking of World Order* (New York: The Free Press, 2002), p. 200.

14. Graham E. Fuller, *A World without Islam* (London: Little Brown, 2010).

15. John F. Burns and Alan Cowell, 'Britain split on a fix for "moral collapse"', *International Herald Tribune*, 16 August 2011, p. 4.

16. Marion Van Renterghem, 'L'Allemagne brise à son tour le tabou du débat sur l'islam', *Le Monde*, 19 October 2010, p. 8.

17. *Focus*, 9 October 2010.

18. Marion Van Renterghem, 'L'Allemagne brise à son tour le tabou du débat sur l'islam', *Le Monde*, 19 October 2010, p. 8.

19. Judy Dempsey, 'Turkish leader provokes criticism in Berlin', *International Herald Tribune*, 1 March 2011, p. 3.

20. 'David Cameron's warning', *Wall Street Journal*, 10 February 2011, p. 11.

21. James Kirkup, 'Muslims must embrace core British values, says Cameron', *Daily Telegraph*, 5 February 2011, p. 1.

22. Bernard Lewis, *What Went Wrong?* (London: Phoenix, 2004), p. 84.

23. Graham E. Fuller, *A World without Islam* (London: Little Brown, 2010).

24. 'Sense about sharia', *The Economist*, 16 October 2010, p. 14.

25. The term 'Eurabia' was actually coined by British essayist Gisèle Littman-Orebi, a.k.a. Bat Ye'or.

26. Richard Bernstein, 'German terror fight hits political impasse', *International Herald Tribune*, 5 May 2004, p. 3.

27. Bernard Lewis, *From Babel to Dragomans* (London: Phoenix, 2004), p. 155.

28. IFOP survey, *Le Monde*, 5 January 2011.

29. Alan Cowell and Michael Slackman, 'Germany raids Islamist sites', *International Herald Tribune*, 15 December 2010, p. 4.

30. Stephen Castle, 'Political earthquake shakes up Sweden', *International Herald Tribune*. 21 September 2010, p. 3.

Chapter 8

1. Rosemary McClure, Chris Erskine, Jen Leo and Judi Dash, 'Best airport for napping between flights? Singapore's Changi', *Los Angeles Times*, 16 August 2009.
2. *International Herald Tribune*, 24 December 2010.
3. Stefan Theil, 'How Europe's new goals will pay off', *Newsweek*, Special Issue, p. 15.
4. Column by Paul Krugman, *International Herald Tribune*, 30–31 July 2005.
5. Mark Leonard, *Why Europe Will Run the 21st Century* (London: Fourth Estate, 2005).
6. Katrin Bennhold, 'Continent guards its right to leisure', *International Herald Tribune*, 19 July 2011, p. 1.
7. Ibid.
8. Rioufol, 'Les 'néoréacs', ces nouveaux modernes', *Le Figaro*, 7 January 2011, p. 15.
9. Sandrine Morel, 'L'Espagne peine à sortir d'un modèle économique construit sur la bulle immobilière', *Le Monde*, 19 October 2010, p. 5.
10. 'A great burden for Zapatero to bear', *The Economist*, 22 January 2011, p. 33.
11. 'After the fall', *The Economist*, 17 September 2011, p. 66.
12. 'Estonian exceptionalism', *The Economist*, 16 July 2011, p. 30.
13. *Le Monde*, 17 August 2005.
14. Giulio Tremonti, *Rischi Fatali* (Milan: Mondadori, 2005).
15. Dambisa Moyo, *How the West Was Lost* (Allen Lane, 2011), p. 84.
16. Koshore Mahbubani, 'What Asia can teach The Indebted West', *Newsweek*, Special Issue, p. 26.
17. Maia de laBaume, 'French professors find life in U.S. hard to resist', *International Herald Tribune*, 22 November 2010, p. 6.
18. 'A machine running smoothly' and 'Angela in Wunderland', *The Economist*, 5 February 2011, p. 64 and p. 11.
19. 'Unbalanced Germany', *The Economist*, 8 August 2009, p. 7.
20. John Vinocur, 'Caution lost in German swagger', International Herald Tribune, 19 October 2010, p. 2.
21. From a letter to the readers of *Newsweek* by Sidney Harman, Chairman of Harman Newsweek LLC and Klaus Schwab, Founder and Executive Chairman of World Econmic Forum, published in *Newsweek* in 2011.
22. Katrin Bennhold, 'In Norway, equality key to prosperity', *International Herald Tribune*, 29 June 2011, p. 2.
23. 'France's lost decade', *The Economist*, 5 February 2011, p. 61.

24. Christine Lagoutte, 'Les métiers qui ont résisté dans la crise', *Le Figaro*, 25 October 2010, p. 23.
25. 'Labour pains', *The Economist*, 6 November 2010, p. 58.
26. Warwick Lightfoot, 'How Big Government Killed Britain's Regions', *Wall Street Journal*, 13 January 2011, p. 12.
27. 'Shrinking time off', *International Herald Tribune*.
28. Bret Stephens, 'What comes after "Europe"?', *Wall Street Journal*, 19 September 2011.
29. Charles Roxburgh, 'Europe's ongoing revolution', *Newsweek*, 29 November 2010, p. 18.
30. Elisabetta Povoledo, "Work or play? In the EU, trading income for time off", *International Herald Tribune*, 19 July 2004.

Chapter 9

1. 'L'antimatière prete à se devoiler', *Sciences et Avenir*, January 2011, p. 8.
2. Melania DiGiacomo, 'Nel G20, persi 20 milioni di posti', *Corriere della Sera*, 27 September 2011, p. 13.
3. Robert Winnett, 'Risk of new banking crisis', *Daily Telegraph*, 5 March 2011, p. 1.
4. Dambisa Moyo, *How the West Was Lost* (London: Allen Lane, 2011), p. 95.
5. Sewell Chan, 'A toxic mix of greed, mistakes and recklessness', *International Herald Tribune*, 27 January 2011, p. 16.
6. Niki Kitsantonis, 'A world turned upside down', *International Herald Tribune*, 23–24 October 2010, p. 11.
7. Jacques Attali, *Tous ruinés dans dix ans?* (Paris: Fayard, 2010), p. 208.
8. Jean-Michel Demetz, 'Irlande, Le Tigre au régime sec', *L'Express*, 22 September 2010, p. 53.
9. 'A parable of two debtors', *The Economist*, 16 April 2011, p. 51.
10. Marie de Vergés, 'La longue dérive d'un pays aux faiblesses structurelles', *Le Monde*, 11 April 2011, p. 12.
11. Gaia Pianigiani, 'Dysfunction holds back Italian growth', *International Herald Tribune*, 29 July 2011, p. 18.
12. Sandro Iacometti, 'I soprusi delle banche costano 45 miliardi alle microimprese', *Libero Mercato*, 24 December 2010, p. 23.
13. 'A wind of change blows into Italy', *Financial Times*, 16 August 2011, p. 8.
14. Philip Blenkinsop, 'Is Belgium doomed to be "Greece of the North"?', *International Herald Tribune*, 27–28 November 2010, p. 17.

Chapter 10

1. Erik Kirchbaum, Reuters, 4 March 2010.

2. Marcus Walker, 'New debate over Eurobonds emerges in Germany, France' and 'What the Eurobond would look like', *Wall Street Journal*, 16 August 2011, p. 4.

3. 'The union within the union', *The Economist*, 12 February 2011, p. 34.

4. Anthony Rowley, 'Japan does a China in EU rescue', *Business Times*, 12 January 2011, p. 2.

5. Gilles Leblanc, 'Quand la Chine fait son marché en Europe', *Le Figaro*, 7 January 2011, p. 14.

6. Liz Alderman, 'In EU, China finds debt and deals', *The International Herald Tribune*, 3 November 2010, p. 17.

7. Paul Carrel, David Millken, Pedro Nicolaci da Costa, Mark Felsenthal and Alan Wheatley, 'Crisis has rewritten the manual for central banking', *International Herald Tribune*, 25 March 2011, p. 15.

8. Alison Mutler, 'Curses! Romania's witches forced to pay income taxes', Yahoo! News, 6 January 2011.

9. William Underhill, 'Britain: back from the dead', *Newsweek*, 4 October 2010, p. 20.

10. 'Ouch!', *The Economist*, 23 October 2010, p. 20.

11. Philip Aldrick, 'Families to be £1,500 a year worse off', *Daily Telegraph*, 2 August 2011, p. 1.

12. Pierre-Antoine Delhommais, 'Nous sommes tous des Terre-NEUviens', *Le Monde*, 22 November 2010, p. 18.

13. George Soros, 'How Germany can avoid a two-speed Europe', GeorgeSoros.com Newsletter, 22 March 2011.

14. Matthew Saltmarsh and Jack Ewing, 'E.C.B. acts further to ease banks' cash crunch', *International Herald Tribune*, 22 September 2011, p. 17.

15. 'Fighting for its life', *The Economist*, 17 September 2011, p. 63.

16. Liz Laderman, 'G-20 seeks 'big bang' solution for banks', *International Herald Tribune*, 15–16 October 2011.

17. Floyd Norris, 'Credit raters may be right on Euro debt', *International Herald Tribune*, 15 July 2011, p. 18.

18. Jeffrey Sachs, 'Greece can be saved – here is how to do it', *Financial Times*, 1 July 2011, p. 9.

19. Alain Salles, 'La Grèce decide de prendre le virage de l'énergie photovoltaique', *Le Monde*, 17 September 2011, p. 8.

20. Floyd Norris, 'Why fight inflation if you need it?', *International Herald Tribune*, 12 August 2011, p. 18.

21. Dimitris Kontogiannis, 'Anger grows at austerity pain', *Financial Times*, 24–25 September 2011, p. 3.
22. Gordon Brown, 'Saving the Euro zone', *International Herald Tribune*, 16 August 2011, p. 6.
23. James Kirkup, 'Financial crisis the worst the world has ever faced', *Daily Telegraph*, 7 October 2011, p. 1.
24. Stephen Castle, 'Continent girds itself for new bank brush fires', *International Herald Tribune*, 6 October 2011, p. 1.
25. David Jolly, Nelson D. Schwartz, Louise Story and Landon Thomas Jr., 'France and its banks feel heat of market's skepticism', *International Herald Tribune*, 11 August 2011, p. 15.
26. Based on market data, 'Fighting for its life', *The Economist*, 17 September 2001, p. 63.
27. Vittorio Da Rold, 'Moody's "vede" il default greco', *Il Sole 24 Ore*, 26 July 2011, p. 3.
28. Nouriel Roubini, 'Mission impossible: stop another recession', *Financial Times*, 8 August 2011, p. 9.
29. Open Europe Blog, 1 August 2011.
30. Otmar Issing, 'Slithering the wrong kind of union', *Financial Times*, 9 August 2011, p. 9.
31. Oliver Sarkozy, 'Europe's dithering over banking risks 2008 again', *Financial Times*, 25 October 2011, p. 9.
32. Mike Dolan, 'Worrying ourselves into a crisis', *International Herald Tribune*, 20 October 2011, p. 20.
33. Stephen Castle, Jack Ewing and Gaia Pianigiani, 'Merkel wins big vote on euro plan', *International Herald Tribune*, 27 October 2011, p. 1.
34. Gerrit Wiesmann, 'Business wary of foreign help', *Financial Times*. 28 October 2011, p. 4.
35. Gordon Brown, 'Saving the Euro zone', *International Herald Tribune*, 16 August 2011, p. 6.
36. Chris Giles, Alan Beattie, Richard Milne, and Michael Mackenzie, 'Global economy pushed to brink', *Financial Times*, 24–25 September 2011, p. 1.
37. Matthew Saltmarsh and Jack Ewing, 'E.C.B. acts further to ease banks' cash crunch', *International Herald Tribune*, 22 September 2011, p. 11.
38. Gordon Brown, 'Europe's real problems', *International Herald Tribune*, 12 July 2011, p. 8.
39. Bruno Waterfield and Robert Winnett, 'Euro under siege as now Portugal hits panic button', *Daily Telegraph*, 16 November 2010, p. 1.
40. Mark Leonard, *Why Europe Will Run the 21st Century* (London: Fourth Estate, 2005).

41. Otmar Issing, 'Slithering to the wrong kind of union', *Financial Times*, 9 August 2011, p. 9.

42. Stephen Castle, 'Economic rifts, exacerbated by crisis, seen as threat to Euro', *International Herald Tribune*.

43. Steven Erlanger and Stephen Castle, 'The EU leader who sees quietness as a strength', *International Herald Tribune*, 9–10 October 2010, p. 3.

44. George Soros, 'Europe should rescue banks before states', *Financial Times*, 15 December 2010.

45. Fraser Nelson, 'The plates are shifting-and the PM risks being stranded', *Daily Telegraph*, 28 October 2011, p. B10.

46. David Owen and David Marsh, 'A blueprint to rejuvenate a debt-ridden Europe', *Financial Times*, 11 October 2011.

Conclusion

1. Dominique Moisi, *The Geopolitics of Emotion* (New York: Anchor Books).

2. Ibid., p. 97.

3. *The Clash of Civilizations and the Remaking of World Order* (New York: The Free Press, 2002), p. 311.

4. *The Expanding Middle: The Exploding World Middle Class and Falling Global Inequality*, Goldman Sachs, Global Economics Paper No.170,. July 2008.

5. Dambisa Moyo, *How the West Was Lost* (London: Allen Lane, 2011), pp. x, 14, 37, 179.

6. Bret Stephens, 'What comes after "Europe" '?, *Wall Street Journal*, 19 September 2011.

7. 'In the Brussels bunker', *The Economist*, 17 September 2011, p. 28.

8. 'Poverty across Europe : a comparison between countries', *Science Daily*, 31 October 2008.

9. *Le Monde*. Reporting on a survey from APEC, 5 October 2010.

10. Mark Leonard, Why Europe Will Run the 21st Century (New York: Fourth Estate, 2005).

11. Robert J. Samuelson, 'The end of Europe', *Washington Post*, 15 June 2005.

12. Max Gallo, 'Jean-Pierre Chevènement face au destin de la France', *Le Figaro*, 13 January 2011, p. 16 (translated by the author).

13. Michel Barnier, 'Poland's solidarity message to Europe', *Financial Times*, 1 July 2011, p. 8 (translated by the author).

14. Michel Barnier, 'Comment ne pas être Européen ?', *Le Monde*, 7 July 2011, p. 14. (translated by the author).
15. Nick Witney, 'The death of NATO', *Europe's World*, autumn 2008.

Epilogue

1. Stephen Castle, 'EU leaders set to admit austerity is insufficient', *International Herald Tribune*, 30 January 2012, p. 1.
2. *The Economist*, 'Self-induced sluggishness', 7 January 2012, p. 9.
3. Daniel Henninger, 'Bain capital saved America', *Wall Street Journal*, 18 January 2012.
4. *The Economist*, 'And then there was one', 21 January 2012, p. 31.
5. *The Economist*. 'Down a notch', 21 January 2012, p. 29.
6. Steven Erlanger, 'Downgrade of France raises heat on Sarkozy', *International Herald Tribune*, 16 January 2012, p. 1.
7. Paul Krugman. 'Economic amnesia and the austerity debacle', *International Herald Tribune*, 31 January 2012, p. 6.
8. Larry Elliott and Jill Treanor, 'Soros: euro crisis might wreck EU', Guardian.co.uk, 25 January 2012.
9. Patrick Jenkins, David Oakley and Ralph Atkins, 'Banks set to double crisis loans from ECB', *Financial Times*, 31 January 2012, p. 1.
10. Elliott and Treanor, 'Soros: euro crisis might wreck EU'.
11. Rachel Donadio and Harvey Morris, 'Some relief for Rome in markets, but not for Monti', *International Herald Tribune*, 29 December 2011, p. 1.
12. *The Economist*, 'Happy new year', 27 January 2012, p. 21.
13. Raphael Minder, 'Joblessness in Spain hit 22.8% at end of year', *International Herald Tribune*, 28–29 January 2012, p. 8.
14. John Arlidge, *Newsweek*, 30 January 2012, p. 37.

BIBLIOGRAPHY

Allègre, Claude, *Peut-on encore sauver l'Europe?* (Paris: Plon, 2011).

Attali, Jacques, *La crise, et après?* (Paris: Fayard, 2008).

——, *Tous ruinés dans dix ans?* (Paris: Fayard, 2010).

Blainey, Geoffrey, *A Very Short History of the World* (Harmondsworth: Penguin, 2004).

Bruckner, Pascal, *La tyrannie de la pénitence* (Paris: Editions Grasset et Fasquelle, 2006).

Cooper, Robert, *The Breaking of Nations* (London: Atlantic Books, 2004).

Cox, Brian and Jeff Forshaw, *Why does E = mc2* (Cambridge, MA: Da Capo Press, 2010).

Cresus, *Confessions d'un banquier pourri* (Paris: Fayard, 2009).

Ferguson, Niall, *The War of the World* (Harmondsworth: Penguin, 2007).

——*The Ascent of Money* (Harmondsworth: Penguin, 2009).

Friedman, George, *The Next Decade* (New York: Doubleday, 2011).

Friedman, Thomas, *Longitudes and Attitudes* (Harmondsworth: Penguin, 2003).

Fuller, Graham E., *A World without Islam* (New York: Little Brown, 2010).

Gombrich, E. H., *A Little History of the World* (Harvard: Yale University Press, 2008).

Heisbourg, François, *L'épaisseur du monde* (Paris: Editions Stock, 2007).

Huntington, Samuel P., *The Clash of Civilizations'* (New York: Free Press/Simon and Schuster, 2002).

Inlacik, Halil, *Turkey and Europe in History* (Istanbul: Eren Press, 2006).

Leonard, Mark, *Why Europe will Run the 21st Century* (New York: Fourth Estate/HarperCollins, 2005).

Lewis, Bernard, *What Went Wrong?* (London: Phoenix, 2004).

——, *From Babel to Dragomans* (London: Phoenix, 2004).

Kagan, Robert, *Paradise and Power* (London: Atlantic Books, 2004).

Kennedy, Paul, *Preparing for the Twenty First Century* (Fontana Press/Harper Collins, 1994).

Kleveman, Lutz, *The New Great Game* (London: Atlantic Books, 2004).

Maalouf, Amin, *Le dérèglement du monde* (Paris: Editions Grasset et Fasquelle, 2009).

Marx, Karl and Friedrich Engels, *The Communist Manifesto* (Arcturus Publishing Limited, 2010).

Mazower, Mark, *Dark Continent* (Harmondsworth: Penguin, 1999).

Moisi, Dominique, *The Geopolitics of Emotion* (New York: Anchor Books, 2010).

Moyo, Dambisa, *How the West Was Lost* (London: Allen Lane, 2011).

Nye, Joseph S. Jr., *Soft Power* (Perseus, 2004).

Pinder, John, *The European Union* (Oxford: Oxford University Press, 2001).

Ramonet, Ignacio, *Géopolitique du chaos* (Paris: Gallimard, 1999).

Pocket World in Figures (London/Harmondsworth: The Economist/Profile Books, 2011).

Reid, T. R., *The United States of Europe* (Harmondsworth: Penguin, 2004).

Rifkin, Jeremy, *The European Dream* (Harmondsworth: Penguin, 2005).

Roberts, J. M., *The New Penguin History of the World* (Harmondsworth: Penguin Books, 2004).

Tremonti, Giulio, *Rischi fatali* (Milan: Arnoldo Mondadori Editore, 2005).

Newspapers, magazines and websites

El Pais
Financial Times
Foreign Affairs
Il Corriere della Sera
Il Giornale
International Herald Tribune
Le Figaro
Le Monde
Los Angeles Times
Newsweek
Science & Vie
The Economist
The Guardian
The Times
Time
Wall Street Journal

INDEX